Choosing Ethnic Identity

MIRI SONG

polity

First published in 2003 by Polity Press in association with Blackwell Publishing.

Editorial office:
Polity Press
65 Bridge Street
Cambridge CB2 1UR, UK

Marketing and production:
Blackwell Publishing Ltd
108 Cowley Road
Oxford OX4 1JF, UK

Published in the USA by
Blackwell Publishing Inc.
350 Main Street
Malden, MA 02148, USA

A catalogue record for this book is available from the British Library.

Library of Congress Cataloging-in-Publication Data

Song, Miri,
Choosing ethnic identity / Miri Song.
    p. cm.
    Includes bibliographical references and index.
    ISBN 0-7456-2276-3 — ISBN 0-7456-2277-1 (pbk.)
    1. Ethnicity. 2. Group identity. 3. Minorities—Race identity. 4. Racially mixed people—Ethnic identity. 5. Ethnic attitudes. 6. Race awareness.
I. Title.
GN495.6 .S65 2003
305.8–dc21   2002010898

Typeset in 10.5 on 12pt Sabon
by Graphicraft Limited, Hong Kong
Printed in Great Britain by MPG Books Ltd, Bodmin, Cornwall

This book is printed on acid-free paper.

Contents

Acknowledgments

This book started life soon after the birth of my first son, Charlie, and its completion has followed the birth of his brother, Theo. Amidst the blur of sleepless nights and domestic chaos, I relied upon the support (and tolerance) of Murray Smith, who also read and commented on large parts of this book – not bad for a film scholar! Because this book explores debates about ethnic identity in both the USA and Britain, I am thankful for the interest of colleagues on both sides of the Atlantic. In Britain, I am especially indebted to Martin Bulmer, who encouraged me to both begin and complete this project. John Solomos also provided friendly advice and support. I also thank my colleagues at the University of Kent for providing me with the space to complete this book, and in particular Frank Furedi, Jan Pahl, Kate Reed, and John Jervis, for their interest in my work. David Herd, Abi Cooper, Cal Anton-Smith, Guy Reynolds, Alison Packer, Pamela Kea, and Guy Roberts-Holmes provided encouragement and excellent company during the writing of this book. Without the help (and good food) provided by Elsie "Jan" Smith and Richard Smith, this book would have taken even longer to write. In the USA, as busy as they were, Paul Spickard and Steve Gold were generous in sharing their thoughts and comments. Lane Kenworthy deserves special thanks for discussing chapter 7 with me. I thank my parents and siblings, and in particular my brother Paul Song, for his interest in my work and for keeping me well supplied with newspaper clippings about the USA.

Introduction

Guy Perron: Isn't Hari Kumar the permanent loose end? Too English
for the Indians, and too Indian for the English?
Nigel Rowan: That's rather Sarah's view. Frankly, I think he's more
interested in being just his own type of Indian.

The Jewel in the Crown

The concept of ethnic identity is in wide usage today. In what ways
is it important to people's sense of themselves, and to what extent
can we say that people are able to "choose" their ethnic identities
in contemporary multiethnic societies, such as the USA and Britain?
Notions such as adopting an identity, or self-designated terms such
as "Black British" and "Asian American," suggest the centrality of
agency and choice for individuals. However, the actual range of
ethnic identities available to individuals and the groups to which
they belong may not be wholly under their control, as the quote
above suggests. Nor do the ethnic and racial designations applied to
people necessarily match the ethnic identities held by individuals and
groups themselves. This book explores the ways in which ethnic
minority groups and individuals are able to assert and negotiate
ethnic identities of their choosing, and the constraints structuring
such choices.

Making sense of people's ethnic identities entails a broader understanding of identity per se. As Jeffrey Weeks (1990: 88) has noted,
"Identity is about belonging, about what you have in common with
some people and what differentiates you from others. At its most
basic, it gives you a sense of personal location, the stable core to your
individuality. But it is also about your social relationships, your complex involvements with others." Various analysts have stressed the
complexity of people's identities, since they are informed not only
by race and ethnicity, but also by other axes of identification, such
as gender, class, sexuality, age, and religion (Bradley 1996; Barot,
Bradley, and Fenton 1999). Nevertheless, this book focuses specifically upon the meanings and dynamics surrounding ethnic identity.
I also focus on the representations of groups because of their constitutive role in the formation of ethnic and racial identities.

The assertion of identities has a dual function, both expressive and instrumental, and much is at stake in the determination of an ethnic identity (Ogbu 1990). The ability of groups to claim or re-create their own self-images and identities, against the backdrop of ethnic and racial labeling by the dominant society, is not only important in terms of self-determination; it can also have important implications for people's self-esteem and sense of well-being. In late modernity, individuals are said to be engaged in a reflexive project of the self (Giddens 1991). A fundamental part of this reflexive project is the ongoing formation and shaping of identity, and for many ethnic minorities in particular, the assertion of ethnic identity is a central part of their everyday lives. The assertion of ethnic identity comprises an important aspect of a person's habitus (Bourdieu 1984).

The ability to exercise, or even enjoy, an ethnic identity of one's choosing is not simply a personal matter – it is a highly politicized issue which cannot be taken for granted. Claims to an ethnic identity may be significantly limited by various forms of overt and covert oppression. Fanon (1963) comes to mind, in his illustration of how the ravages of colonialism broke down the ability of the colonized to believe in, much less exercise, a separate and precious inner sense of self. The issue of ethnic identity is also of central importance in contemporary societies because the struggles associated with "identity politics" are collective processes in which groups and individuals within them grapple with particular forms of recognition and legitimacy in the wider society (Calhoun 1994). Being able to assert an ethnic identity of one's choosing is also an important component of a contemporary politics of citizenship, which addresses issues of "difference," belonging, and the multifarious ways in which people now participate in social life (Hall, Held, and McGrew 1992: 176).

Concerns about both legal and illegal immigration and the potential change to "national character" have meant that assertions of ethnic and racial difference, and minority rights more generally, are often perceived as problematic and threatening to the wider society (see Soysal 1994; Joppke 1996). Given the significant growth of minority populations in parts of the USA, such as California, the possibility that White Americans will no longer comprise a numerical majority, or dominate various institutions without challenge, has led to a crisis in White identity (Omi and Winant 1996: 475). In the context of the post-Civil Rights era, ordinary White Americans have increasingly questioned the idea that ethnic minority people continue to suffer from various forms of racial discrimination, and the idea that White people are necessarily more privileged, vis-à-vis minority groups (Marable 1995). In a major national survey of racial attitudes of White Americans since World War II, a substantial majority of White Americans disagreed with the proposition that Black people are still treated badly in the USA, and they opposed government interventions to desegregate schooling or residential areas (Schuman and Steeh 1996). In particular, during the Reagan administrations of the 1980s, there was retrenchment of Affirmative Action (or "positive discrimination" in Britain) policies, on the grounds that it was White people who suffered racial discrimination on the basis of their race.[1]

In Britain, the recognition that the country is becoming increasingly multiethnic is often characterized as being problematic. Drawing on ideologies and discourses about difference, Margaret Thatcher once famously spoke of her concerns about immigration in a television interview: "I think it means that people are really rather afraid that this country might be swamped by people of a different culture. The British character has done so much for democracy, for law, and done so much throughout the world that if there is any fear that it might be swamped, then people are going to be rather hostile to those coming in" (Solomos 1993: 187). The growing support for the British National Party (BNP) in British elections and the recent disturbances between White and Asian youths in Northern cities also suggest that a tense racial politics provides the backdrop to many debates about the social and political significance of ethnicity and ethnic and racial difference.

Relatively few books on ethnic identity, race, and racism draw on a wide range of studies from more than one country. Drawing on studies from the USA and Britain allows us to analyze what disparate groups in these two countries have in common, in terms of the politicized processes and dynamics associated with the negotiation and assertion of ethnic identities. While I focus on studies of groups in the USA and Britain, I do not look at the broader global politics of race (e.g. the complex racial politics in societies such as Brazil or Jamaica), which is beyond the scope of this book.

Although the processes and politics surrounding ethnic identity formation and assertion are highly contextual, and while the treatment of immigrants and ethnic minority groups is historically distinctive in the two countries, a focus upon the experiences of groups in the USA and Britain is especially revealing. There is still a great deal in common, transatlantically, especially in terms of discourses about race, identity politics, and the two-way flows of popular culture (Gilroy 1993) – despite the undeniable differences in the countries' histories, institutions, and populations. This book relies upon discussion of groups in the USA and Britain, but is not meant to be a systematic comparison of ethnic minority groups' experiences in the two countries.[2] Rather,

Choosing Ethnic Identity explores the politics and dynamics of ethnic identity assertion in a much more fluid way, drawing on the experiences of various groups from both countries. Except for where I introduce a new term or concept, for the sake of simplicity, I do not use scare quotes around words such as "race," "Black," or "mixed race." This is not intended to deny the contested usage of such terms.

Outline of chapters

In chapter 1, I review the debates about the basis and meanings of ethnic attachments and identities. The continuing significance of ethnicity in the USA and Britain, and the intertwining of ethnicity and race, are also discussed in this chapter. Furthermore, I critically explore the idea that ethnic minorities can, albeit in limited ways, exercise "ethnic options."

In chapter 2, we consider what it means for ethnic minority groups to possess ethnic options. Very little is known about how different groups can be said to possess and to exercise choices about their ethnic identities. By focusing in particular on the comparative experiences and positions of African Americans and Asian Americans in the USA, it is argued that, rather than representing polar opposite experiences, these groups encounter and grapple with racialized images and stereotypes of themselves which are both positive and negative. It is difficult to conclude that some groups possess more ethnic options than others in any straightforward way.

In chapter 3, the tensions and the politics surrounding individuals' negotiation of ethnic identities, as members of ethnic groups, are explored. Groups are collectivities which must negotiate the meanings and images associated with themselves. Within groups, there is dissension and debate about these issues, and individual members of groups must negotiate their own desired identities in relation to the images and meanings associated with their group. This chapter examines the ways in which they can establish criteria for membership, including the ways in which they can demand "authentic" behavior from their individual members. It also considers the strategies which individuals adopt in claiming particular identities.

In chapter 4, we explore the question of how we should theorize and categorize the ethnic identities of mixed race people. This question is especially pertinent, given the significant growth of mixed people and relationships in both Britain and the USA. The debates surrounding the theorizing of mixed identities reveal the complex, politically contested dynamics involved in people choosing their ethnic identities.

For instance, mixed people can be subject to pressures to affiliate primarily with one race over another, and to prove their ethnic and racial authenticity. In both countries, there has been growing debate about whether mixed people, regardless of their particular parentage, share their mixedness in common.

How does the internal diversification of ethnic minority groups shape the ways in which they negotiate and assert their ethnic identities? Chapter 5 examines the impact of class differentiation and ongoing patterns of immigration for the formation of ethnic groups in the USA. For instance, what it means to be Black and African American has been hotly debated in light of the growth of the Black middle class in the USA and the growth of Black immigrant communities which want to distinguish themselves from African Americans. This chapter also discusses the debate about who is and is not Black in Britain. We consider the implications of internal group differentiation and the tensions regarding the ways in which groups attempt to represent themselves in relation to the wider society.

Chapter 6 looks at how the dynamics surrounding ethnic identity have been fundamentally shaped by generational change: that is, by the emergence of second (and even third) generations in Britain and the USA. This chapter considers whether the second generation can be said to possess more choices concerning the assertion of their ethnic identities than do their immigrant parents. Much of the recent literature on the second generation has stressed the strategies they employ in their claims to their ethnic identities, especially given their heightened consciousness of everyday experiences of racism and exclusion. It is argued that second-generation individuals forge and conceive of their ethnic identities within the context of globalization and the emergence of diasporic communities around the world.

It would be difficult to make sense of how ethnic minority groups and individuals negotiate and assert their ethnic identities without addressing current beliefs and understandings about groups' opportunities and constraints, including their experiences of racism and racial disadvantage. In chapter 7, we examine how the idea of racial hierarchy informs our understandings of the positions, privileges, and experiences of ethnic minority groups, including their ability to assert ethnic identities of their choosing. In both the USA and Britain, there are growing debates about the legitimacy of understanding groups' positions and experiences in terms of their placement along a racial hierarchy.

Chapter 8 poses two key questions: can we, and should we, transcend the language and philosophy of race and racial difference? Is it possible that we are heading for a "post-ethnic" or "post-racial" world?

I

Ethnic Identities: Choices and Constraints

The continuing significance of ethnicity

In recent years, there has been a great deal of attention, both academically and popularly, to the meanings, experiences, and politics surrounding ethnic identity. "Ethnicity" and notions of cultural difference and marginality are "in," as shown by the proliferation of studies concerning ethnic identity from the 1990s onwards (Sharma, Hutnyk, and Sharma 1996). In part, this is due to the fact that the racial and ethnic landscapes of many Western societies such as the USA and Britain have been undergoing major changes in the late twentieth and early twenty-first centuries. The 1990 US Census revealed that nearly one in every four Americans is of African, Asian, Latino, or Native American ancestry (Omi and Winant 1996: 474). In Britain, the size of the ethnic minority population has grown in the last decade. There were an estimated 4 million ethnic minorities in mid-2000, or 7.1 percent of the total population. This compares with 3.1 million, or 5.5 percent of the total population in 1991 (Scott, Pearce, and Goldblatt 2001).[1] Furthermore, in 1998, the *Guardian* newspaper featured a front-page heading heralding the emergence of "beige Britain," in light of the significant growth of mixed race relationships and individuals (Parker and Song 2001a). These major demographic changes have impacted upon the ways in which we understand concepts such as ethnic identity and race.

But what are ethnic identities, and why have they remained important? The answers to these questions are by no means simple or straightforward. There is no one universally accepted definition of ethnicity used by academics or by ordinary people. According to Martin Bulmer (1986: 54): "An 'ethnic group' is a collectivity within a larger society having real or putative common ancestry, memories of a shared past, and a cultural focus on one or more symbolic elements which define the group's identity, such as kinship, religion, language, shared territory, nationality or physical appearance. Members of an ethnic group are conscious of belonging to the group." One important aspect of this definition is that it is a group's belief in its common ancestry and its members' perception and self-consciousness that they constitute a group which matter, and not any actual evidence of their cultural distinctiveness as a group.

There has been much debate about the basis and meanings of ethnic attachments and allegiances. A "primordial" understanding of ethnicity suggests that it exists naturally, due to common heritage, and is basically an extension of blood ties (Geertz 1963). According to Pierre van den Berghe (1978), much of ethnic identity is predetermined at birth, and is not actively chosen or acquired over one's lifetime.

However, many recent analysts of ethnicity have argued that ethnicity has no natural or objective existence as such, and have stressed its socially constructed, rather than primordial, nature (see Barth 1969; O. Patterson 1975; Wallman 1978; Hein 1994; Lal 2001).[2] Primordial views of ethnicity are now largely criticized for positing a culturally essentialist view of ethnicity, in which the characteristics and cultures of ethnic groups are seen as static and unchanging. As Yancey, Ericksen, and Juliani (1976) have argued, ethnicity is emergent, and ethnic groups can change their boundaries and criteria for membership. According to "situational" theorists of ethnicity, ethnic solidarity and ethnic attachments are not constant or guaranteed, because they can fluctuate over time (Wallman 1978; Nagel 1994). Ethnicity can be activated in particular times and situations by material and other interests; that is, people can use their ethnic affiliations and ties as resources in a variety of contexts, in response to current needs, or in terms of competition with outside groups (A. Cohen 1974; Yancey, Ericksen, and Juliani 1976; O. Patterson 1975).

The exploration of ethnic identities is of prime importance today, because ethnic identities are not simply and gradually eroding in significance, as some analysts in the past predicted. Whether in the case of the enduring ethnic identities of immigrant populations or the various nationalist movements which are motivated by strong feelings about a group's ethnic distinctiveness (Calhoun 1994), such as manifest by the Quebeqois secessionist movement in Canada and the "ethnic cleansing" that occurred in the former Yugoslavia, there is much, varied evidence of the importance of what we call "ethnic identity" and "ethnicity." If anything, ethnicity and ethnic differentiation have been resurgent throughout the world (Banton 1997; Cornell and Hartmann 1998).

In *Economy and Society*, Max Weber (1968) predicted that ethnicity would decline in the context of modernity, which he saw as marked by the rationalization of human action and organization; ethnic attachments were considered "communal" and were not expected to thrive in modern societies, which would gradually displace such putatively traditional relationships. American theories of assimilation were based on the experiences of White European immigrants to the USA. Over the centuries, the USA had absorbed immigrants from various parts of Europe, and they had gradually gained their rights and become accepted into the wider society, in spite of the significant nativist hostility and prejudice they had encountered upon their arrival (see Warner and Srole 1945; M. Gordon 1964). Thus, while Italian, Irish, Polish, and German immigrants, to name a few, initially encountered scorn and prejudice, successive generations of these White immigrants were gradually accepted as bona fide Americans (see Alba 1990; Waters 1990). Based on the experiences of White European-ancestry immigrants to the USA, the straight-line assimilation model predicted that non-White immigrant groups and ethnic minority groups would also be able to assimilate into the mainstream fabric of America, once they had learned the English language and adopted American ways of living and behaving. It was believed that this, in turn, would contribute to the reduction of discrimination and prejudice against them. In this way it was believed that such groups' ethnicity would gradually wane in significance (M. Gordon 1964).

However, many empirical studies now make clear that a straight-line theory of assimilation does not apply to the case of many non-White immigrants or ethnic minority groups in either the USA or Britain. For instance, African Americans tended to be excluded in considerations about assimilation, which were modeled on the experiences of White European immigrants (Glazer 1993). African American culture was perceived to be pathological, thus preventing African Americans from entering into the mainstream culture and values of the USA (see Myrdal 1944). Theories of assimilation were also criticized for treating immigrant individuals as the passive objects of the "host" environment, rather than as active agents who can creatively adapt and negotiate their ethnic identities.

There is increasing evidence that there is no uniform linear process by which successive generations of immigrant groups are integrated into the wider society; nor is there any conclusive evidence that their ethnic identities are necessarily diluted in a straightforward way over time. In contrast with the straight-line model, the segmented assimilation model argues that many post-1965 immigrants may achieve economic and social mobility through the retention of their immigrant cultures and community ties (Portes and Zhou 1993). Furthermore, embracing one's ethnic identity may be associated with higher self-esteem and the ability to deal with discrimination (Chavira and Phinney 1991). Many analysts on both sides of the Atlantic claim that ethnicity continues to be not only a central aspect of minority peoples' identities, but also a fundamental basis for divisions in most contemporary societies.

Ethnic distinctiveness has endured even when identifiably distinctive cultural practices associated with particular groups have declined (Cornell and Hartmann 1998). For instance, most third- and fourth-generation descendants of Armenian immigrants to the USA do not regularly engage in culturally distinctive practices which would be considered "Armenian," but, nevertheless, have tended to uphold a strong sense of their Armenian heritage (Bakalian 1993). Significantly, although these American-born Armenians do not use the Armenian language in their everyday interactions, or eat Armenian food on a regular basis, or necessarily partner with Armenian people, they still feel Armenian. This example reveals that what it *means* to be Armenian is subject to change, and is re-created and reinvented over time. Ironically, in the case of many White Americans of European heritage, the fact that they have assimilated so well has meant that many of them wish to claim a European ethnic ancestry, such as Norwegian or Italian, which makes them feel distinctive and special – and not just "ordinary" Americans (Waters 1990).

However, unlike most White ethnics, many ethnic minority people are often attributed not only ethnic, but also racial, labels and images by others – whether or not these labels and images accord with their own ethnic and racial identities. Central to the process by which ethnic minority people are labeled and categorized is the notion of "race" and the processes involved in racialization.

The intertwining of race and ethnicity

We have briefly examined what is meant by ethnicity. But what is race? The concept of race has tended to refer to a biologically (and genetically) distinct subpopulation of a species (Cornell and Hartmann 1998). In Western societies such as Britain and the USA, notions of race and of racial difference were premised upon classification systems which posited the relative superiority and inferiority of particular groups, with White people considered the superior race. According to this way of thinking, race was associated with distinct hereditary characteristics, so that differences in intelligence and sexuality, for instance, were to be understood to be racial in character (Cornell and Hartmann 1998). Based on a racial classification system which emphasized inherent differences between the races, White people's concerns about racial mixing, especially concerning the putative contamination of the White race (see Stonequist 1937), were widespread in both the USA and Britain throughout the nineteenth and the first half of the twentieth centuries (Furedi 2001). While the existence of race used to be legitimated on pseudo-scientific grounds, it is now recognized as the arbitrary grouping of dissimilar people based upon phenotypical differences such as skin color and hair type (King 1981; Lewontin, Rose, and Kamin 1984).

Although the terms "ethnicity" and "race" are sometimes used interchangeably and together, some analysts have offered analytical distinctions between the two: Pierre Van den Berghe (1978), for example, makes a clear-cut distinction between the two terms. "Race" is said to be "socially defined but on the basis of physical criteria," whereas an ethnic group is "socially defined on the basis of cultural criteria." In a more sophisticated formulation, Martin Bulmer (1986) notes that "ethnicity" is a more "inclusive" term than "race," because while "race" is predicated (however spuriously) on biological membership of a particular group, ethnic groups are generally seen as having more fluid and blurred boundaries (Wallman 1978). This is because members of ethnic groups can change the boundaries of ethnic group membership – since they are socially constructed and negotiated boundaries.

However, the apparently neat and sensible distinctions drawn above start to blur when we consider that, like ethnicity, race is a social construct without an objective existence of its own – race too is a form of "imagined grouping" (Goldberg 1992). Even people's perceptions of other people's physical markers, and the determination of which racial categories they belong to, are subjective. In this way, racial categories such as White, Black or Asian have no enduring meanings. Moreover, some of the groups identified in the past as races – for instance, Jewish people – are now commonly referred to as ethnic groups (Sollors 1989). A number of analysts have argued that, as a social construct, race has no fixed meaning, and is constructed and transformed sociohistorically through competing political projects (see Omi and Winant 1994; Goldberg 1990).

Accompanying the delegitimation of biologically based beliefs about racial differences has been the wider usage of the term "ethnicity." However, just as race can be reified, understandings of ethnicity can also suffer from reification and static, essentialistic characterizations of particular ethnic groups (Gilroy 2000). The reification of ethnicity results from the belief that ethnic groups are somehow endowed with a given set of cultural values and practices – rather than conceiving of ethnicity as something which is continually in process, negotiated, renewed, and subject to a variety of social, economic, and political forces (Steinberg 1981).

The neat analytical distinction between race and ethnicity tends to overlook the slippery and often blurred boundaries between the two terms, and the contingent and changeable ways in which ethnic and racial identities can be experienced, attributed, and claimed. Thus, while I use the terms "ethnic identity" and "ethnicity" in this book, this usage is meant to incorporate the complex intertwining of race and ethnicity. In many American and British discussions of race and ethnic identity, it is actually very difficult to disentangle these two terms, because the meanings and images associated with each tend to bleed into the other.[3] In order to achieve a complex understanding of what we call "ethnic identity," in multiethnic societies such as the USA and Britain, we cannot neatly and completely jettison the notion of race (see chapter 8).

Racial assignment

The seeming omnipresence of race and racial consciousness in many social interactions is difficult to ignore. As Vilna Bashi has pointed out in relation to the USA, "one does not choose between ethnic labels and racial labels. Individuals have *both* ethnic and racial identities, *at one and the same time*" (1998: 962). Bashi continues: "Racial identities are obtained not because one is unaware of the choice of ethnic labels with which to call oneself, but because one is not allowed to be without a race in a racialized society" (1998: 966). Here, the author notes that people possess both ethnic and racial identities, but suggests the primacy of race and racial categorization in the experiences of non-White ethnic minorities in the USA.

Although the notions of race and racial categories, as a scientific basis for differentiating between human beings, have been largely refuted, this has not resulted in the expulsion of this idea from our minds or from academic and political debates and discourses. This is because of the enduring social and political power of race and racial designations in contemporary societies. However arbitrary or non-sensical racial categories may be, our perceptions and understandings of race continue to fundamentally shape people's lives and interactions in contemporary multiethnic societies. Race has a real existence to the extent that, although the meanings associated with it differ across societies, it is part of our common parlance and a marker used by both ordinary individuals and institutions alike.

This is especially evident in the ways in which people attribute racial, as well as ethnic, characteristics and identities to each other. As Michael Omi and Howard Winant (1994) have argued, race, in addition to sex and age, is one of the first things that is noticed about someone. Upon seeing someone for the first time, we may consciously or unconsciously categorize them in racial terms. For instance, in Britain, one might immediately register the entrance of someone who appears to be "Asian" (meaning of South Asian origin), though we may or may not have any conception of this person's ethnicity or religious background. Although this Asian person may consider herself to be second-generation Pakistani British, her specific ethnicity may not be recognized or legitimated in many of her interactions with others.

Although there is a growing tendency in Britain to pejoratively distinguish Muslims from other Asians (as the British National Party leader Nick Griffin has done in the aftermath of the riots in the Northern cities in the spring and summer of 2001), Asians are still often regarded in racial, as opposed to ethnic, terms. Racial categorizations of people can sometimes, though not always, "trump" or override ethnic designations. That is, people's ethnic identities may be subsumed within broader racial identities which are imposed by others. For instance, West Indian immigrants in the USA may find themselves labeled Black, first and foremost because the White majority may not recognize their ethnic identities as Jamaicans or Trinidadians, but rather see them in racial terms, as Black people. While many Black Jamaicans, Trinidadians, and Haitians think of themselves in these specific ethno-national terms, they can also be highly aware of being seen as Black in many social contexts in the USA. As argued earlier, we cannot always or easily separate race and ethnicity, because people's ethnic identities are often informed and shaped by the ways in which they are racially categorized.

Various analysts have argued that racialized minority groups experience "racial assignment" (Cornell and Hartmann 1998). That is, in most White majority societies, minority groups have tended to be arbitrarily placed in racial categories, vis-à-vis the dominant White group. Racial assignment by the wider society involves a form of "othering," which objectifies and essentializes subordinate groups in relation to a limited set of characteristics (Bhabha 1990a). In this way, the power to mark and classify certain groups is a significant exercise of symbolic power (Hall 1997).[4] As a result, a number of analysts have observed that members of many ethnic minority groups are often limited in the assertion of their desired ethnic identities (Waters 1990, 1996).

Central to the process by which ethnic minority groups are labeled and categorized by others is the institutionalization of race and racial difference (Dominguez 1998). The existence and institutionalization of seemingly natural racial categories belies the fact that race and the recognition of racial categories reflect a system of power which constructs and gives meanings to racial groups on the basis of recognized physical differences (Banton 1997; R. Miles 1989). Under South Africa's apartheid regime, the South African government officially recognized four races: White, African, Colored, and Asian (Cornell and Hartmann 1998: 22). This institutionalization of four races determined a stratified order in which White South Africans were the privileged elite, and the Africans were the poorest, most disadvantaged group, despite the fact that the Africans were the numerical majority in the country.[5]

As in South Africa, in both the USA and Britain, the historical use of racial categories has been arbitrary and changeable, and they have been employed in such a way as to convenience and privilege the dominant (White) population. Non-White ethnic minorities are especially subject to forms of racial assignment because, while most White people in the USA and Britain represent the norm, which requires no racial marking of them as human beings, race acts as a marker which tends to differentiate and essentialize ethnic minorities in a denigrating fashion.

Exercising ethnic options

In comparison with non-White people subject to forms of racial assignment, Mary Waters (1990) has argued that many White people in the USA possess an array of "ethnic options." Earlier generations of immigrants to the USA, such as the Irish and those from southern and eastern parts of Europe, such as Italians, were denigrated and regarded as distinct, unassimilable races. However, in the contemporary USA, groups such as Italian and Irish Americans are seen (along with those of English, Scandinavian, or German backgrounds) as belonging to a White race (Waters 1990; Lieberson 1988; Steinberg 1981). For most White Americans, their European ethnic heritage is no longer central to their sense of selves or to their everyday lives. Rather, White Americans think of themselves primarily in national terms, as Americans.

According to Waters, the adoption of ethnic identities by Americans of European descent, such as Irish Americans or Italian Americans, is optional, because they are able to invoke their ethnicity when, and in the ways, they wish. In other words, White Americans' ethnicity is purely symbolic (Gans 1979), and its celebration is without real social costs. For instance, White Americans of Irish heritage may like to celebrate St. Patrick's Day, or frequent an Irish bar, but their Irishness does not figure centrally in their lives. They can enjoy and be proud of their Irish heritage, but this is episodic and, for the most part, superficial (Waters 1990). Richard Alba (1988), who has characterized Italian American ethnicity as being in the "twilight" of ethnicity, and Zenner (1988), who has argued that Jewishness is largely a matter of individual preference, have made similar arguments about the directions of White American ethnicity. That is, ethnicity is not something that influences these groups' lives unless they want it to.

Such an argument could be extended to the case of many White English people, who, if they wish, may invoke other European heritages, such as French, German, or Scandinavian ancestry. Like their White American counterparts, White English people can simply claim an English or British identity, which draws upon a dominant understanding of English and British nationality. Unlike the USA, however, Britain is characterized by specific nationalist movements by White minorities (such as the Welsh, Irish, and Scottish), who assert distinctive ethnic heritages and identities (Jenkins 1997).

Nevertheless, in both countries, ethnicity for many White Americans and Britons (and especially White English) may be said to constitute a "passive," as opposed to an "active" identity (Bradley 1996). In contrast with most White people, members of non-White minority groups are likely to experience their ethnicity as an active identity because, as Bradley notes, "active identification often occurs as a defence against the actions of others or when an individual is conscious of being defined in a negative way. Active identities are promoted by the experience of discrimination" (1996: 25–6). Using this distinction between active and passive identity, many racialized minorities are constantly aware of (and made to feel) their ethnic identities in a variety of social situations, whether it be walking into a predominantly White lecture hall or simply walking down the street.

The experiences and meanings of ethnicity can differ substantially for members of various groups; ethnicity is not uniformly important or a fundamental part of everyone's lives. A distinction which Stephen Cornell and Douglas Hartmann make is useful here: "A comprehensive or 'thick' ethnic or racial tie is one that organizes a great deal of social life and both individual and collective action. A less comprehensive or 'thin' ethnic or racial tie is one that organizes relatively little of social life and action" (1998: 73). In the case of Italian Americans in the USA, ethnicity today is experienced as a relatively "thin" identity because, although it may be celebrated and significant in some respects, it doesn't tend to fundamentally structure their lives today (1998: 74).

Waters has argued that non-White minorities cannot exercise ethnic options in the same way as White Americans, because racial identities are constantly imposed upon non-White minorities.

> The symbolic (white) ethnic tends to think that all groups are equal; everyone has a background that is their right to celebrate and pass on to their children. This leads to the conclusion that all identities are equal and all identities in some sense are interchangeable – "I'm Italian-American, you're Polish-American. I'm Irish-American, you're African-American".
>
> (Waters 1996: 449)

Waters concludes that "all ethnicities are not equal, all are not symbolic, costless, and voluntary" (1990: 160). For racialized minorities such as Asian Americans and African Americans, their identities, and their lives more generally, are significantly shaped by their race and their national origins. While White Americans of European descent can be said to celebrate "individualistic symbolic ethnic identities," racialized groups are faced with a "socially enforced and imposed racial identity" (Waters 1996: 449). While racialized groups must constantly contend with stereotypes of themselves, White people tend to be represented in White culture as being complex, changing, and infinitely varied individuals (Dyer 1997).

However, the suggestion that ethnic minority people possess few or no ethnic options needs further exploration and thought. In this book, I critically explore the idea that ethnic minorities, broadly speaking, are able, although in limited ways, to exercise ethnic options. While it would be difficult to deny the structuring force of dominant racial discourses and stereotypes as they are applied to many ethnic minority groups and individuals, Waters's analysis is perhaps too categorical in polarizing the ethnic options of White people and those of racialized ethnic minorities. What need more exploration are the diverse ways in which ethnic minority groups and individuals negotiate and work at asserting their desired ethnic identities.

Assertions of ethnic identity and choice

How do ethnic minority groups challenge undesirable regimes of representation or assert ethnic identities of their choosing? Not only are representations of groups constantly subject to change because of shifts in meaning, but members of groups vulnerable to racial stereotyping can invert or manipulate the associations and meanings of particular ethnic identities. For instance, in Hanif Kureishi's novel *The Buddha of Suburbia* (1991), which chronicles the experiences of Kareem, the teenage son of a White English mother and an Indian father in suburban Britain, Kareem's father develops an avid interest in Buddhism. As a bored civil servant by day, he dons a turban by night and adopts a Buddhist pose with his English friends and neighbors who come to observe his "Buddhist" practices. What unfolds is that Kareem's father knowingly provides a performance of Indianness. This performance of being both Indian and Buddhist is all the more outrageous because his father is no Buddhist, but rather raised as a Hindu; that is, he adopts the persona of what he thinks White Britons conceive of as a "real" Indian. This example suggests that people can "play" with the stereotypes they encounter.

Ethnic minority groups (and the individual members of these groups) are active in re-creating and reinventing the meanings and practices associated with themselves. Much of the recent research on ethnicity underlines its socially constructed and highly politicized nature; for instance, analysts such as Werner Sollors (1989) and Joanne Nagel (1986) have referred to the "invention of ethnicity" and the "political construction of ethnicity," respectively.

In addition to Waters's notion of ethnic options, other recent scholarship on ethnic identity, such as that on mixed race people, has highlighted the idea of choice and of choosing ethnic identity (see Leonard 1992). For instance, the historian David Hollinger has argued for a "postethnic" perspective, which emphasizes the importance of individuals' voluntary affiliation with ethnic groups, rather than racially prescribed categorizations of people: "A postethnic perspective denies neither history nor biology, nor the need for affiliations, but it does deny that history and biology provide a set of clear orders for the affiliations we are to make" (1995: 13).

There is now more interest and emphasis on the *active* ways in which people may shape and assert their own ethnic identities, and the strategic ways in which they invoke their ethnicity. For instance, some analysts such as Ann Swidler (1986) have talked about how cultural practices and resources provide a kind of "tool kit" of symbols, stories, and rituals which can be used by individuals in a variety of ways, including their efforts to solve a range of problems they encounter. Social psychologists also point to the use of "social creativity strategies," which involve the development of new forms of intergroup comparisons that will create positive, rather than negative in-group identity (see Murrell 1998: 196). And although the choices around ethnic identity are limited, and are structurally bounded, there is a recognition that choices are still made. According to Joanne Nagel, "Since ethnicity changes situationally, the individual carries a portfolio of ethnic identities that are more or less salient in various situations and vis-à-vis various audiences. As audiences change, the socially-defined array of ethnic choices open to the individual changes" (1994: 154). The notion of being able to choose one's ethnic identity is a useful tool for examining the ways in which minority groups and individuals negotiate and participate in these processes.

Much theorizing on ethnic identity in the past has been problematic because of the emphasis upon lineage and one's past and origins. What is striking about much of the new work on ethnic and racial identities is the insistence upon the present, and the changeability of identity formations through time – for example, over one's lifetime, and in different geographical spaces and contexts – despite the often long shadow of the past.

Influenced by postmodernism, the themes of assertion and choice concerning ethnic identity are timely, given both the discrediting of old paradigms and the emergence of new scholarship which stresses the situational, contingent, and changeable aspects of identity formation and maintenance (Back 1995). According to Stuart Hall, for instance, "Cultural identity . . . is a matter of 'becoming' as well as 'being'. . . . Far from being eternally fixed in some essentialized past [it is] subject to the continuous play of history, culture and power" (Hall 1990: 225).[6]

While the postmodernist stress upon choice and the conceptualization of people's identities as relatively free-floating have been welcome in terms of dismissing static and essentialist notions of identity, there has not been enough consideration of the dynamics which both open up and constrain people's identities – hence my focus upon assertion and choice, and the ways in which such choices are negotiated by a multitude of factors at work in the larger society.

It is widely understood that a complex and changing spectrum of racial exclusion and prejudice, which is based upon the recognition of racial and ethnic differences, still exists in White majority societies such as Britain and the USA (Solomos and Back 1994). Various forms of exclusion and discrimination, rather than ebbing away, are persistent, albeit constantly changing, and are important in shaping ethnic minority people's sense of their ethnic and racial identities. While there is no one accepted definition of racism in either Britain or the USA, there is fairly wide agreement that racist acts and ideologies take multiple forms and are constantly mutating over time (Goldberg 1990).[7]

Many analysts have observed the emergence of "cultural racism" (Barker 1981). Rather than invoke politically incorrect views of biological superiority and inferiority as the basis of racial difference, it is now much more common for people to marginalize or exclude ethnic minorities by invoking the notion of cultural difference (e.g. Margaret Thatcher's stated fear of being "swamped by people with a different culture"). This is done by using narrowly drawn discourses of nation and patriotism. For instance, some years ago, Black British cricket players' allegiance to their British team was questioned in a sports magazine because they were Black. The questioning of their loyalty and commitment was aptly captured in the headline to an article about the ensuing controversy: "Please try harder" (*Guardian*, 4 July 1995). As Paul Gilroy has argued in *There Ain't No Black in the Union Jack* [the British flag] (1987), being Black *and* British is often conceived of as being mutually exclusive. Ethnic identities are thus importantly, though not exclusively, informed by experiences of racial prejudice and discrimination.

Nevertheless, the recognition of the power of racial categories and designations should not result in the belief that ethnic labels and identities are simply blotted out by the master status known as race. Although ethnic minority people are subject to often denigrating experiences associated with racial categorization, racial assignment is actually key to understanding the formation and *assertion* of ethnic identity: racial meanings and discourses, in this sense, inform (though not exclusively) people's understandings of their ethnic identities and of who they are more generally (Cornell and Hartmann 1998).

Experiences of racial discrimination and stereotyping over time can result in the reinforcement of ethnic identities (Ogbu 1990; Jayaweera 1993). But an understanding of the formation and maintenance of ethnic identities solely in terms of racial exclusion and denigration is overly deterministic. As important as they are, experiences of racial discrimination do not tell us everything about the ways in which ethnic identity is experienced by people; it is much more complex than that.

By focusing on the concepts of agency and choice, I do not mean to suggest a simplistic, unfettered, and individualistic understanding of choice. I use the term "agency" to emphasize the interaction between micro-level (an individual's actions, for instance) and macro-level (the wider society) processses (Giddens 1984). Individual agency impacts upon social structure and processes, and vice versa. Actors are able to create projects or find solutions to deal with structures that constrain their choices and intentions (Ortner 1996). Such an approach avoids the pitfalls of conceiving of either an unfettered actor or an actor without agency, who is simply a product of her subject position in social life.

The following chapters examine groups' ethnic options, which are negotiated collectively, and the ways in which individual members of groups go about asserting their ethnic identities vis-à-vis their coethnics and the wider society. The notion of negotiating ethnic identity is useful in making sense of the real limitations and structures which bear on such processes, and the politicized interaction between groups and individuals in the determination of their own and others' ethnic identities. By emphasizing the negotiation and assertion of ethnic identity, we are also reminded that even relatively disadvantaged ethnic minority people are active agents who participate in the shaping of their own ethnic identities.

2

Comparing Minorities' Ethnic Options

Do ethnic minorities have ethnic options?

Ethnic minority groups are subject to various forms of racialized definitions and representations of them in the wider society. The state plays a key role in the process of ethnic labeling and the construction of ethnic and racial categories (Spickard 1989; Omi and Winant 1994; Nagel 1994). Racialized groups must also contend with dominant representations of them in the media and in forms of popular culture, which can play a constitutive role in the formation of their identities (hooks 1992). For example, in Britain, the moral panic surrounding the representation of Asian youth and "gangs" is gendered, and it is young Asian men who are widely branded as being trouble-making "fundamentalists" who, it is imagined, will go and join Al-Qaeda if given half a chance (Alexander 2000). In comparison with young men, whose public presence on the streets is closely and worryingly watched (Keith 1995), young Asian women in Britain are constantly depicted in the setting of the domestic, "private" sphere, as victims of oppressive expectations that they enter into arranged marriages (Alexander 2000).

The dominant images and meanings associated with specific groups are also important because they can be internalized by groups themselves. For example, in a study of a multiracial high school in Chicago, Grace Kao (2000) found particular group images and stereotypes associated with Black, White, Hispanic, and Asian students: Hispanic students were often associated with manual labor, Asian students were perceived as being quiet and not athletic, and Black students were perceived as wanting to have fun and being good at certain sports, such as track. These group images had profound implications for these students' academic aspirations and achievements. Group images also tend to define areas of competency in relation to other school activities, such as sports and drama, and can influence students' choices about the areas in which they participate. Only White students were not significantly affected by group stereotypes, and they did not have to worry about fitting into a particular group image (Kao 2000: 428). By comparison, non-White students were aware of whether their behaviors and aspirations "fit" or diverged from the stereotypes applied to their particular ethnic group. Thus dominant stereotypes can serve as behavioral scripts for subordinated minority groups, so as to become self-fulfilling prophecies (Sidanius and Pratto 1999: 44).

Nevertheless, as I argue in this chapter, rather than simply being the products of racial assignment, minority groups' images and identities form in interaction between assignment, which is imposed by others in the wider society, and assertion, which is a claim to ethnicity made by groups themselves (Cornell and Hartmann 1998; Nagel 1994; Waters 1990; Espiritu 1992). While they are not impervious to the debilitating effects of negative stereotypes and imagery, racialized minorities can and do play key roles in resisting unwanted meanings and images associated with them (Kibria 2000; Omi and Winant 1994; Solomos and Back 1996; Fernandez-Kelly and Schauffler 1994; Hall 1997).

For example, groups can engage in a variety of "disidentifying" strategies (Goffman 1963: 44), which can be employed in order to "break up an otherwise coherent picture"; the use of disidentifiers disrupts the often stereotypical assumptions people make about one another, on the basis, say, of race or gender. Also, a number of "trans-coding" strategies are possible in challenging dominant representations of race, including taking an existing term or category and reappropriating it with new meanings (Hall 1997: 270). One such strategy is to substitute a range of positive images of Black people, Black life and culture (e.g. "Black is beautiful") for some of the negative imagery which is used in the popular representation of Black people.

Ethnic minority groups actively participate in efforts to counter and reshape the meanings and images associated with their ethnic identities. In this sense, I argue that minority groups can possess ethnic options (Waters 1990). Most people can grasp the idea of *individuals* making choices about their ethnic identities, based upon an array of factors which structure an individual's choice, such as their ethnicity, class, gender, nationality, etc. To discuss individual ethnic options without reference to group options, however, makes no sense whatsoever, given how important group membership is in structuring or limiting individual options.

The notion of minority group options is theoretically complicated because while groups are, at one level, comprised of individual members exercising ethnic options, as an aggregate concept, group options cannot adequately be understood as simply the sum of individual members' options (see chapter 3 for a discussion of group dynamics). There has been very little elaboration of what ethnic options actually are. No one has addressed what it actually means for *ethnic minorities* to possess ethnic options. Remember that Mary Waters's (1990) analysis centers on White Americans' possession of ethnic options, by virtue of their privilege and economic power as White people (see chapter 1). Thus a comparison of the ethnic options of various groups is an important area of study.[1]

Ethnic options are presumably constituted by the nature and range of choices available to a group. Since ethnic minority groups differ according to many variables, it would seem reasonable to think that some groups may have a wider range of choices about their ethnic identities than others. It may also be reasonable to think that ethnic options are shaped by the kinds of ethnic labels and stereotypes associated with particular groups. Furthermore, to possess ethnic options in any real sense must mean that groups are actually able to claim at least some images and identities they desire, in a variety of social contexts and especially in public spaces. In other words, the ethnic identities asserted by groups need to be recognized and validated by the wider society – otherwise, the term "ethnic options" carries no real weight or significance.

In this chapter, we examine what it means for an ethnic minority *group* to possess ethnic options. In what ways are groups' ethnic options similar or different from one another? Many factors are likely to shape a group's ethnic options. For instance, various ethnic categories are characterized by differing degrees of stigma or advantage attached to them (Nagel 1994). By focusing on the experiences of African Americans and Asian Americans in the USA, this chapter examines the ways in which ethnic minority groups encounter and manipulate a range of ethnic identities. We will also consider whether some groups can be said to possess more ethnic options than others.

Differential ethnic options?

These questions arise because of a growing body of research, particularly in the USA, in which such comparisons among ethnic minority groups are being made. In particular, the ethnic options of Asian Americans and African Americans have recently received attention from various scholars. In her study of second-generation Chinese Americans' and Korean Americans' ethnic identities, Nazli Kibria (2000; 2002) implies that Asian Americans may possess *more* ethnic options (though this is not the terminology used) than African Americans. Two types of arguments have been made by her and other analysts to suggest this. First, in comparison with African Americans, who are said to possess few or no ethnic options to speak of, Kibria argues that Asian Americans have recourse to ethnic and national backgrounds, for instance as Korean, Chinese, Japanese, or Vietnamese people. Kibria notes that, "As an immigrant group, Asian Americans have not experienced the forced obliteration of ethnic differences that has been part of the historical experience of African Americans" (2000: 93). Unlike African Americans (whose ethnic ties with Africa were wrested from them), Asian Americans are regarded as "authentic ethnics" by the wider society (Kibria 2000). For instance, they are expected by the wider society to maintain distinctive cultural practices (including speaking an Asian language) and to be knowledgeable about various aspects of East Asia. This expectation applies even to third- or fourth-generation Asian Americans, who are often believed to be newly arrived immigrants (Tuan 1998).

Although both African Americans and Asian Americans suffer forms of racialization imposed by the wider society, in certain situations, Asian Americans are able to counter racialization as Asians by claiming a particular ethnic heritage. For instance, Kibria relates how one Chinese American woman, Meg, who was working as a youth counselor in a predominantly African American neighborhood, made a point of saying that she was of Chinese, not Korean, heritage (2000: 84–5). Meg made this distinction because she was concerned about being mistaken as Korean, and thus incurring hostility from African Americans in light of the various tensions and conflicts reported between Korean American shop owners and African American customers in cities such as New York and Los Angeles (see Min 1996; Abelmann and Lie 1995). Kibria argues that Meg, in this instance, was able to transcend racialization as simply Asian and to assert her Chinese ethnicity in a way which bettered her relationship with African American youths.

Kibria's work (1997, 1998) on Asian Americans' ethnic identities has been important and insightful in highlighting the often contradictory and multiple pressures they face in the framing and assertion of their ethnic identities. On the whole, I do not disagree with her valuable analysis of Asian Americans' ethnic options. However,

Kibria's (2000) more recent work is premised upon a seemingly innocuous notion – that African Americans possess few or no ethnic options. Although her discussion centers primarily upon Asian Americans, I am interested here in probing the suggestion that Asian Americans possess more latitude and choice than do African Americans in the assertion of their desired ethnic identities.

By pointing to the ways in which recourse to ethnic ancestry can be a resource, Kibria is not suggesting that Asian Americans can then unproblematically and easily assert the ethnic identities of their choosing. There is important documentation of the "ethnic bind" that Asian Americans encounter: while they wish to establish themselves as bona fide Americans, they are also expected by the wider society to be authentically ethnic. Nevertheless, there is a clear contrast between them and African Americans, who are characterized as being unable to claim a specific ethnic ancestry; in this way, African Americans, it is suggested, cannot capitalize on their ethnic backgrounds in the way that Asian Americans, in some situations, are able to do.

Other analysts have also implied that African Americans possess few or no ethnic options, albeit in different ways, by pointing to this group's racialization as Black. Though she does not explicitly compare African Americans with Asian Americans, Joanne Nagel makes a similar point to that made by Kibria: "And while blacks may make intra-racial distinctions based on ancestry or skin tone, the power of race as a socially defining status in U.S. society makes these internal differences rather unimportant in interracial settings in comparison to the fundamental black/white color boundary" (1994: 156). Mary Waters (1996) and Mia Tuan (1998) also highlight the case of African Americans as *the* paradigmatic example of racial assignment in which they possess few or no ethnic options. Although Tuan does not suggest that Asian Americans possess a wider range of ethnic options than African Americans, she notes that "Since ethnicity has long since faded as a salient marker for blacks, the issue of ethnic options is irrelevant" (1998: 6–7). Tuan suggests that African American people effectively have no *ethnic* options to speak of because their *racial status* is paramount in the eyes of mainstream American society, and the attribution of race effectively trumps Black people's ethnic status. Unlike African Americans, for whom racial identity is allegedly key, and for whom "the issue of ethnic options is irrelevant" (1998: 7), Asian Americans are attributed both racial and ethnic qualities. Asian Americans are regarded as a distinct racial group, but they are also seen as possessing a distinctive ethnicity as well. This is evidenced by the fact that some Asian Americans, particularly immigrants, retain distinct ethnic practices, for instance in terms of language, food, or forms of socializing. Recent research also suggests that young Asian American professionals may retain various forms of ethnic attachment despite a high level of social assimilation into a predominantly White world of employment and friendships (see Min and Kim 2000).

But is it in fact the case that ethnic options are "irrelevant" for African Americans, as argued by Tuan (1998)?[2] If one accepts that ethnic options are indeed irrelevant for African Americans, one would then reasonably conclude that they have few or no ethnic options to speak of. Unlike Kibria, whose argument suggests that Asian Americans have recourse to ethnic identities and heritages not available to African Americans, Tuan's argument is based on the contention that race simply overcomes African Americans' ethnic options.

The second reason advanced for the greater ethnic options of Asian Americans is that certain assumptions about Asians' ethnic options are derived from the fact that they occupy a relatively privileged socioeconomic status in the USA. There is a fairly widespread consensus there that, broadly speaking, White people are at the top of the racial hierarchy, African Americans at the bottom, and Asian Americans, who are regarded as a "model minority," somewhere in between the two groups (Kibria 1998; Feagin 2000; Bashi and McDaniel 1997). Many comparisons have been put forward concerning the differential positionings of Asian Americans, such as those of Korean, Japanese, and Chinese heritage, who are widely perceived to be successful, and of African Americans, many of whom are seen as mired in poverty and welfare dependency (see e.g. Sowell 1981; D'Souza 1995) – although, as Mitch Duneier (1992) has observed, employed working-class African Americans tend to be overlooked, not to mention middle-class African Americans.

Asian Americans have been regarded in some circles as "honorary whites" (a view refuted by Tuan 1998), whose trajectory is said to be similar to that of White European immigrants, as recently suggested by Andrew Hacker (1997). One reason for this is that Asian Americans, on average, have a higher annual family income than White Americans, and certainly higher incomes than African Americans, Hispanics, and Native Americans.[3] Generally speaking, Asian Americans experience lower rates of residential segregation than African Americans (Massey and Denton 1993), and many second-generation Asian Americans have been successful in entering higher education and professional occupations. Furthermore, Asian Americans are said to benefit from their positive image as a model minority who exhibit a strong work ethic and strong family values. This overall (but quite generalized) picture of success has fostered the notion that Asian

Americans may be situated somewhere in between the privileged, dominant position of Whites and the disadvantaged position of many, though not all, Black people.[4]

Nazli Kibria has recently argued that Asian Americans' social mobility (according to various socioeconomic indicators) affords them "some latitude in how to organize and express their ethnic identity" (2000: 80). This important point is not elaborated. While it appears to be sensible, it is by no means obvious or widely understood. It is not clear just how Asian Americans' social mobility enhances their over-all ethnic options when we consider the limitations surrounding the assertion of those options.

Many American studies have shown that African Americans have suffered some of the most pernicious forms of racial discrimination (see Feagin 2000; Duneier 1992; S. Small 1994; Gold and Phillips 1996; Waters 1996), whether it be in the realm of racial violence, employment, university life, or getting served in a restaurant. The reason put forward is that, unlike most other groups, African Americans have suffered slavery and its long aftermath, including Jim Crow laws (Woodward 1966). The African American experience is distinct from the kinds of racial oppression suffered by other groups (see chapter 7). Various analysts have argued that forms of "racial apartheid" apply in the organization of American society (see Hacker 1992). In *American Apartheid*, Douglas Massey and Nancy Denton have argued that, "black segregation is not comparable to the limited and transient segregation experienced by other racial and ethnic groups, now or in the past. No group in the history of the United States has ever experienced the sustained high level of residential segregation that has been imposed on blacks in large American cities for the past fifty years" (1993: 2).

It is not my intention here to dispute the distinctiveness or severity of racial discrimination experienced by African Americans in the past or the present. However, the logic of claims about the relatively privi-leged position of Asian Americans in socioeconomic terms would seem to suggest that Asian Americans are able to exercise ethnic options of their choosing more easily than their African American counterparts. But is this actually the case?

Though the nature of these various authors' arguments differ, they tend to imply one common conclusion: that African Americans possess fewer ethnic options than do Asian Americans. In the remain-der of this chapter, I put forward four reasons why such a conclusion is problematic and, at the very least, inconclusive. In doing so, I draw occasionally on studies of ethnic minority groups in Britain to illustrate my points.

The efficacy of asserting ethno-national distinctions

Nazli Kibria (2000) has asserted that Asian Americans have recourse to specific ethno-national distinctions, which enhances the kinds of choices they have in asserting their desired ethnic identities. The ability to assert a desired ethnic identity is an important element, it would seem, of a group's so-called ethnic options. However, I would question the efficacy of Asian Americans' claims to a specific ethno-national background – though, as with other groups, they can be active in asserting their desired identities in a variety of ways. There are many situations and contexts in American and British society in which recourse to specific ethnic backgrounds is either ignored or ineffective, as noted by Kibria herself. In Britain, for example, being Pakistani, as opposed to Indian (or being Sikh, as opposed to Muslim), simply does not register in many situations in the wider society (Modood 1996). In relation to Asian Americans, possibly the best-known example of this concerns the killing of Vincent Chin (a Chinese engineer killed by disgruntled White unemployed automobile workers who assumed he was Japanese – and thus to blame for the decline of the American auto industry). His murder reminded many Asian Americans of their vulnerabilty to being racialized as generically "Asian." The homogenizing racialization of disparate ethnic identities and labels renders them largely synonymous and interchangeable. While there may be certain instances, like that of Meg, discussed earlier, in which Asian Americans may be able to assert a specific ethnic background with some success, on balance, there is still very little empirical evidence as to just how effective such disidentifying strategies actually are in countering the common racialization of Chinese, Japanese, Korean, and Vietnamese people.

   Mia Tuan (1998: 155) has also noted that while many Asian Americans can exercise some flexibility and choice regarding the retention or discarding of certain cultural practices, this flexibility is largely confined to their *personal lives*. In other words, Asian Americans' freedom to exercise their ethnic options (especially their claims to being Americans) is quite limited in most public arenas and in most interactions with non-Asians. If the exercising of ethnic options is largely limited to people's personal lives, this is a significant constraint on their so-called ethnic options. In this respect, the experiences of racialization which Asian Americans are subject to are very similar to those experienced by African Americans and Black immigrants to the USA. Studies of Black immigrants from the Caribbean and Latin America have found that, despite these immigrants' efforts at resisting the racial label "Black," their claims to specific ethnic and national backgrounds were not recognized in many situations in the wider society (Waters 1994; Fernandez-Kelly and Schauffler 1994).

Economic power and ethnic options

As discussed earlier, Nazli Kibria has argued that the relative social mobility enjoyed by Asian Americans has provided them with "some latitude in how to organize and express their ethnic identity." Many scholars have made the reasonable assumption that a group's ability to exercise its ethnic options is importantly shaped by the overall socioeconomic position of that group. Needless to say, ethnic minority groups have not fared equally well in terms of their material circumstances, as evidenced by a variety of socioeconomic indicators, such as entrance into higher education or success in obtaining desirable jobs and housing. In Britain, a review of socioeconomic indicators suggests that a complicated picture is emerging among ethnic minority groups. For instance, Chinese and Indian men have earnings which are far closer to (if not greater than) those of White men, in comparison with more economically disadvantaged groups such as Pakistanis, Bangladeshis, and African Caribbean men (Modood et al. 1997). But can we then conclude that Chinese and Indian men in Britain are more able than Pakistani, Bangladeshi, and African Caribbean men to "organize and express their ethnic identity"?

The assumed automatic connection between economic privilege and the possession of ethnic options needs further investigation (see chapter 7). It is easy to see how class privilege works, but how does this privilege translate itself into an increased ability to exercise one's ethnic options? In a study of Hispanic young people's identities in the USA, Portes and MacLeod (1996) found that class was an important factor in determining the adoption or rejection of the panethnic category "Hispanic" – a term which can carry pejorative connotations in the USA. The category "Hispanic" includes people of diverse origins, including people of Puerto Rican, Mexican, and Cuban heritage (Lopez and Espiritu 1990). By comparison with those of Puerto Rican and Mexican heritage, many individuals of Cuban heritage in the USA are middle class (many of them are exiles from the Castro regime). Interestingly, many of the Cuban young people studied asserted their Cuban, as opposed to Hispanic identities, while those of Puerto Rican and Mexican origin (who are generally of lower socioeconomic status) were more likely to call themselves Hispanic. In general, respondents from groups of higher average socioeconomic status and longer residence in the USA were more likely to reject the panethnic label "Hispanic." This finding suggests that immigrant groups who are better off are more able to resist "the symbolic violence of unwanted outside labels" (Portes and MacLeod 1996: 536).

It is possible that middle-class people experience less racism, generally speaking, than their working-class counterparts, and may more easily avoid unwanted designations and labels. In their study of mixed young people of Black and White heritage in London, Tizard and Phoenix (1993) found that reports of experiencing racism, which could influence the formation of ethnic identity, were more commonly reported among their working-class respondents than their middle-class respondents.[5] Although the suggestion that middle-class ethnics are more able to exercise their ethnic options than their working-class coethnics (because they are more privileged and less subject to forms of racism) may seem reasonable, there is little empirical evidence on this issue, to date. While middle-class status may help to provide a social buffer to *some* forms of racism, its effects upon identity formation are still quite indeterminate. It is also possible that class resources make more of a difference for some ethnic minority groups than for others.[6]

In practice, despite their relatively privileged socioeconomic position, many Asian Americans, unlike African Americans (or Native Americans), are not accepted as "real" Americans (Kuo 1995; Tuan 1998; Kibria 2000; Espiritu 1992). Thus Asian Americans are often denied a key ethnic option – that of being American. The "success" image of Asian Americans does not reflect their genuine acceptance into mainstream society by the dominant White group (Hurh and Kim 1989: 531). Contrary to classic assimilation theory, which posited that immigrants who fully integrated into the American mainstream would be fully accepted into American society (see M. Gordon 1964; Warner and Srole 1945), being successful in higher education and in the labor market has not automatically led to social acceptance for many Asian Americans. While they are lauded as a model minority, Asian Americans are not taken seriously in public life, and some are even vulnerable to the accusation that they are agents of a foreign power (C. Kim 1999), as in the case of the Asian American scientist Wen Ho Lee.

Just as being in elite professional jobs has not shielded many African Americans from various forms of racism and anxiety about racial marginalization and discrimination (Benjamin 1991), so being in high-level elite posts has not meant acceptance as "real" Americans for Asian Americans; nor has it precluded persistent anxiety about racial discrimination and stereotyping (Tuan 1998; Min and Kim 2000).

Rising levels of anti-Asian violence, which typically involves the characterization of Asian Americans as an unwanted foreign presence, seriously undermine the notion that Asian Americans lead lives which are comparable to those of White Americans. Asian Americans' success in material and educational terms, as well as the success of the Pacific Rim economies, has stoked up sentiments about an "Asian invasion" (Tuan 1998). It is possible, of course, that there may be regional variations (based upon the duration and size of Asian American settlement and the racial and ethnic mix of specific regions) in the degree to which Asian Americans are accepted as bona fide Americans.

Another example of how Asian Americans are not seen as "real" Americans arose in the course of the long O. J. Simpson murder trial, during which third-generation Japanese American judge Lance Ito received a great deal of unflattering media attention. On a radio show, New York Senator Alfonse D'Amato ridiculed Ito's handling of the trial by speaking in singsong pidgin, caricaturing the way in which a newly arrived Asian immigrant learning English would speak. As Tuan points out, Ito, who was "born and raised in the land of the Beach Boys, who speaks little Japanese and is married to a white ethnic woman" (1998: 3), is mocked as a foreigner. Since Ito speaks English in much the same way that a White Californian speaks, such treatment, we can only assume, derives from Ito's appearance as an Asian man and his name, Ito. Unlike the forms of racial discrimination suffered by African Americans (which do not usually include allegations of foreignness or of not "belonging" in the USA), Asian Americans constantly battle with the commonplace belief that they are newly arrived ("fresh off the boat") immigrants who are therefore foreign (Tuan 1998).[7]

Similarly, in a study of Chinese families running take-away businesses in Britain, Song (1999) found that reports of racial stereotyping and denigration by Chinese young people were common, both in and outside the take-away business. Although many of these Chinese families were economically middle class and successful, and although many Chinese young people were entering university and professional fields, their stories of life in Britain revealed how narrowly their ethnicity as Chinese people in Britain was depicted and understood. These young people constantly struggled with the view that Chinese people were both strange and servile, and "belonged" in the take-away business (see also Parker 1995). And although Britons of Indian heritage, in comparison with the South Asian population as a whole, are now a successful group in socioeconomic terms (Modood et al. 1997), they too must struggle to assert their desired meanings of Indian identity in Britain, including their status as bona fide Britons.

In these examples, class privilege is mediated by these families' experiences of immigration and the particularities of Chinese and Indian settlement in Britain, in addition to Britain's colonial pasts in Hong Kong and the Indian subcontinent. In these cases, as in others which remain to be documented, the relationship between economic power and the possession of ethnic options, though tangible, needs refinement and qualification.

Although ethnic options are clearly shaped by economic privilege or disadvantage, one cannot read off a group's ethnic options automatically on the basis of its socioeconomic status (see chapter 7). A group's ethnic options should not be conceptualized as simply extensions of its material resources or political power. A group's ethnic options are negotiated by members of the group, both in relation to each other and in relation to the wider society. Put another way, the ability to exercise ethnic options is highly complex, and not merely epiphenomenal to various material indicators of oppression or privilege. Even groups who are relatively disadvantaged in terms of socioeconomic indicators, such as African Americans, can arguably exercise a diverse, albeit limited, range of ethnic options – despite the view held by some that African Americans' racial status as Black people predominates, and dwarfs any ethnic attributes or identities they may possess.

Groups may encounter different kinds of barriers and difficulties in asserting the meanings and images they want associated with themselves, and economic power surely enhances the variety of ways in which they are able to do this. However, we know little about the actual opportunities and limits involved in the exercising of ethnic options, even for minorities who are relatively privileged. Middle-class status does not automatically open all doors; nor does it ensure all forms of social acceptance, which are important in the assertion of desired ethnic identities. Economic power must make some difference, but the question is, what difference? More empirical investigation of this question is needed. I now turn to two additional arguments: the need to broaden our understanding and conceptualization of ethnicity and the importance of going beyond superficial readings (and presumed effects) of ethnic labels and images.

Broadening the conceptualization of ethnicity

As discussed above, Nazli Kibria and Mia Tuan suggest (though in different ways) that African Americans, in effect, possess no ethnic options – they are simply reduced to their racial status as Black people. I question the suggestion that Asian Americans necessarily possess more ethnic options than African Americans by pointing to the *very narrow conceptualization of ethnicity* underlying this suggestion. In the USA, ethnicity tends to be understood, at least among sociologists, in terms of a person's ethnic origin and heritage, and the distinctive cultural practices associated with that origin.

The suggestion that African Americans effectively have no ethnic options because of their racialization as Black people, based upon "the forced obliteration of ethnic differences" accompanying diverse African people's enslavement, is problematic. Kibria (2000) rightly notes that the attribution of authentic ethnicity to Asian Americans, though oppressive in many instances, can also provide them with valuable forms of ethnic capital, including ethnic networks, ties, and resources (see Zhou and Bankston 1994; Portes and Zhou 1993). This is an important point, but there is no consideration of how African Americans may possess forms of ethnic and cultural capital, as discussed below.

As in the case of African Americans, who are said to be described primarily in terms of their race rather than their ethnicity, some analysts in Britain have implied that African Caribbeans lack the potentially positive resources associated with ethnicity. For instance, Kenneth Pryce argued that some troubled West Indian youth in Britain have failed to succeed partly because of the inability of "West Indians in general to develop a distinctive culture of their own that is strong enough to counteract the disorienting effects of poverty and the frustrations of social rejection" (1979: 112A). By comparison, Pryce argues that Indian and Pakistani youth in Britain have not suffered the same kind of "psychic and cultural confusion," because of their reliance on a distinctive language and religion and a strong family system. While one cannot dispute that a strong sense of ethnic ties and family support help to provide a buffer against the worst effects of racism, the assertion, in effect, that Indian and Pakistani youth have a distinctive culture and ethnicity, while African Caribbeans do not, is unfounded and erroneous (Alexander 1996).

Although North American analysts such as Tuan and Kibria do not mean to suggest that African Americans possess no culture, the notion that, while all minority groups are raced, some are seen to possess ethnicity while others are not, results in a crude and overly simplistic conceptualization of ethnicity, one that is understood primarily in terms of ethnic lineage and other people's attributions of foreignness. Such a simplistic conceptualization of culture and ethnicity, which is suggested by the point that African Americans have been deprived of knowledge of their African heritage, would suggest that ethnicity is something which is "traditional," and some-how "preserved" from "the old country," rather than something that is constantly created and re-created (Ang 1994; Alexander 1996). Surely, despite the violence with which African Americans were deprived of their African roots, they have built on and created mean-ings, ethnic identities, and cultural practices which are both related to and independent of their African origins. Indeed, contemporary Black culture and ethnicity have drawn importantly upon the slave experience itself (Gates 1988; Gilroy 1993).

Furthermore, evidence of distinctive cultural practices (such as a distinctive language or the eating of traditional ethnic foods – prac-tices which African Americans are not usually associated with) is not actually required to make an ethnic group "real" or to make an ethnic identity a lived experience. Ethnic identity arises from, and is re-created by, historical and lived experiences as well as from adher-ence to what are seen as traditional cultural practices from "the old country."

Reading the most recent American literature on ethnic minority groups, one might think that African Americans have always and solely been understood by analysts as a racial, not an ethnic, group. But this is not the case. Back in 1979, Ronald Taylor put forward an important argument about the historical emergence of black ethnicity in the USA. He argued against the tendency to regard African Amer-ican identity and experience solely in terms of racial oppression and exploitation (or predominantly in terms of "internal colonialism," as famously argued by Blauner (1972)), to the neglect of their experiences of migration, urbanization, and intergroup conflict – all of which contributed importantly to the emergence of a distinctive Black *ethnicity* (see also Glazer and Moynihan 1963).

African Americans (and African Caribbeans in Britain, though in rather different ways) assert particular meanings, practices, and images which are meant to convey Black identity and ethnicity – and these can vary according to both class and regional differences. Although there are many shared meanings and practices associated with a Black identity in the African diaspora (Gilroy 1993), there are also multiple, diverse manifestations of Black ethnic identity in both the USA and Britain. For instance, some Black people may play up being "bad" (through forms of speech, dress, music) as an independ-ent assertion of their identities, as Black people, by highlighting their divergence from the norms of Whiteness and conventional ideals of "success" (Lott 1994; Ogbu 1990). This is evident, for instance, in the image put forward by some Black rap bands such as Public Enemy and Niggas with Attitude (now defunct), who have fostered controversial reputations. Another example of this is the embracing of the counter-ideology and culture provided by reggae music and Rastafarianism in the Black diaspora. In Britain, Pryce (1979) found that some young Black men embraced the shock value of long dread-locks, and even the wearing of rags, in the effort to be as Black as possible. The assertion of such a Black identity, as an expressive means of coping with undesirable identities, is linked with instru-mental responses to a disadvantaged minority status (Ogbu 1990). Another means of playing up one's Blackness is, for instance, the practice of re-naming, in which Black people's slave surnames are discarded for African names or the use of distinctly Black first names, such as "Sheronda, Lichelle, and Aretha" (Russell et al. 1992: 69). Some African Americans also choose to speak with a distinctly Black accent (Davis 1991). These are all, in my view, examples of African Americans exercising their ethnic options (although these options are clearly limited). And whether it be in scholarly or popularized writ-ings of an Afrocentric bent, or in the practice of celebrating Kwaanza, there are ongoing debates among Black people about Black culture and about what it means to be Black – all of which constitute elements of their ethnic options. Therefore, while it would be true to say that African Americans are often racialized in ways over which they have no control, the notion that they possess fewer (if any) ethnic options, in comparison with Asian Americans, is both overly simplistic and erroneous.

Furthermore, in the USA, the tendency to make very clear analytical distinctions between the terms "race" and "ethnicity" has contributed to the overly narrow conceptualization of ethnicity discussed above. For instance, in a recent study of Asian American professionals' ethnic and racial identities, Pyong Gap Min and Rose Kim make the follow-ing distinction between ethnic and racial identities: "Whereas their ethnic identity is related closely to the ethnic subculture practised in their parents' home and in their parents' home country, their racial identity stems from the consciousness of their non-white status in a white dominant society. To state it alternatively, their racial identity is related closely to the perception that as non-whites they are not fully accepted in American society" (2000: 751). This definition of ethnic identity, which is based upon notions of "ethnic subculture" and "their parents' home country," is consonant with the narrow conceptualization of ethnicity I criticize above. Although such ana-lytical distinctions between racial and ethnic identities can be helpful in understanding the source and formation of such identities, such distinctions can also be rather wooden, and can discount the slippery, blurred boundaries between racial and ethnic identities, and the ways in which the meanings and experiences associated with these identities can shade into one another.

The complex dynamics of ethnic labels and images

In order to critically assess the comparisons made between Asian Americans' and African Americans' ethnic options, we need to look at the nature of the images and labels applied to these groups. As noted earlier, Nagel (1994), among others, has argued that various ethnic categories are characterized by differing degrees of stigma or advantage. Not only have different minority groups encountered variable treatment by the state, as well as differential forms of discrimination, but they also suffer disparate kinds of expressive or symbolic discrimination (Ogbu 1990). Stereotypes, which are by definition reductive and crude, are an integral part of how racialized regimes of representation operate (Hall 1997; Gilman 1985).

Another reason why some analysts may assume that African Americans do not possess ethnic options is that many of the images and labels applied to this group appear to be negative. Given the persistence of stereotypes about Black people and criminality (Hall et al. 1978), African Americans in the USA and African Caribbeans in Britain have often noted the way in which White people clutch their belongings as they walk by, or the fact that they are often monitored for theft in stores. One particularly tenacious stereotype of Black people is that they comprise a dangerous "underclass," who are not only lazy and on welfare, but also criminally minded (Morris 1994; Song and Edwards 1997). In many White majority societies, such as the USA and Britain, representation of the major segment of the Black population, which is both "decent" and law abiding, tends to be passed over in favor of the sensationalistic image of most Black people (particularly men) as dangerous, shifty hustlers. African Americans and Asian Americans have been racially stereotyped by the wider society, generally speaking, as "bad" and "good" minorities, respectively. Conservative American analyst Dinesh D'Souza (1995), for instance, has made comparisons between allegedly successful Asian Americans and welfare-dependent African Americans. Asian Americans and African Americans have tended to be depicted in a wholly antipodal manner, particularly in terms of their cultures and their overall success in American society (Abelmann and Lie 1995; C. Kim 1999; Prashad 2000). However, both groups are often subject to double-edged meanings and images, and this complicates the everyday experiences of Asian Americans and African Americans.

As noted by both Tuan and Kibria, the wider society's allegedly positive perception of Asian Americans has always been ambivalent and rather uneasy – at one moment, Asian Americans may be paragons of the American Dream, and at another, they may be ruthless and cunning, as "Orientals" are wont to be, not least because they are seen to be both an economic threat in the Far East and high achievers who threaten to gobble up places in elite universities (Lowe 1996; Takagi 1992).[8] Because Asian Americans may have to endure unappealing stereotypes, such as being stolid and humorless, overly ambitious, or inscrutable, in addition to more positive characterizations, such as being intelligent and competent, Kibria (1997, 2000) found that her Asian American respondents were highly aware of the unflattering aspects of the model minority image, and that they tried hard to distance themselves from such characteristics, particularly by displaying behaviors which were contrary to the stereotype (see also S. Lee 1996; Tuan 1998). Some might say that the widespread image of scientifically or mathematically oriented Asian American students with bad haircuts is hardly damaging, but such a "nerdy" image has real and painful ramifications for Asian American young people, in particular, who are anxious to gain social acceptance from their peers (S. Lee 1996).

It is also possible for ethnic labels and images to be rather ambiguous, or inflected in changeable ways. Nagel (1994) notes that ethnic minorities are subject to both formal and informal kinds of labeling. Informally ascribed ethnic labels, in everyday life, can differ from formally ascribed ethnic labels, which are usually institutionalized by the state. Many analysts in the USA tend to overlook not only informal kinds of ethnic labeling, but also informal everyday kinds of ethnic identity assertion and cultural practice. Related to this point about the need to examine both formal and informal modes of identity ascription and assertion, the received wisdom about what constitutes a "good" and a "bad" group image/stereotype is questionable, because it relies upon very superficial readings of what is good and bad. It fails to consider the double-edged nature of many group images: that "bad" can, in certain contexts, appear to be "good" in some ways (e.g. being radically oppositional or even a bit dangerous can be cool), or that "good" can, in certain contexts, appear "bad" (e.g. being a reliable, hard-working person can also appear conformist, unimaginative, self-serving, etc.).

Apparently good and bad images can, upon closer examination, reveal unexpected benefits and liabilities for various groups. An exploration of these double-edged meanings and images is integral to the broader conceptualization of ethnicity I employ (and which

I argue is central to understanding the notion of groups' ethnic options). Part of the difficulty in comparing the ethnic options of Asian Americans and African Americans is that, usually, little distinction is made between informal and formal modes of ascription, for in "real life" these often shade into each other.

Ironically, the assertion of "bad" oppositional identities has, in some ways, enhanced some Black people's ethnic identities and images. African Americans in the USA and African Caribbeans in Britain have gained a cultural kudos that coexists uneasily with the very real forms of racial oppression they still suffer. In many spheres of social life, Black people have gained a great deal of popularity and attention, as evidenced by forms of cultural synthesis and White youths' appropriation of Black music, dress, and speech (see S. Jones 1988; P. Cohen 1988; Hewitt 1986). Citing the "significant growth in black-white sociability and cultural synthesis, especially among young people," Modood points to "the high esteem in which black cultural styles are held, in the hero-worship of successful black 'stars' in football and sport, music and entertainment" (1996: 9). Despite the criticisms by Ellis Cashmore (1997) and Paul Gilroy (2000) that White-dominated corporations have commodified forms of Black culture in self-serving ways, this has not blunted the positive (though not all popular associations with Blackness are positive) status and associations of Black identities and cultures.

Mindful of the negative discourses surrounding Black men in Britain, for instance, some British analysts such as Roger Hewitt (1986) and Claire Alexander (1996) have emphasized the emancipatory and imaginative implications of oppositional cultural practices and identities asserted by Black people (see also Gilroy 1987).[9] By comparison, the Chinese in Britain, who are generally regarded as a non-troublesome, high-achieving group, consistently tend to be stereotyped as "square," conformist, and uncreative (see Parker 1995).

While the growth of "Asian Kool" in Britain is now also visible, as evidenced by the popularity of South Asian artists, such as Corner Shop, or the bindi-wearing, Asian-influenced Madonna, Virinder Kalra and John Hutnyk question whether such media and artistic exposure has a straightforward positive effect upon the social and political status of Asians as a racialized minority group, and if music can be involved in social struggles that actually achieve forms of "payback" (1998: 340): "What we find significant is that at the same time that Asian Kool proliferates with its high visibility, in the forgotten corners of the UK, the industrial estates, housing commissions and 'ethnic enclaves,' police repression, racist violence and day-to-day exploitation remain a matter of course" (1998: 344). While we should not exaggerate the importance of such visibility in popular culture in effecting social and political change, nor should we underestimate its significance. At the very least, the recognition of minority groups as a social force with reverberations in the wider society, especially in relation to the younger population, enhances their status in the public realm.

Although the term "cultural capital" is typically associated with the possession of elite, mainstream tastes and cultural practices (Bourdieu 1984), certain Black cultural styles and practices can constitute an important form of cultural capital for Black people in a variety of situations. But, as in the case of Asian Americans, both African Americans and African Caribbeans have been subject to double-edged connotations associated with being Black. As Phil Cohen has noted, "Blacks are simultaneously admired for their 'gangsta' reputation whilst being denigrated for their violence and street criminality" (1996: 20). To recognize the "street cred" possessed by young Black people in particular is not to neglect the very real consequences of racially based discrimination and marginalization, which contribute to (though not exclusively) the creation of vibrant Black youth cultures.

While we must not be overly sanguine in our formulations of Black people's status and experience by virtue of their cultural kudos, equally, we should not discount the positive ramifications of possessing such forms of cultural capital, particularly in the case of economically disadvantaged Black people.[10] For example, in a study of low-income African American youth, Prudence Carter (2000) argues that, in addition to the attainment of conventional cultural capital, which is important for mobility within the opportunity structure, "non-dominant" forms of Black cultural capital are critical to Black youth's "social prestige" and sense of belonging within African American communities (see also Young 1999). I would argue that the possession of such cultural capital is, in fact, an important ethnic option for African American and African Caribbean people, particularly for young Black men.

Not more or less ethnic options

Assertions of ethnic identity and processes of self-invention necessarily engage with dominant representations and discourses about minority groups in the wider society. The persistence and strength of group stereotypes, and their ability to shape group members' aspirations and behaviors, are central to understanding the continuation of racially segregated social spheres, such as peer and friendship networks. While White dominance and power are still undeniably important in structuring the opportunities and constraints experienced by groups of color, it is important to remember that ethnic minorities' interactions with others are not wholly determined by the dominant (and sometimes undesirable) images held of them by the wider society, and that minority people contest and negotiate their desired ethnic identities. By critically assessing the suggestion that some minority groups may possess more ethnic options than others, I have tried to raise some key questions about what we mean by the notion of ethnic minority groups possessing ethnic options in the first place.

Because the dynamics around the assertion of ethnic identity are complex and often changeable in multiethnic Western societies today, it is difficult to conceive of one minority group as possessing, in any straightforward fashion, more (or, for that matter, better or worse) ethnic options than another. True, groups may possess *different* kinds of ethnic options, but "different" does not easily translate into measures of more or less, or better or worse, options.

I would argue that the suggestion itself – that some ethnic minorities may be said to possess more ethnic options than others – is a misguided one, and one which does not facilitate a full or subtle understanding of ethnic options. I question the received notion that Asian Americans necessarily possess a wider array of ethnic options than African Americans. The very terms in which the comparison is set are problematic. To try to measure or quantify the possession of ethnic options in a clear-cut way (via the wrong-headed language of more or less) is not possible. I suspect that this is one reason (in addition to the political sensitivities surrounding the issue) why some analysts, such as Kibria, imply the comparison without actually using the language of "more" or "less." Given both the existing (and limited) theoretical knowledge and consensus about what it means, in practice, to possess ethnic options in the first place, and the many, multiple dimensions which underly the assertion of ethnic identity, I do not think it is possible, *with any exactitude*, to make claims about one minority group having more or less options than another group. Specific measures of particular ways of having options (though there is no recognition of, or consensus on, what these are) would yield different measures and results.

The language of more and less ethnic options, by comparison, *can* be applied, and does make sense, in the comparison between White Americans and ethnic minority Americans, because the differences between Whites and non-Whites, generally speaking, are still so stark. In the case of Asian Americans and African Americans, such a comparison would necessarily be tentative as regards the "results" of comparing the two groups – not because of theoretical fence sitting or sophistry, but because of the difficulty and *vastness* of both the theoretical and the empirical questions involved.

To the extent that ethnic identities and options are importantly shaped by the dominant images and labels applied to disparate groups, it is difficult to portray the representation of either African Americans or Asian Americans in wholly positive or negative terms. In reviewing the representations and characterizations of Asian Americans and African Americans, I have demonstrated that both these groups are subject to doubled-edged meanings and images associated with them. More attention needs to be given to the ways in which the possession (or lack) of cultural capital, including the practice of popular cultural forms by particular groups, has mediated groups' range of ethnic options, as well as their selective inclusion and exclusion across many social contexts. Even if we were to accept that the ethnic options which African Americans possess are more negative than positive in their consequences (though this would depend on the particular situation and the desired goal), then (rather than suggesting that African Americans do not possess an array of ethnic options) it would be more accurate to make the more specific claim that Asian Americans, generally speaking, possess more advantageous ethnic options than African Americans. This latter, more specific claim, however, raises different, though related, theoretical and empirical questions which would require further study.

Easy distinctions and assumptions made about the nature and effects of "good" and "bad" racial images and labels, and their implications for a group's ethnic options, need to be problematized and further studied. The many complexities surrounding the dynamics of race and racisms mean that the ways in which groups gain prestige, or are denigrated, or exercise their ethnic options, are not necessarily straightforward or mapped easily in relation to other groups.

3

Negotiating Individual and Group Identities

Individuals and the meaning of ethnic identity

In the last chapter, I argued that ethnic minority groups must work at asserting their desired identities, given that the nature and range of their ethnic identities are limited by the dominant discourses, representations, and images which are attributed to them by the wider society. However, ethnic minorities are not simply the passive recipients of imposed identities; rather, they can actively respond to negative and unwanted images and identities in various ways. Thus Joanne Nagel defines ethnic identities as "the result of a dialectical process involving internal and external opinions and processes, as well as the individual's self-identification and outsiders' ethnic designations – i.e. what *you* think your ethnicity is, versus what *they* think your ethnicity is" (1994: 154). Here it is implied that "they" constitute people outside one's own ethnic group.

However, in addition to dominant representations and stereotypes attributed to groups, an individual's ethnic identity is also fundamentally shaped by interactions with one's coethnics – the members of one's own ethnic group. Just as an individual's sense of self may not necessarily mesh with the dominant stereotypes and images attributed to her group by the wider society, her sense of self may not accord perfectly with coethnic designations of what it means to possess a particular ethnicity. On the one hand, membership within a group entitles one to participate in the group's culture and politics; it gives one a claim to distinctive ways of talking, dressing, interacting, eating, and so on. On the other hand, membership involves obligations; for instance, coethnic members may expect a degree of conformity or similarity in expressions of ethnic identity (Zack 1996:

143). Minority individuals may be expected to demonstrate commitment to their group and to a particular notion of group identity through certain behaviors and cultural practices, and it may be difficult for individuals to flout group norms which they do not wish to uphold.

Espousing a "postethnic perspective," David Hollinger argues that people's affiliations with an ethnic or racial group should be wholly voluntary, as opposed to prescribed: "Individuals should be allowed to affiliate or disaffiliate with their own communities of descent to an extent that they choose, while affiliating with whatever nondescent communities are available and appealing to them" (1995: 116). However, such a scenario is rather utopian, since the issue of affiliating with a particular group is unlikely to be determined by an individual's desires or choices alone.

There are a number of ways in which coethnics can mediate individuals' ethnic identities. One way is by making individual members aware of the normative values and behaviors expected of them, as group members. However, what it means to be a group member is continuously contested through collective debates about group culture and identity. In this way, individual agency regarding the assertion of ethnic identity is constrained and influenced by the politics of recognition and authenticity practiced within minority groups, just as it can be compromised by White racist stereotyping – though the dynamics of these two processes differ.

It is often assumed that members of an ethnic group share, by definition, similar cultural values, practices, and identities. The concept of the group experience, which assumes a certain homogeneity of experience for individuals of a common ethnicity, is itself problematic. Every group's culture is complex, diverse, and constitutive of a wide variety of practices and intellectual and cultural traditions, which may espouse differing values and positions. No group's culture is static or unidimensional; rather, it is always contested and in flux. Culture is also subject to processes of translation, so it is difficult to locate a stable essence of any one culture (Bhabha 1990b).

Given the relatively widespread acceptance of multicultural rhetoric in many Western societies, ethnic minority groups, generally speaking, are seen to possess a right to their particular cultural practices, though the exercising of such a right may be limited in terms of public policies (Kymlicka 1995). However, the recognition of group rights raises a number of questions, such as, what is a group's culture? Who defines its primary elements? (Anthias 1998). While there may be some shared meanings about ethnicity which are quite durable, in relation to a shared history or a racialized minority status, ethnic groups are made up of members, who are diverse with respect to gender, class, and age; hence there is unlikely to be an easy consensus about the meanings and images associated with a particular ethnic identity.[1]

Individual members of an ethnic group may possess different understandings of their ethnic identities, and may manifest their ethnicity in disparate ways. Related to this, within ethnic groups, individuals may experience and respond differently to the racisms and forms of racial assignment they encounter. For instance, in the case of Asian Americans who are racially labeled as Asian by most other Americans (regardless of their specific ethnic origins and nationalities), Nazli Kibria still found that the "effects of racial assignment on identity formation were mediated by the diverse ways in which individuals interpreted the experience of racial labelling" (1997: 540). As Michael Thornton has pointed out, the process of ethnic or racial labeling greatly oversimplifies how race or ethnicity are actually experienced: "There is no intrinsic personality related to race; what develops is a complex interaction between individual and social definitions. Individuals are expected to locate themselves 'accurately' within established racial structures. . . . ideally, individual choice and social designations are psychologically satisfying for the individual and socially approved" (1992: 323). A complex understanding of the experiences of racial discrimination must take into account both the cumulative character of an individual's experiences of discrimination and the group's accumulated historical experiences as perceived by the individual (Feagin 1991). Therefore, individual interpretations of commonly shared racialization experiences can result in a variety of individually negotiated ethnic identities or ways of combating racism.

Rather than conceiving of minority individuals as simply buffeted between the wider society and their coethnics, we need to see them as agents who actively negotiate their desired ethnic identities in relation to both insiders and outsiders in a multitude of contexts. Within limits, minority individuals can contest the meaning of a particular ethnic identity, including the terms of ethnic group membership. For instance, what does it mean to be Chinese in Britain today? Does it mean speaking a Chinese dialect and partnering with a Chinese person? Or does it mean being informed by both Chinese and British identities and cultures? In this chapter I am primarily interested in how *individuals* negotiate the normative range of behaviors and lifestyles which are often prescribed within ethnic groups. Individuals who diverge from the remit of accepted and normal practices, as defined by the group collectively, can be subject to disapproval, and the authenticity of their ethnic identities may be called into question.

Groups and the maintenance of ethnic boundaries

In order to understand the ways in which individuals' ethnic options are shaped and constrained by group norms and practices, we must first consider the nature of ethnic groups. While there is no one definition, an ethnic group "is a segment of a larger society whose members are thought, by themselves or others, to have a common origin and to share important segments of a common culture and who, in addition, participate in shared activities in which the common origin and culture are significant ingredients" (Yinger 1994: 3). Ethnic groups are real to the extent that they are socially and politically recognized and constructed by their members and by the wider society. An ethnic group exists only where its members possess a conscious sense of belonging to it. In this way, ethnic groups don't exist outside a politicized process of (self-) recognition.

What holds an ethnic group together? A number of analysts have emphasized the instrumental and economic concerns underlying ethnic ties and interactions (see A. Cohen 1974; Glazer and Moynihan 1975). According to Orlando Patterson:

> Ethnicity can only be understood in terms of a dynamic and contextual view of group allegiances. What is critical about an ethnic group is not the particular set of symbolic objects which distinguishes it but the social uses of these objects: Ethnic loyalties reflect, and are maintained by, the underlying socioeconomic interests of group members.
>
> (1977: 101)

It is undeniable that ethnicity can be invoked in instrumental and changeable ways. Nevertheless, Patterson overlooks the continuing importance of the symbolic content of an ethnic group, for the cultural content of a group forms the basis for contestations about what is distinctive about the group vis-à-vis other groups. I agree that a static description of seemingly enduring group attributes is a dead end. However, ethnic groups constantly engage in politicized and often heated contestations about their cultural content, and the function of ethnic identity is not always reducible to "the group's optimization of its socioeconomic position in the society" (O. Patterson 1977: 102). It is, in fact, more plausible that ethnic groups are motivated by both socioeconomic and political interests, as well as by non-instrumental concerns about their representation and boundaries in relation to the wider society. While political or economic interests encouraging ethnic cohesion may change over time (see A. Cohen 1974), emotive beliefs about a group's culture can be very strong and enduring

(Cornell and Hartmann 1998). In addition to the shared interests underlying ethnic solidarity, beliefs about the existence of some kind of shared culture, or what Anthony Smith (1990) calls an "ethnic core," cannot be dismissed.

A distinct ethnic identity is central to groups' efforts to differentiate themselves from other groups. The idea of ethnic boundary keeping has been a key way of conceptualizing the processes of group differentiation and identity (Barth 1969; Wallman 1978). Barth (1969) argued that ethnic boundaries, rather than withering away, endured in multiethnic contexts; cultural interaction among different groups was the basis for the recognition of ethnic boundaries. The discourse of "difference" is central to our understandings of ethnic boundary keeping, and difference is often invoked to exclude and marginalize outsiders and others. White Europeans had a great deal to gain by imposing strict boundaries between themselves and non-European groups. Without the imposition and enforcement of racial boundaries and categories, imperialist expansion and the subordination of groups, such as Native Americans in the USA or Indians under colonial British rule, could not have occurred. However, difference can also be celebrated as a source of diversity and hybridity, and can be a means of emancipating subordinate identities (Said 1978). For some marginalized minority groups, difference can be embraced, at least on the terms that they, as opposed to the wider society, attempt to dictate.

Ethnic groups may want to uphold their boundaries for a variety of reasons, particularly if they are a minority group in the wider society. The drawing and maintenance of ethnic boundaries is also integral to various forms of nationalisms such as in the former Yugoslavia and in the Basque region of Spain. In such nationalist movements, the determination of a group's identity is centrally linked to its objectives concerning autonomy (Calhoun 1993). But on what specific *criteria* are ethnic boundaries drawn? Ethnic groups are not automatically or "naturally" unified around the social markers which define and demarcate their ethnicity, whether these markers be language, religion, physical appearance, or modes of dress.

Cultural survival

Threats to ethnic boundaries, which are important for the definition of a group's ethnic identity, can engender highly emotive protest and opposition, especially if there are concerns about cultural survival.[2] Movements concerning cultural survival can be especially potent in the case of a dwindling, disadvantaged minority group whose traditions and heritage are perceived to be threatened by the group's immersion in the dominant society and culture. Such appeals have been made in relation to quite disparate groups, such as Native Americans or recent Korean immigrants in the USA, who may be fearful of losing their traditional cultural practices. Policies to "civilize" and assimilate Native Americans in the early 1900s included the uprooting of young people from their tribal communities and their placement in boarding schools where they were expected to learn the English language and the dominant values more generally (Schulz 1998). In the case of many tribes, such as the Navajo, the ability to speak the Navajo language, and an understanding and appreciation of Navajo spirituality and oral traditions, are highly valued as key aspects of Navajo identity (Schulz 1998).

Intermarriage is often regarded as a threat to the integrity of an ethnic group (see chapter 4). This is because intermarriage is perceived to be one of the most concrete ways in which the ethnic purity and cultural content of ethnic groups is threatened (Merton 1941).[3] In a study of second-generation Korean American and Chinese American ethnic identities, Nazli Kibria found that some respondents expressed concerns about intermarriage. As one Korean American respondent put it,

> After listening to my parents and thinking about it, I've pretty much decided that I will marry Korean. I want to keep my lineage [pause] . . . I don't want to say pure because that kind of has a negative connotation, but I don't want to mix. I know it sounds racist, but a lot of it has to do with the fact that this society doesn't accept us at some deep level. I feel like it's important to marry Korean because no matter how American you think you are, by the fact that your hair is black and your skin is yellow and you have Korean blood, you are different. Plus biracial children have a lot of problems fitting in.
>
> (1997: 531)

In addition to concerns about disrupting the purity of Korean lineage and culture, this respondent explained that another reason for maintaining ethnic boundaries via endogamy is that it provides an important bulwark against racial oppression and the myriad forms of racial exclusion experienced by ethnic minority groups.

Opposition to intermarriage among some African Americans also manifested itself with the rise of the Black Power movement in the 1960s, when African Americans not only shunned the need to integrate into White society, but were militant in asserting the integrity and values of African American history, culture, and people (Spickard 1989: 303). While many Asian and African Americans today are not opposed to inter-racial relationships, such relationships can be controversial.[4] In addition to opposing intermarriage, there are a number of other ways in which ethnic minority groups may attempt to shape and regulate their ethnic boundaries and the meanings, images, and practices associated with their ethnic identities. For instance, some ethnic minority people oppose trans-racial adoption, which has usually involved White parents adopting ethnic minority children (see Kirton 2000).

Although both men and women are subject to pressures to adhere to dominant group norms and practices, the pressures on individuals to promote cultural survival may be gendered. Because ethnic boundary keeping tends to rely on rules about appropriate behavior in relation to marriage, family relationships, and sexuality, women are particularly subject to scrutiny concerning their intimate friendships and relationships and their behavior more generally. Because they are often treated as emblems of the nation and as "culture carriers," women are expected to transmit forms of cultural heritage and practices to their children, whom they socialize and care for (Anthias and Yuval-Davis 1992; Schulz 1998).[5] In these ways, women are regarded are extensions of ethnic group integrity and identity. Given their symbolic importance as the bearers of ethnicity and national identity, women's ethnic options can be constrained by sexist images of them and by the patriarchal expectations imposed upon them by men (Josephides 1988). The expectation that women fulfill the role of cultural transmission (as well as biologically reproduce for the group) may be especially acute in the case of subordinated minority groups, who may regard the protection and cultivation of their culture as key to their survival as a group.

While I am not suggesting that most individuals within ethnic minority groups support separatist positions in relation to intermarriage or trans-racial adoption, it is important to recognize that ethnic minority groups themselves can be active in boundary-keeping practices and in the maintenance of exclusionary discourses about ethnic membership and "purity" (though the motivations for such boundary keeping can vary). In effect, these boundary-keeping practices work to define and to limit the identity and life-style options of individuals vis-à-vis the groups to which they belong, because individuals are subject to collectively negotiated pressures to identify and behave in particular ways.

Debates about ethnic and racial authenticity

Given some groups' concerns about boundary keeping and cultural survival, debates about ethnic and racial authenticity can arise in relation to ethnic minority individuals. In his influential book,

Imagined Communities, Benedict Anderson (1983) argues that modern national identities evolve in conjunction with the creation of "imagined" political communities with national boundaries which involve processes which define who does and does not belong within the community. Some understandings of "community" have tended to uphold the illusion of cultural homogeneity, fixed modes of identification, and consensus within groups who are seen to constitute a community (Alexander 1996).

While an emphasis on community and togetherness can be very positive and important for ethnic minority people, by providing both emotional and material forms of support, this very emphasis can also generate expectations about the cultural content of an ethnic group, including the meanings and practices around ethnic identity as they are articulated in everyday life. Unlike the case of White ethnics such as Italian Americans, for whom ethnic identity is "private and voluntary, intermittent and undemanding," and for whom "such an ethnic identity is, in other words, *a personal style*, and not the manifestation of membership in an ethnic group" (Alba 1988: 153, my emphasis), individuals' membership in ethnic minority groups can be binding and entail much more than a "personal style." Indeed, in the case of non-White minorities, the ability to assert a personal style can be impinged upon not only by racial assignment in the wider society, but also by the norms and expectations of coethnics.

Despite the fact that people are often aware of the dominant and normative cultural practices and values associated with their groups, one reason why there is no clear-cut consensus about the cultural content of an ethnic group is that the meanings of culture and ethnicity are fluid and contested, rather than fixed, even though some members of ethnic groups may *believe* that a group's ethnic identity and its concomitant cultural practices are perennial, clearly defined, and utterly distinctive. While some degree of individual latitude concerning one's identity and life-style is possible, there are dominant modes of behavior which are prescribed either implicitly or explicitly by certain groups, and pressures to adhere to "normal" behavior (whatever this may be) may be quite significant. Expectations concerning dominant modes of behavior are linked with groups' understandings of ethnic and racial authenticity.

"Scripts of behavior"

Kwame Anthony Appiah (in Appiah and Gutmann 1996) has made the observation that ethnic and racial identities are often associated with particular "scripts" of behavior, which stipulate (both implicitly and explicitly) certain forms of behavior and/or adherence to particular values.[6] For instance, in a study of Peruvians of Japanese descent, Ayumi Takenaka (1999) found that the Japanese Peruvian community (known as "Nikkei," distinguishing them from Japanese people in Japan and other Peruvians in Peru) selects members and imposes a code of behavior by establishing written and unwritten rules. Nikkei identity and group membership rely upon a set of values which reflect a specific set of community relations and expectations about conformity of behavior.

Although the word "script" seems to imply a performance of sorts, I use it more generally to refer to widely recognized norms of behavior. While some people can happily adhere to expected rules of behavior, where the script of behavior is not at odds with their own values and life-styles, others can be said to *perform* certain scripts in the sense that they are succumbing to pressures to adhere to such scripts.

Integral to the function of these scripts are discourses about racial or ethnic *authenticity*. For instance, questions about a Black person's authenticity can arise in charges of being a "coconut" or an "oreo" in the USA (or a Bounty Bar in Britain) – Black on the outside, but White on the inside. Such an allegation would be leveled at a Black person who was seen to be acting White. As discussed in chapter 2, some African Americans may consider oppositional identities and behaviors to be in keeping with what it means to be African American. Such individuals can be critical of Black people who embrace conventional, White norms of success (Ogbu 1990; Waters 1994; Kao 2000). For example, African American students who succeed academically in school, and who use standard English, can be accused by their peers of acting White or of being "Uncle Toms." Such successful Black students may be accused of not being Black at all. In Tom Wolfe's recent novel, *A Man in Full* (1998), which surveys race relations in 1990s Atlanta, a successful African American lawyer named Roger White is known as Roger "Too" White because he works in an elite White law firm, and because of his apparent acceptance of mainstream norms of success. He is therefore suspiciously regarded as a "beige brother" by some of his more Black "brothers and sisters." As such, Roger "Too" White is constantly aware of the ways in which he feels subject to tests of ethnic authenticity by his Black coethnics, particularly poor, working-class Black people in Atlanta. The dilemma faced by people such as Roger "Too" White provides an example of how some Black and other ethnic minority people may feel pressure to adhere to certain norms of behavior which are collectively upheld by their coethnics.

Scripts of behavior tend to rely upon a "you are what you are" essentialism which conceives of an individual only in terms of his or her ethnic or racial designation. One could go as far as to say that such scripts also rely on crude stereotypes. Stereotypes are important for ethnic boundary keeping, because they tend to be invoked in the maintenance of social and symbolic order; stereotypes tend to fix boundaries, symbolically, by excluding those elements which are not considered desirable or which do not belong (Douglas 1966). The depiction of middle-class Black people as White sell-outs may be unwarranted. The fact that a middle-class Black professional may work primarily with White people, for instance, does not mean that the person will socialize mainly with White people outside work. Studies of the Black middle class, in fact, show that they often lead a kind of double life, in which they uphold White norms and standards in the workplace, and take refuge in their homes and Black social spaces (such as predominantly Black bars or restaurants), where "they can return to the comfort of their private lives and 'de-robe', in a sense, switching to ethnic African-American symbolic and interactional styles" (Neckerman, Carter, and Lee 1999: 954).

Scripts of behavior, as upheld by group members, appear to be formed in interaction with dominant representations and discourses about groups in the wider society. For instance, the norms associated with acting "Black" derive partly from racial representations of Black people in the wider society, even if the oppositional meanings associated with acting Black may be regarded in a positive light among Black people. Similarly, the expectations that some Asian Americans may have of one another – for example, that Korean Americans will speak the Korean language and carry on forms of Korean cultural heritage – correspond with the wider society's representation of Asian Americans as foreign and distinguished by their cultural distinctiveness.

Notions of what constitutes authentic behavior can, of course, differ across groups. Unlike the case of many African Americans, being successful in higher education or the labor market is in keeping with, not in contravention of, (dominant) Korean American and Chinese American scripts of behavior. For example, some of the British-born Chinese young people I interviewed seemed concerned or embarrassed when I asked them if they spoke a Chinese dialect; such individuals were concerned that they would be seen as "not really Chinese" if they were not fluent in a Chinese dialect (Song 1999; Ang 1994). Furthermore, the strength of expectations concerning adherence to scripts of behavior may vary across groups. Grace Kao (2000) found that in a multiethnic high school, Black and Hispanic students were particularly concerned to demonstrate their ethnic ties and loyalties, in comparison with Asian students. In addition to the fact that there were not as many Asian American students, it is possible that Asian students felt less pressure to demonstrate ethnic loyalty with coethnics because they are not generally associated with oppositional repertoires of behavior, such as acting Black (Ogbu 1990).

Markers of ethnicity are key components of a group's script of behavior, and groups negotiate the terms and symbols of ethnic membership and authenticity differently.[7] Although there may be competing scripts of behavior within groups, given the diversity of people within every ethnic group, most people are aware of which behaviors and practices are considered normal or typical in relation to themselves and their coethnics.

African Americans and discourses of authenticity

As discussed earlier, concerns about a group's ethnic heritage and authenticity may be especially pressing for groups whose cultural traditions have been suppressed historically, as in the case of Native Americans and African Americans. For instance, Afrocentric thought is an important intellectual and political response to the historical denigration of African Americans and their cultural uprooting as slaves from Africa.[8] One of its key proponents, Molefi Asante, has argued that an Afrocentric perspective is a necessary counter to the White Eurocentric thought and values which have dominated the academy and everyday thinking in the USA. Afrocentrism is said to be fundamental for the restoration of "African agency": "If we have lost anything, it is our cultural centeredness; that is, we have been moved off our own platforms. This means that we cannot truly be ourselves or know our potential since we exist in a borrowed space. . . . [W]ithout this kind of centeredness, we bring almost nothing to the multicultural table but a darker version of whiteness" (Asante 1998: 8). Although Afrocentric principles cannot be said to be dictating debates about the direction of African American culture and thought, some of the key ideas, especially those concerning African American authenticity, crop up in wider discussions about the need to value and celebrate African American culture and history.

Within the context of revaluing and celebrating the cultural and intellectual heritage of subordinate groups, in recent years various scholars have commented upon the intense pressure brought to bear upon many African American people to uphold racial unity and solidarity. One way of upholding racial unity is to abide by collectively prescribed scripts of behavior. To subordinate the goal of racial unity to individual needs or preferences may be perceived as selfish and disloyal. In the case of African Americans, the long-standing emphasis upon racial unity has evolved out of the very real need to "stick together" in relation to the common experiences of racism, albeit in changing forms over several centuries.

One reason why discourses of racial or ethnic authenticity can exert such power is that it is often understood that there is a *moral* basis for racial unity and solidarity, particularly in the case of historically persecuted groups (see Appiah 1990). For instance, some (though by no means all) Jewish people believe that they should support Zionist movements, and such a belief may be an important part of their Jewish identity. Such an expectation by some Jewish people is likely to stem fundamentally from their sense of a shared history, as a people who have suffered pogroms and myriad forms of discrimination. In this sense, discourses of authenticity can effectively draw upon moralistic expectations of what is entailed in group membership. The attribution of disloyalty to a group member can be justified as a necessary, ethical need to protect the integrity of the group, whose culture and traditions are vulnerable and have been historically reviled (Zack 1996).

Given the vicissitudes commonly experienced by many African Americans, either by themselves or by their forebears, it is hardly surprising that an emphasis upon mutual cooperation and solidarity has emerged among them. Crossing cultural boundaries and behaving in ways which are regarded as White – for instance, in terms of speech or educational excellence – can be threatening to minority identity and security, as well as to their solidarity (Ogbu 1990). Therefore, by engaging in behavior which is deemed to be White, some African American individuals risk not only condemnation, but also ostracization by their coethnics. This is clearly a difficult dilemma, particularly because minority individuals may be fearful of losing the support of their own groups, and do not want to have to "choose sides." According to Michael Dyson, "The desire to promote love, friendship, and mutual cooperation among black folk is a laudable cultural goal, especially in light of the vicious and paralyzing forms of self-hatred and mutual contempt that have riddled black culture from its origins in slavery . . . [However] an enabling solidarity should not appeal to *truncated understandings of authentic racial identity* or place an ideological noose of loyalty around the necks of critical dissenters from received ideas about racial unity" (1994: 221, my emphasis).

The valorization of racial unity may be problematic for individuals, because the commitment to racial unity demands that minority individuals toe what is perceived to be the politically and socially necessary line, or script of behavior, regardless of their own beliefs, values, and experiences. Adopting such a script can affect every dimension of social life, including who one's friends are, or how one presents oneself in the wider society. One key test of being, for instance, a "real" African American may be one's willingness to demur from any public criticism of another Black person (however differently they may be discussed behind closed doors).

Such prohibitions and prescriptions of behavior have clear implications for the pressures that ethnic minority people may feel when they make key life decisions or negotiate their cultural practices in their daily lives. As an advocate of "an oppositional African American cultural criticism," Dyson argues not only for the need to celebrate and support Black cultural forms, but also for the importance of freely passing critical judgement on various cultural expressions and political activities, whether they be forms of popular music, preaching, or Black nationalist politics. To silence critical discussion around disturbing events, such as the furore surrounding the alleged rape of Tawana Brawley in New York City,[9] on the grounds of not airing "dirty laundry" in front of White society, is problematic and misguided. To expect such behavioral uniformity, in the name of racial unity and solidarity, is to essentialize (however unwittingly) Black people all over again. Like Dyson, Appiah argues against such an ideological noose: "Racial identity can be the basis of resistance to racism, but even as we struggle against racism – and though we have made great progress, we have further still to go – let us not let our racial identities subject us to new tyrannies" (in Appiah and Gutmann 1996: 104).

Nevertheless, it would be misleading to characterize scripts of behavior and pressures to uphold racial or ethnic unity in solely negative and oppressive terms. This is because members of minority groups, whether they be African American or any other minority group, can also derive benefits from adhering to collectively prescribed norms of behavior. Adherence to a group's dominant values and norms, particularly if they differ from those held by the wider society, can provide group members with an important sense of belonging and self-determination. Not only can adherence to group norms provide a sense of unity and membership, when they may not be accorded a sense of full membership in the wider society, it can also provide people with a sense of security about who they are. Another way in which adhering to particular scripts of behavior may be a positive experience is that members of ethnic minority groups, such as African Americans, may believe that they are *entitled* to engage in the cultural modes and practices associated with their particular group. Boundary maintenance and adherence to scripts can also be about the ownership of a group's culture.

However understandable it may be that some minority individuals wish to uphold beliefs and norms regarding ethnic and racial authenticity, the entire notion of authenticity is flawed, because it relies on a static understanding of ethnicity and culture, when in fact cultures not only overlap, but are in a continuous process of hybridity (Bhabha 1990a).

Individualized ethnic options

Group notions of ethnic or racial authenticity, as illustrated by the expectation that members adhere to particular scripts of behavior, can be at odds with understandings of individual authenticity. Individuals' efforts to adhere to norms of allegedly authentic behaviors can pose difficulties, because they can directly conflict with a person's wish to be *true to themselves* – something which can only be achieved by some degree of detachment and autonomy from group pressures and norms (C. Taylor 1994).[10] In the case of African Americans, some individuals who are comfortable with speaking "proper" English may still feel compelled to speak Black English in the company of other Black people, even though they may, ironically, feel fake in doing so. By adhering to the expectation that they speak Black English, they become insincerely "authentic" – that is, inauthentic to themselves.

Thus an individual may find herself caught between the dominant norms and behaviors of the group to which she belongs and the potentially different priorities and meanings she values in relation to her own individual identity. If she takes the emphasis upon the undeniable uniqueness and originality of each individual to an extreme, acceptance of a group's norms and behaviors may seem unconscionable and a weak acceptance of conformism. As socially embedded beings, however, few people may be able to live with a real disregard for group esteem or approval; they are therefore inevitably subject to the very real pressures to abide by certain written and unwritten rules – we do live in the public gaze. Furthermore, as discussed earlier, for many minority individuals, their group membership itself constitutes an important part of their individual identities.

Though subject to pressures to follow prescribed scripts of behavior, individuals are able to engage in certain practices which may afford them some control and flexibility in the assertion of their desired ethnic identities. Individuals can be creative about the ways they negotiate their identities, although this creativity is bounded by their resources and their location in specific social and historical times and places. According to Barbara Lal, the actor learns to "do" ethnic identity insofar as she routinely employs reason and exercises choice: "The internal processes of interpretation, reflection and decision-making go on even in circumstances in which significant constraints of various sorts limit the kinds of activities the actor can reasonably hope to undertake" (2001: 160).

Nevertheless, the ability to assert an identity of one's choosing is never constant or assured; it is always variable and situationally dependent. While the use of creative strategies may alter the cognitive and affective framework of the individual, her social status within the larger society may remain unchanged (Murrell 1998: 197). I discuss below some of the ways in which individuals may try to negotiate their desired ethnic identities. While the options discussed below are not necessarily mutually exclusive, each will be discussed separately for analytical purposes.

Adherence to dominant scripts of behavior

Some individuals may *choose* to conform to dominant norms and scripts of behavior associated with a group, and may do so for a variety of reasons. For some people, strict adherence to such scripts and clear observance of ethnic boundaries may provide a strong, positive sense of belonging and kinship with other coethnics. Upholding prescribed scripts of behavior may be particularly attractive to members who feel rejected or who have experienced persistent forms of racial discrimination and exclusion in the wider society. Alienating experiences of racism, in the case of some individuals, may encourage the need for strong and oppositional ethnic self-definition. Although racism is not the only basis for ethnic identity formation, it can be important in shaping people's ethnic boundary-keeping practices and the desire to maintain ethnic and cultural purity – if only as a bulwark against racist denigration and marginalization. Even if some individuals do not feel particularly marginalized or oppressed in relation to the wider society, they may still value the maintenance of tight boundaries on the grounds of cultural preservation or group solidarity, and regard normative scripts of behavior as a means of achieving it.

"Opting out" of an ethnic group

Like Hollinger (1995), who espouses the importance of people voluntarily affiliating with specific ethnic groups, Joseph Raz (1994) defends a "right of exit" from a group, even if, according to the wider society, an individual's parental heritage firmly locates her within it. Nevertheless, putting such a right into practice is not easy. Some individuals may try to opt out of an ethnic group by employing a variety of disidentifiers (Goffman 1963: 44) – for instance, by adopting non-traditional life-style practices, choosing friends and partners outside their assigned ethnic group, or fully integrating into mainstream cultural practices. These individuals may attempt to disidentify with their group and disrupt other people's assumptions about their ethnic identities. Although there may be various motivations for wanting to opt out of a group, efforts to do so would be one way of dealing with the stigma of group membership – albeit an extreme strategy involving the denial of one's heritage and group affiliation (Goffman 1963).

In my study of Chinese families running take-away food businesses in Britain, I found that children (many of whom were born and raised in Britain) in these families differed in the kinds of ethnic identities they adopted (Song 1999). The Chinese take-away and working together as a family were important emblems of Chinese cultural identity in Britain, given the high proportion of Chinese families operating such livelihoods. However, some individuals were more interested and invested in their Chinese heritage than others, and siblings tended to feel differently about their families' reliance on the Chinese take-away food business. While many young people supported the widespread expectation among Chinese families that children should "help out," others found these norms oppressive. Therefore, some of the young people in these families tried to distance themselves as much as possible from their family's Chinese take-away businesses. For instance, in one family, Simon explained that his brother Colin's aversion to working in the take-away stemmed from Colin's attitudes toward being Chinese: "He's a White man. He has Black friends and White friends, but not Chinese friends. And now he lives in 'x'. It's all White. There isn't even a Chinese take-away down there" (Song 1999: 151). According to Simon, Colin has tried to opt out of being Chinese by distancing himself completely from any association with Chineseness.

In another Chinese family, David was seen by his sisters as a pariah in the family. This was because, like Colin, he distanced himself as much as possible from the running of the take-away business and from all things deemed Chinese. According to his sisters, David reportedly hated any associations with his Chinese heritage. He had moved away from the family as soon as he turned sixteen, partnered with a White woman, and did not associate with other Chinese people. Since David was not interviewed, we do not know if he would agree with his sisters' characterization of him. We cannot assume that David was straight-forwardly and wholly ashamed of being Chinese. Though this is pos-sible, he may simply have felt oppressed by *both* the dominant, racist British stereotype of Chinese people (as being servile people who worked only in take-aways) and the dominant norms of behavior expected by Chinese families in Britain, including the expectation that children should faithfully help out in the family business.

While opting out is a radical measure, one reason why individuals like Colin and David may have attempted to do so is that there are still very narrowly defined understandings of what it means to be Chinese in Britain. As David Parker notes in his study of young Chinese people in Britain, a dominant notion of Chineseness "allows for few departures from that norm in terms of language use, interethnic friendships and relationships" (1995: 176). To depart from these symbolic markers of Chineseness is to have your Chineseness ques-tioned. So if a person perceives that there is too little room for maneuver, opting out may appear to be a reasonable response.

However, the ability to opt out is limited by the fact that other Chinese people, and the majority of British people, may refuse to acknowledge David as anything other than Chinese, given his physical appearance. Many of these young people, including David's sisters, did not think it was possible to opt out of Chineseness, since their racialization as Chinese (based upon their physical appearance) immediately marked them out from White Britons. Opting out is rarely a complete solution, because in order to *successfully* opt out of a group, one must be able to opt into, and gain membership in, another group.

Manipulation of individual identity within a group

I have argued throughout this chapter that minority individuals are, to some extent, capable of subverting or manipulating both dom-inant stereotypes and images attributed to them by the wider society, as well as scripts of behavior imposed by their coethnics. Thus, on an individual level, while not being wholly unfettered, people are not entirely shackled in their possibilities either. By "manipulation" I do not mean that individuals are necessarily always conscious of the presentation or assertion of their identities (though they are in some situations). Both of the possibilities discussed above (whether one adheres to a script of behavior or opts out of a group) are premised upon an essentialist understanding of what it means to "be" of a particular ethnicity. Rather than adopt either of these extreme positions, which appear to provide rather neat and conclusive identity outcomes, there are other possible articulations of individual ethnic identity. There is a continuum of possibilities regarding an individual's stance, vis-à-vis their ethnic group(s) and the wider society.

Rather than adhere to a prescribed script of behavior or opt out of a group, some individuals may attempt to fashion a personalized stance toward ethnic group membership. One example of how someone may adapt an existing script is illustrated in a study of some young Black West Indians in Britain who are, in Pryce's (1979) parlance, "in-betweeners," who are neither "hustlers" nor "proletarian respectables." While rejecting the life-styles and values associated with both "hustlers" and "proletarian respectables," such individuals wanted a stable job and security without sacrificing their Black identities and becoming "sell-outs" to White society: "In-betweeners have resolved their dilemma by an ideological and highly self-conscious manipulation of their life-attitudes. In their life-style, the stable law-abiding idea of material success through conventional work has been retained, and is still valued and adhered to. However, full conformity to the overall stable law-abiding way of life is attenuated by an active preoccupation with expressive values and the need to be loyal to one's roots in terms of 'black culture' and 'black pride'" (Pryce 1979: 242). In-betweeners value group membership as West Indians, but try to assert their own version of what it means to be West Indian. By refusing to succumb to either polarity, as exemplified by "hustlers" and "proletarian respectables," they can be law abiding, steadily employed, *and* still be Black.

Another way of carving out an individualized ethnic identity is by claiming a *partial* identification with either the majority culture and society and/or one's own ethnic community. For example, David Parker found that some Chinese young people in Britain adopted a "subjectivity of conditional belonging," in which they felt a partial identification with Britain, despite their experiences of being marginalized: "This qualified sense of investment in Britain is one of the defining features of a subjectivity of conditional belonging. This involves a willingness to stay in this country, but on condition of being able to contribute to redefining the grounds on which identifications are made" (1995: 199). Some of these Chinese young people claimed a sense of localized belonging – say, in terms of a regional Geordie or Liverpudlian identity – while feeling no investment in a wider national British identity (Gilroy 1987). For many Chinese young people, while Britain is not unproblematically home, neither is Hong Kong, despite their ancestral roots there. Furthermore, conditional belonging involves a belief in open formations of identity, such that, for example, what "Chinese" means changes over time, and is not traceable back to a sole origin. To espouse an open formation of Chineseness, or any other ethnicity for that matter, is to reject not only narrowly defined and racist definitions of British nationality, but also the legitimacy of any kind of fixed script of behavior attached to any ethnic minority group.

The notion of conditional belonging is useful, because it illustrates how partial, fragmented, and multifaceted the experience of "belonging" can be. What is also striking about the idea of conditional belonging is that individuals who feel this way are staking a claim; they are refusing to accept the view that they do not belong in Britain because they are Chinese. In relation to the African Caribbean population in Britain, Stuart Hall also communicates this sentiment: "Fifteen years ago we didn't care whether there was any black in the Union Jack. Now not only do we care, we must" (Hall 1987: 30). At the same time, assertions of conditional belonging point to the ways in which African Caribbean and Chinese people resist any easy and blithe notion of belonging in multicultural Britain – for the reality is that such belonging is not total, uncontested, or unambiguously embraced. To belong in Britain, as second- or third-generation minority people, is often complicated and necessarily partial (see chapter 6).

Although ethnic minority individuals cannot fully control the ways in which they are ethnically or racially constructed by others (including other coethnics), they can, according to Roger Hewitt, retain both "the interiorised sense of self and belonging and the external blazonry of group affiliation, membership" (1992: 34). In such a situation, one's "interiorised sense of self" may diverge somewhat from one's persona as a member of a group. Anne Wilson (1987) makes a distinction between "primary" and "secondary" levels of racial identification in her discussion of mixed race children in Britain. While the primary level of racial identification is one which is largely shaped by other peoples' attributions of racial identity – for example, as Black – Wilson argues that the secondary level of identification is conceived of as a more private form of identification, in which mixed race children are able to acknowledge both sides of their dual heritage. The bifurcation of public and private identities (and associated behaviors and practices) involves a compartmentalization of identity. For instance, David

Parker found that some Chinese young people experienced their lives and identities in their homes as predominantly Chinese, while they felt primarily English in the public spheres of school and employment – "so rather than a hybrid, blended combination of British and Chinese identities, many segment the different identifications" (1995: 182).

As illustrated by these examples, some analysts have articulated a kind of dual and complementary structure to the ways in which people conceive of their ethnic identities. Thus the conceptualization of a more private, interiorized sense of identity, which is held apart from imposed identities and from public shows of group affiliation, suggests some scope for agency and control concerning the individualized maintenance of ethnic identities. The key difficulty with the notion of a privatized identity is that it begs the following question: how meaningful is such an identity if it is not recognized or legitimated in social interactions with others? Some would argue that in order for ethnic identity to thrive, it must rely on validation by others.[11]

With the exception of the two extreme positions – strict adherence to a script and opting out – the potential ways in which individuals may manipulate their ethnic identities are not mutually exclusive. Various means of articulating aspects of ethnic identity may be employed simultaneously. For instance, depending on the specific social situation, it is possible that someone who asserts a conditional sense of belonging in, say, east London, may also assert both public and private articulations of ethnic identity in specific situations.

This chapter has shown that there is a potential tension between individual assertions of ethnic identity and collective determinations about the meanings, cultural practices, and identities associated with particular ethnic groups. The specificities of a person's life experiences do not simply mirror group experience, just as collective identities are not simply reducible to the sum of various individual experiences (Brah 1996: 124). What is difficult for many minority individuals is the assertion of difference and ethnic identity on their own terms. Although pressures to adhere to particular scripts of behavior may be experienced by individuals across various ethnic minority groups, the substantive nature of such scripts is likely to differ across disparate groups. Furthermore, concerns about ethnic and racial unity may be especially intense in certain groups, such as African Americans, who evidence not only a distinctive historical experience, but also a significant degree of class diversification as a group (see chapter 5).

4

The Growth of Mixed Race People

Who is mixed race?

At a conference in 1992 sponsored by the Multi-Racial Americans of Southern California, there was debate about who qualified as a "mixed" person (Weisman 1996). In one session, a White-looking participant argued for her right to claim a multiracial identity based on her Black ancestry some generations back. But how many generations back should one go? It is widely known that most African Americans in the USA have some White ancestry in their family trees, though the White ancestor may have been the slave master from a previous century. This scenario at the conference highlights some of the thorny issues involved in the assertion of ethnic identities. Although the above woman may claim a multiracial identity (based on some Black ancestry), others may not recognize her claim to such an identity.

An exploration of how ethnic minority groups and individuals exercise their ethnic options would be incomplete without examining the experiences of so-called "mixed race" or "multiracial" people – terms I will use interchangeably in this chapter.[1] The very presence of multiracial people challenges many of the assumptions of how racial life is organized – for example, that people are inherently distinct and separable in terms of their racial backgrounds. The existence of multiracial people requires a profound rethinking not only of existing racial categories and their legitimacy, but also of the everyday belief that there are such things as "pure" and distinct races (Parker and Song 2001a).

The growth of multiracial people in both the USA and Britain reflects the increasing incidence of inter-racial cohabitation and relationships in both countries (Alibhai-Brown and Montague 1992; Root 1992; Frankenberg 1993). Although only 1.8 percent of all marriages in the USA were inter-racial in 1990 (Thornton 1996), this figure does not tell us about cohabiting couples or young couples who are dating – a number which is surely higher (S. Small 2001).[2] In the USA, Native Americans, Hispanics, and Asian Americans – particularly women in those groups – exhibit fairly high rates of exogamy (Snipp 1997: 672). A recent study found that Britain has one of the highest rates of inter-racial relationships in the world, with a rate ten times the European average (Parker and Song 2001a: 2). In Britain, 50 percent of Caribbean men (and 30 percent of Caribbean women) born in Britain, who are married or cohabiting, have a White partner (Parker and Song 2001a: 2).

In the past, mixed relationships were prohibited in the USA by anti-miscegenation laws, which applied to White–Chinese couples, as well as to White–Black couples. These laws were made unconstitutional in 1967, in the ruling *Loving v. Virginia* (Spickard 1989: 374). By comparison, there were no legal restrictions on mixed marriages in Britain; this could have been because, until the 1950s, there were relatively few Black people in Britain (Tizard and Phoenix 1993: 3). Much of the research on mixed relationships in Britain is now quite dated, and has tended to focus on African Caribbean–White partnerships (e.g. Dover 1937; Collins 1957; S. Patterson 1963; Benson 1981; see Alibhai-Brown and Montague 1992 for a more recent look at mixed relationships in Britain).

In Britain, the Fourth National Survey of Ethnic Minorities (FNSEM) queried both White and ethnic minority people about how they would feel if a close relative of theirs were to marry an ethnic minority person or a White person, respectively (Modood et al. 1997). Across all age groups, 71 percent of White respondents reported that they "would not mind," while 14 percent reported that they "would mind very much." In the case of ethnic minorities asked about a close relative marrying a White person, people of Caribbean and Chinese origin were the most tolerant of intermarriage, with 84 percent of each group saying that they "would not mind," and only 7 percent of Caribbeans and 8 percent of Chinese saying that they "would mind very much" (Modood et al. 1997: 315–16). By comparison, 40 percent of Pakistanis in the study reported that they "would mind very much" if a close relative were to marry a White Briton (but 41 percent said that they "would not mind"). Like Caribbean people in Britain, African Americans in the USA are more tolerant of intermarriage with White people than vice versa (Spencer 1997). Overall, it appears that mixed marriages are more common in Britain than in the USA, particularly between young Black and White people (Berthoud 1998).

So, most debate and scholarship about mixed people in both countries has focused upon people of White and Black heritage – despite the fact that in Britain there are more mixed people of Asian–White heritage than African Caribbean–White heritage (Phoenix and Owen 1996). And in the USA, Black–White mixture dominates thinking around mixed race, although groups such as Japanese Americans have much higher rates of intermarriage with White people (Montero 1981). The predominant focus upon people of Black and White parentage as representative of inter-racial relationships reflects the fact that such unions were historically seen as most threatening to the White population, especially in the USA. Although they are fewer in number, we should not lose sight of multiracial people who do not have a White parent, such as someone with Latino, Black, and Native American heritages, or someone of Asian, Black, and Mexican heritages, who defy binary conceptions of mixedness and the "one drop rule" (Mahtani and Moreno 2001).

Today, mixed unions exemplify not only boundary transgressions, as discussed in the last chapter, but also choice, agency, and love. Nevertheless, the offspring of such relationships are still subject to racial ideologies and rigid forms of categorization. Logically, one might expect that mixed race people possess a greater number of ethnic options than do monoracial minorities, simply by virtue of having parents of different ethnic backgrounds. But to conceive of mixed people's ethnic options in this way would be overly simplistic and erroneous. We would be mistaken to think of mixed people as automatically, or necessarily, possessing more options than monoracial people. Despite the significant constraints they experience, I argue in this chapter that there is evidence that multiracial people are increasingly assertive about choosing their ethnic identities on their own terms.

Racial ambiguity

People of so-called mixed race reflect the arbitrary and contested logic of racial distinctions (Parker and Song 2001b). Such people have historically tended to fall outside the prevailing set of racial categories. As such, mixed people may feel that they have to choose sides in relation to their multiple backgrounds; this is because, rather than recognizing or legitimating the multiplicity of heritages, the politicized discourse around racial identity tends to be dual and exclusive in nature – for example, one is regarded as Black *or* White, rather than Black *and* White. Their racial ambiguity means that they may be subject to both implicit and explicit expectations of others to justify and explain their very existence – "what" are you?!

One common supposition about all mixed people, regardless of ancestries, is that they are somehow not whole beings; rather, they are often described as being fragmented (Root 1996; Mahtani 2001) – one-half this, or one-quarter that. Notions of blood quantum have been fundamental to such thinking. For instance, the terms "mulatto" and "octoroon" have been used to refer to people with one-half and one-eighth African American heritage, respectively; while in Britain, the antiquated term "half-caste" has been used in relation to individuals of White and African Caribbean or White and Asian heritage.

The racial ambiguity of mixed people has been manipulated by White groups to ensure their dominance in racial classification systems (Spickard 1992). Historically, in White majority societies such as the USA, blood quantum was used to determine people's status and rights. For instance, the one drop rule, the rule of hypodescence, was legally upheld in many states until about the mid-twentieth century (Spickard 1989; Davis 1991). Even if one's ancestry was only one-thirty-second Black, that person was officially recorded as Black.[3] While the one drop rule has been primarily applied to people of White and African ancestry, it was also invoked in the case of people of mixed Japanese and White ancestry, who were put into internment camps during World War II, as a result of the Japanese bombing of Pearl Harbor (Spickard 1989).

Many contemporary analysts now reject the traditional terms applied to multiracial people which rely on notions of blood quantum and have pathological overtones, but there is no consensus about the appropriate terminology to use in relation to such people. For instance, some analysts have argued that the term "mixed race" (or even "multiracial" or "biracial") should be dropped altogether, since the term implies that there are indeed such things as races, in favor of more neutral terms such as "mixed parentage" (see J. Small 1986). Nevertheless, terms such as "half-caste," "mixed race," and "colored" are still very much in use in the so-called real world.

Contemporary thinking about the problems faced by mixed race individuals has been influenced by sociological and anthropological theorizing from the 1920s and 1930s on the "marginal man," who could be either a cultural or a biological hybrid. The forms of maladjustment associated with such people, such as an unbalanced mental state, race consciousness, and intense insecurity, all supposedly stemmed from their inability to fit fully into any one group (see Stonequist 1937; R. Park 1928; Furedi 2001).[4] Until relatively recently, it was largely assumed that, because of their racial ambiguity and marginal status, mixed individuals inevitably suffered from confusion about their ethnic identities, as well as from low self-esteem (A. Wilson 1987; Tizard and Phoenix 1993; Ifekwunigwe 1999). Problems were thought to arise as a result of the mixed person's efforts to incorporate two allegedly incompatible and inherently different ethnic backgrounds, cultures, and values. Like the children of minority immigrant groups, studies of whom have stressed their being "between two cultures" (e.g. Watson 1977; Anwar 1998), mixed race children were believed to be inherently in between, not really belonging to any group. The often posed question, "But what about the children?", is one that many mixed couples have had to endure from supposedly well-meaning strangers, as well as family and friends (Mass 1992; Nakashima 1996).

It is clearly impossible to generalize about all mixed people's experiences. Since we do not tend to question claims that many monoracial minorities have suffered from difficult feelings and experiences concerning their ethnic identities and minority status, it would be fatuous and unrealistic to deny that *some* multiracial people experience forms of confusion or negative (and positive) feelings in relation to their mixedness – just as some monoracial minority individuals may. Although some contemporary studies (see e.g. Lyles, Grace, and Carter, 1985; Gibbs and Moskowitz-Sweet 1991) still regard the developmental processes encountered by mixed children and adolescents in primarily problematic terms, some recent studies of mixed people reveal a different picture.

A study of the identities of mixed (Black and White) adolescents in Britain found that just under 50 percent of the 58 young people interviewed thought of themselves as "Black"; the rest considered themselves to be "brown," "mixed," or "colored" (Tizard and Phoenix 1993: 159; see also A. Wilson 1987; Katz 1996). Nevertheless, the researchers observed that some of these young people possessed multiple racial identities, and some regarded themselves as *both* Black and mixed race (or even half-caste). Tizard and Phoenix's main finding of interest, however, was that, of the 60 percent of the sample which exhibited a positive racial identity, nearly three-quarters saw themelves as mixed rather than Black. Although roughly 20 percent of the sample wished that they were White, or Black, rather than mixed, those who had positive racial identities and who saw themselves as mixed were proud of their mixed heritage, and saw more advantages than disadvantages to their mixed status (Tizard and Phoenix 1993: 161).

This is an important finding because it has been asserted for some time that only young people who saw themselves as (monoracially) Black would feel positive about themselves, while those who did not identify in this way would exhibit the classical symptoms of the marginal man discussed above (see also Lal 2001).

In recent years, some authors have challenged the view (discussed in chapter 3) that the growth of mixed race people will somehow dilute the ethnic content and boundaries of minority groups, at least in any straightforward way. For instance, studies of people of Japanese and White American parentage have found that such individuals do not necessarily lose their sense of Japanese ethnic identity. Rather, according to Mass, "they may be more aware of their Japanese heritage because they have to struggle to affirm and come to terms with their dual racial background" (1992: 266). In Mass's comparison of multiracial White–Japanese individuals and monoracial Japanese Americans, there were some instances in which some monoracial Japanese Americans felt *more* fully assimilated into mainstream American society than some mixed Japanese individuals, who possessed a very strong sense of Japanese identity (1992: 268). The fact that many mixed individuals of White and Japanese heritage *look* more White than do monoracial Japanese does not automatically ensure that they will *feel* less Japanese. Feeling Japanese, however, does not ensure recognition of their Japanese identities by other (monoracial) Japanese people or the wider society.

These studies have been important in countering the characterization of mixed people as locked into their marginal, in-between status, by pointing to the diverse identity experiences of multiracial people. Recent studies of multiracial people, particularly in the USA, have stressed the possibility of possessing multiple and fluid identities and of membership in various ethnic groups simultaneously (see especially the anthologies of Maria Root (1992, 1996) and Zack (1995)). But to what extent are mixed race people actually able to choose their ethnic identities? How does their range of ethnic options compare with those of monoracial minorities?

"Passing" and misrecognition

It is commonly believed that there is one particular ethnic ancestry which is the most "essential," defining aspect of a multiracial person. For example, mixed people with some African American heritage are largely constrained to identify as Black, even when they also have White European and Native American ancestry (Waters 1996).

Ishmael Reed and colleagues (1989) have pointed out that if Alex Haley, the famous author of *Roots* (1976), had traced his father's (as opposed to his mother's) ancestry, he would have traveled back many generations to Ireland, not Gambia. It is significant, and not by chance, that Haley emphasized his Gambian as opposed to his Irish heritage. For some mixed people, certain ancestries take precedence over others, whether by choice or through assignment by others. In the case of multiracial people with some Black heritage, the one drop rule still seems to apply in many social contexts. For instance, as a woman of White Jewish and African American heritage, Naomi Zack (1996) notes that her Black ancestry has always taken precedence over her (White) Jewish heritage in the USA. According to Zack, her Whiteness is "obliterated." If Zack were to assert her Whiteness or Jewishness as much as her Blackness, she would most likely be viewed as someone denying her Blackness, rather than as someone affirming her Jewishness or Whiteness. As Mary Waters notes, "If one believes one is part English and part German, one is not in danger of being accused of trying to 'pass' as non-English and of being 'redefined' English by the interviewer. But if one were part African and part German, one's self-identification as German would be highly suspect and probably not accepted if one 'looked' Black according to the prevailing social norms" (1996: 447).

Since there is no *racial* opposition in being a White person of both English and German heritages, the accusation of "passing" would not usually apply to such an individual. However, in the case of someone of German and African parentage claiming a German ethnic identity, such a mixed person can be subject to accusations of passing by both groups. As discussed in chapter 3 in relation to issues of ethnic authenticity, if a coethnic alleges that someone is trying to pass as White (and thus denying their non-White heritage), this would be tantamount to a charge of self-hatred and of being inauthentic to both oneself and to the wider society.[5]

By contrast, in their study of American Pacific Islanders' identities, Spickard and Fong (1995) found that it was common for Pacific Islanders (such as Hawaiians and Samoans) to claim a *multiethnic* identity. Given the history of the Pacific Islands, in which there has been a great deal of intermarriage over the centuries (this is also true for Filipinos, who have been mixed for centuries, following their colonization by Spain), Pacific Islanders have historically tended to construct their ethnic identities in complex and multifaceted ways. An important feature of Pacific Islander multiethnicity is "the common practice of choosing one from among the available identities for emphasis, at the same time holding onto other identities" (Spickard and Fong 1995: 1370). Such widely accepted and relatively uncontroversial assertions of multiethnicity, however, seem to be specific to the history and social climate of Hawaii. Again, as there is no stark racial transgression in the mixing of Hawaiians and Samoans, this assertion of multiethnic identity is less contested than in the case of a Black–White mixed person.

Indeed, the notion of passing has been most commonly discussed in relation to African Americans, although not exclusively to this group.[6] The accusation of passing is pejorative because it implies that someone is pretending to be something that he or she is not. Passing has traditionally been seen as a resource which enables people to circumvent the disadvantages associated with a non-White status. To pass as White, historically, has meant the difference between occupying a subordinate, often despised position and occupying a privileged, powerful position in White majority societies. As is well known, before civil rights legislation was enforced in the USA, African Americans were not allowed to enter White restaurants, attend White universities, or sit in the front of buses. The benefits of passing apply in the labor and housing markets, the marriage market, and in people's access to a whole range of public services. Nevertheless, many people think that passing is morally unjustifiable, because it reifies the existing structures of racial inequality in which White people are first-class citizens, while Black people remain second-class citizens.

The accusation of passing is loaded precisely because of the suggestion that a particular person is claiming an identity or heritage which is somehow *false*. In his discussion of Henry Louis Gates's biographical treatment of writer Anatole Broyard in the *New Yorker*, Paul Spickard criticizes Gates for his implicitly judgmental claim that "Anatole Broyard wanted to be a writer, not a black writer. So he chose to live a lie rather than be trapped by the truth" (Gates, quoted in Spickard 2001: 80). As a light-skinned man, Broyard is said to have passed as White in his pursuit of a career as a writer in New York in the mid-twentieth century. Gates notes that he did not want to be "trapped" into being labeled as a Black writer, as had his contemporaries Ralph Ellison and James Baldwin. So Broyard is said to have pretended to be White, and escaped the shackles of a Black identity. However, as Spickard notes: "why should Broyard's choice be construed as passing for something he was not? His appearance was White, his ancestry was mostly White, he functioned smoothly as a White man in the world without raising serious question, his adult family and friends were White – in what meaningful sense was he not White?" (2001: 81). As Spickard notes, by arguing that Broyard was "passing," Gates invokes an essentializing notion of the one drop rule.

Particularly in the 1950s, when Broyard was establishing his career, his options were limited to being *either* White *or* Black; back in those days, one could not "own" a mixed heritage and also proclaim a Black identity, as some mixed Black people are doing today.

Although some people may pass intentionally, it would be errone-ous to assume that passing is always intentional. Some light-skinned Hispanic, Black, or Eurasian people who are assumed to be White, for instance, may have no wish to pass.[7] While passing can be a resource in certain situations, it can also involve *misrecognition* and thus a potential disjuncture between how someone perceives her own ethnic identity and her identity as seen by others. Thus, even if someone with a White parent and a Mexican parent, for instance, wants to be regarded as Hispanic, her Hispanic heritage may not be readily recognized by others (including other Hispanic people and other minority groups) if she looks White. In this way, passing is not always a straightforward and positive resource, subject to control by the individual.[8]

Even for those individuals who intentionally pass, what is often overlooked is the emotional and psychological cost involved in the effort of passing. For instance, in the critically acclaimed melodrama about racial identity and mother–daughter relationships, Douglas Sirk's *Imitation of Life* (1959), a successful White actress played by Lana Turner relies heavily (both practically and emotionally) upon her Black maid/live-in assistant, Annie. Annie's daughter, Sarah-Jane, is so light-skinned (unlike her mother) that she is usually assumed to be White. As a young girl, Sarah-Jane insists upon being White, and grows up to be a young woman who is determined not to be dis-advantaged and hated for being Black in 1950s America. Sarah-Jane makes every effort to pass – in school, in various social events – and increasingly dissociates herself from her mother, whose very existence threatens the charade she feels she must play. Sarah-Jane leads a difficult life in which she is constantly fearful of being "found out" as someone with a Black heritage. The tragic consequences of her insist-ence upon passing culminate in her running away from home and adopting a new, White identity.

Thus passing needs to be reconceptualized, not as a straightfor-ward, uncomplicated resource possessed and knowingly employed by light-skinned mixed people, but rather as an ethnic option with a heavy cost, and one which mixed people may not always be able to control. The heavy cost of passing is captured in the tired notion of the "tortured mulatto," like Sarah-Jane, who lives in constant fear of discovery as someone with some Black blood. It is an ethnic option which can ensure privileged treatment, but it requires much vigilance and secrecy. As stated before, in the case of light-skinned mixed people who pass unintentionally, they can also suffer from misrecognition as a White person when they wish to be regarded as Black or mixed race.

Monoracial prescriptiveness

On the basis of the discussion above, it is clear that mixed race people can be subject to forms of monoracial prescriptiveness whereby multiracial people may feel pressured to identify themselves in terms of only one racial ancestry (Spickard 2001). This usually involves favoring a particular minority ancestry over other heritages (particularly if they have a White parent). People of White and Black parentage in both Britain and the USA have historically been regarded as Black, and this has been the basis for some contemporary analysts' claims that such mixed people are Black, and *should* see themselves as Black. However, aside from issues concerning agency and the right to choose, such reasoning is simplistic and disingenuous, because some mixed race people can be distinguished from other monoracial Black people (people with two Black parents) – for instance, on the basis of their lighter skin color and their known mixed parentage (Phoenix and Owen 1996; Zack 1996).

Contrary to the assumption that it is only the White majority which does not recognize mixed people as, for example, being of both White and Black heritage (given the historical legacy of the one drop rule in the USA (Spickard 1989)), the recognition of mixed identity has become a controversial topic among various minority groups in Western societies. We must remember that groups do not only deny some people membership; they can keep people *in* the group via "forced inclusion" (Hickman 1998), for instance, by labeling or categorizing someone in a particular way. A mixed race person with some Black ancestry may be said to experience forced inclusion if she is held to the one drop rule by other people – so that, even if she were of both White and Black parentage, she would be expected to identify herself in relation to her Black heritage. This rule has been historically enforced by Whites, but it now enjoys some degree of support among African Americans (Spencer 1997; S. Small 2001). This kind of forced inclusion is problematic, because it may involve the misrecognition of some individuals. As discussed in relation to the notion of ethnic or racial authenticity in the last chapter, individuals can be labeled or attributed ethnic identities which are not consonant with their own sense of identity.

The attribution of a monoracial identity to a mixed race person in effect denies that person's mixed heritage. In fact, it is possible for a mixed person of part-Black heritage to claim *both* mixed and Black identities, as Darryl Slater, aged 32, does, in an interview for the *Guardian* newspaper: "He was born to a Jamaican father and a White, British mother. He says he is both Black and mixed-race. 'Some people have a problem with that and think I have to come down on one side or the other but I think I can contain those contradictions. As far as mainstream British society is concerned I am Black, but sometimes it helps to make the distinction as to what kind of Black that is'" (Younge 1997: 2). Although Darryl notes that the wider society will see him as Black, even if he is only part-Black, he insists upon his prerogative to recognize *both* his White mother and his Black father. His experience of his parents and family relationships, if nothing else, is distinct from that of monoracial Black people.

Conversely, multiracial people with a particular mix of ancestries may be denied membership within a monoracial ethnic group because they are not regarded as, for instance, *fully* Japanese, or fully Indian (and this could also apply to mixed people of White and Black heritage in relation to both the White and Black populations). Although people can "work at" proving their authenticity, a key criterion for ethnic authenticity among many ethnic groups is something that most people cannot change, control, or manipulate: their physical appearance and parental heritage. For instance, some individuals were told that they could not be part-Japanese (if that individual was Japanese-African American or Japanese-White American) because they did not look Japanese (see Hall 1992; Mass 1992).

The following excerpt concerning Ron, a person of White American and Japanese American ancestry, illustrates the exclusion experienced by some multiracial people from monoracial minority communities. Ron was wearing a fuku charm on his necklace (a character meaning good fortune in Chinese and happiness in Japanese) one evening in San Francisco's Japantown. He encountered some acquaintances of Indonesian, Chinese, and Vietnamese backgrounds. These acquaintances told Ron that he should not wear the charm because they alleged that he did not know its meaning (presumably because he was "only" part-Japanese). They brutally attacked Ron after tearing off his necklace. According to Ron:

This happened in Japantown. The place where I have felt the most comfortable. I am Japanese and I have a right to do whatever I want to, especially to wear my necklace. I have heard just about every derogatory, oppressive, and offensive comment from just about every full Asian or Pacific Islander person that I have ever met, and these people are usually supposed to be my "friends". Many ask me, "Why do you want to be a *Real Japanese* so bad?" Ya know, I don't want to be anything. I am who I am. My culture that I have grown up with is Japanese American. What the hell am I supposed to do? I can't be White. I have had White people start fights with me because they think I am Mexican. I can't be full Japanese [because] shit like this happens to me all the time. I can't be Latino [because] I'm not Latino. I'm Hapa.[9] But barely anybody I talk to knows what that is. And anyway, when I am myself – doing many Japanese things – people criticize me and say that I can't do that – I am only *trying* to be Japanese.

(Quoted from Mengel 2001: 108, emphasis original)

Laurie Mengel notes that, "While in White America, Ron's Asian blood cannot make him White, in Asian America, his White blood cannot make him Asian." In this sense, some White people and Japanese Americans (and other Asian Americans more generally) may regard mixed people like Ron as being truly "marginal" (Stonequist 1937). In contrast with invoking the one drop rule, which can entail the forced inclusion of people with some Black ancestry in the category Black, Ron's experiences demonstrate that monoracial minorities can also deny membership to people because they are not "fully" of any *one* heritage. Mengel found that a number of her respondents reported that their relatives considered them to be primarily of one race – but always the one that the relative was not, as in the case of a Korean-Scottish woman: "I feel that both sides of the family seem to regard me as a member of the opposite race." Thus a Scottish relative would consider this woman to be Korean, while a Korean relative would see her as Scottish.

As discussed earlier, Naomi Zack, who is of White Jewish and African American heritage, experienced misrecognition in a multitude of ways (both from White people and from other minorities) because of her indeterminate physical appearance. Moreover, the negotiation of her ethnic identity was complicated by the fact that there is now some antagonism between Jewish and Black groups in the USA.[10] As a result, she finds it difficult to embrace membership in either group. For Zack, holding back from claiming membership in these groups is an ethical decision she has made, in favor of the "existential limbo of not-being" (1996: 151), because to claim membership in one group would implicitly endorse the prejudice and hatred toward the other part of her heritage. Also, it is clear that Zack does not feel that she should *have* to choose between one or the other ethnicity. Being Jewish and being African American should not be mutually exclusive. People like Zack, or the Korean-Scottish woman above, may

be pressured into monoracial boxes not only by the wider population, but also by their own families and by monoracial minority
communities.

As illustrated by Ron's experiences in Japantown, racisms experienced by mixed people are not generally acknowledged. Like some
monoracial minorities, some mixed people may attempt to minimize
their experiences of racism as a coping mechanism (Khan 2001;
Kuo 1995). Such a refusal to acknowledge the racialized experiences
of mixed people can also occur in families, and is not confined to
interactions with others in the outside world (Ifekwunigwe 2001).
Unfortunately, it is not only White people, but also Black, Asian, and
other mixed people, who may perpetrate racist attitudes toward mixed
people of various backgrounds (Khan 2001).

"Choice" and the growth of multiracial autobiography

Recent studies have shown that the process of self-definition, in relation to others, can be lengthy and exhausting for many mixed people,
requiring a whole geography and history of explanation (Mahtani
2002; Mengel 2001). For example, Minelle Mahtani observes, "The
burden of hyphenation, where one is seen as not solely 'Canadian' but
'Canadian and fill-in-your-ethnic-background' is especially heavy for
women of 'mixed race', who further trouble the hyphen by employing and intermingling two or more ethnicities in their own definitions
of their identities, through the coining of labels like 'African-Persian-
Cherokee-European-Canadian' " (2002: 12). In these ways, the mixed
person resists the occupation of a single ethnic space.

Despite (or because of) the pressures on multiracial people to
identify themselves primarily in terms of only one of their ancestries,
many recent writings about multiracial people have emphasized the
ways in which multiracial individuals defiantly assert their desired
identities. Analysts such as Maria Root exhort mixed people to re-
work existing racial dogmas and classifications, which have no place
for them, by declaring multiple racial and ethnic identities. By doing
so, multiracial people are said to be able to create "emotion/psychic
earthquakes in the social system" (1996: 8). Root also advocates "a
bill of rights for racially mixed people": "I have the right . . . not to
justify my existence in this world; not to be responsible for people's
discomfort with my physical ambiguity; to identify myself differently
than strangers expect me to identify; to identify myself differently
than how my parents [and siblings] identify me; to change my identity
over my lifetime – and more than once; to have loyalties and identify

with more than one group of people; to freely choose whom I be-friend and love" (1996: 7). A noticeable tone is the defiance with which Root asserts her rights as a multiracial person. She challenges the fragmenting and fractionalizing of self which she has experienced in her lifetime: "How exactly does a person be one fourth, one eighth, or one half something?" (1996: 3).

In the USA there is now a proliferating body of autobiographical literature which explores the experiences of multiracial individuals (Spickard 2001). A key theme in the growing literature on being multiracial is the issue of agency and choice and the right to choose one's ethnic identities and affiliations. Many of these books chart the personal journeys undergone by the authors in their quest for a validated mixed identity, while navigating forms of racism and the occasionally treacherous politics surrounding racial affiliation and membership (see G. H. Williams 1995; Sollors 1997; Funderburg 1994; Thompson and Tyagi 1996). Some authors, such as Shirlee Haizlip (1994), in *The Sweeter the Juice*, celebrate their mixedness in an unproblematic way, rather than portray mixed identity as a social and personal problem.

Nevertheless, this autobiographical genre often reveals personal pain, doubt, and probing. Kevin Johnson's *How did you Get to be Mexican?* (1999) documents his gradual recognition and acceptance of his Mexican American identity. As the son of a White American father and a Mexican American mother, Johnson tells us that he could have passed as White, and in fact often did pass as White in his childhood and young adulthood in California. However, his confusion and doubts about his ethnic identity came to a head when he attended Harvard Law School, where he felt terribly alienated from the predominantly White, wealthy students in his class. Although he denied his Mexican American heritage when growing up, Johnson tells us that he worried that "real" Latinos at Harvard Law School, those who were politicized about their Latino identity, might reject him (1999: 30).

Because his parents divorced when he was relatively young, Johnson led a difficult split existence. In his life during the week with his Mexican American mother, he and his brother subsisted on food stamps; but at the weekends with his much more affluent father, Johnson inhabited a predominantly middle-class, White world. As an adult, his uncertainties about whether or not he felt part Mexican American stemmed from the derogatory images of illegal Mexican immigrants with which he had grown up. Furthermore, his mother had tried to Anglicize him. In addition to her denial of her own Mexican heritage (she would say that she was Spanish, not Mexican),

Johnson's mother purposely avoided teaching her sons any Spanish. According to Johnson, "Many Latinos have been much more successful [than his mother] at integrating themselves into the Anglo mainstream. Assimilation, however, involves pain and suffering, and my mother was one of its casualties. . . . I am convinced that my mother's psychological traumas were inextricably linked to her assimilation experience and her efforts to be 'white'" (1999: 61).

A further complicating factor for Johnson was his physical appearance, which was, as in the case of many other multiracial people, rather indeterminate. At various times in his life, Johnson reveals that he was mistaken for being Asian American, rather than Mexican American! *How did you Get to be Mexican?* is also valuable because it points to the many contingencies which can be fundamental in the perception of a person's ethnic identity. For instance, the author notes the significance of him having his father's Anglo surname – Johnson: "To some people, I look white enough. But change my name to Kevin Johnson Gallardo or Kevin Johnson Salazar and my social identity would be instantly transformed" (1999: 126). Rather than explicitly and consciously choosing to be Mexican American in a politicized way, Johnson is more illustrative of someone who gradually and painfully grows into his Mexican American heritage.

In addition to biographical and autobiographical works on being mixed race, a growing body of fiction (much of which is autobiographically based) on the subject of mixed race has emerged.[11] For instance, Mira Stout's *One Thousand Chestnut Trees* (1997) tells the story of a young woman of Korean and Irish American heritage, whose interest in her Korean heritage is awakened in her twenties. The book chronicles her ambivalent efforts to find out more about her mother's history and family in Korea, including her mother's traumatic experiences as a young girl during the Korean War. In doing so, the protagonist acknowledges her own Korean heritage. In many ways, this story of initial disinterest in her Korean heritage, denial, confusion, "owning up," and, eventually, complicated acceptance of her dual heritage, exemplifies many of the themes addressed in the autobiographical genre on being mixed race.

In theory, assuming they have some knowledge of, and exposure to, both parents' families and histories, mixed individuals can choose from a variety of ethnic heritages in the formation of an ethnic identity. There are a number of possibilities. Some people may insist upon the recognition of both parents' heritages (and some parents may have multiracial backgrounds themselves). Another possibility is that some elements of a person's ethnic heritage may become more or less salient over time (Spickard 1989; Snipp 1997). While some multiracial individuals refuse to choose one particular ancestry as being more central to their identities than another (like Zack, discussed above), others may do so. For some, this may mean that there is unequal valuation of each parent's heritage (Kich 1992). Lisa Jones, in *Bulletproof Diva* (1994), adopts an openly politicized and explicit stance about *choosing* to be Black, although she has a White mother and a Black father: "That I don't deny my White forbears but call myself African American. . . . That I feel comfortable and historically grounded in this identity. That I find family there, whereas no White people have embraced me with their culture" (in Spickard 2001: 79). While Jones acknowledges her mixed ancestry, and has a good relationship with her White Jewish mother, she embraces her Black identity.

Given some of the difficulties which can arise from straddling two or more disparate groups, some mixed people do choose sides, due to a proactive political decision to identify as a member of a particular group, or because they genuinely feel more a part of one group than the other. Nevertheless, each author's trajectory of ethnic identification is quite distinctive, and while some people may make a personal choice about choosing one ethnic identity over another (like Lisa Jones), others may not consciously make any choices but, rather, gradually drift into a particular identity.

Accounting for mixed race in the Census

The growing emphasis upon choice as illustrated in the autobiographical writings by mixed race authors has also shaped debate about how multiracial people should be represented in the Census in Britain and the USA. The growth of mixed race people and families has raised numerous questions about the adequacy of state policies and official taxonomies of racial and ethnic categorization in accurately counting and capturing the lived experiences of mixed people. As a result, there has been much debate on both sides of the Atlantic about the Census.

In order to address the changes brought about by the increase of multiracial people, the first population censuses of the new millenium in the USA (2000) and Britain (2001) utilized rethought ethnic categories. Generally speaking, the Census question on ethnic origin is extremely important, because it has tended to be adopted as the standard ethnic classification system in all official statistics, and it is widely used by other organizations conducting research or ethnic monitoring (Owen 2001).

In the 2000 Census in the USA, for the first time multiracial people were able to mark all the racial categories they felt applied to them (Office of Management and Budget 1997). In the past, individuals were forced to label themselves in relation to only one ethnic category. Even when individuals ticked as many boxes as applied to their multiple heritages, government agencies in the USA tended to edit down multiple responses to one response (Snipp 1997: 669). For example, in the 1990 Census, questionnaires in which more than one box was ticked were simply assigned a single race.

The 1991 British Census was the first to ask questions about ethnicity, and included nine categories.[12] In Britain's 2001 Census, a "mixed race" category was one of five main ethnic categories available, with four further subheadings within the mixed category: "White and Black Caribbean, White and Black African, White and Asian, Any other mixed background, please describe" (Owen 2001: 147).

The main objective in introducing a "mixed race" box in a Census is to ascertain the ethnic origins of the population. But obtaining that information is not easy. The mere provision of a mixed category in the British 2001 Census does not ensure accurate information about the existence of multiracial people in Britain. According to Richard Berthoud:

First, it is important that *everyone* of mixed origin should be recorded as such. We need to avoid the possibility that some individuals of mixed black-white origin would choose Black, others White and others Mixed. All three categories would then lose their shape. Second, Mixed is not an ethnic origin in its own right. In particular, it seems unlikely that people of mixed black-white heritage would have much in common with those of mixed Indian-white heritage. A single Mixed category would therefore be both unpopular with the people concerned, and meaningless to analysts.

(1998: 62, emphasis original)

Berthoud stresses that the Census is primarily about getting an accurate picture of people's ethnic origins, not about which part of their heritage people identify with most closely.[13] Asking about both parents' ethnic *origins*, rather than query the respondent about her ethnic *identity*, allows us to differentiate between people's ethnic ancestries and the ways in which they conceive of their own ethnic identities. The two may not necessarily be the same.

While some analysts such as Berthoud (1998) oppose a "mixed race" box in the British Census, on the grounds that it may provide inaccurate information about people's ethnic origins, other analysts favor it over the checking of multiple ethnic categories, for politically motivated reasons. The creation of a mixed category may help to officially legitimate the existence of mixed people who wish to be known as mixed (regardless of their specific ethnic mix). Although its introduction may be an important step in recognizing the ethnic diversity and complexity surrounding ethnic identification, others object to a "mixed race" box in the Census because it is believed to be a meaningless, essentializing racial category.

Some people and organizations (such as the National Association for the Advancement of Colored People in the USA) have opposed the creation of a "mixed" box because it would affect the political enumeration and representation of monoracial minority groups such as African Americans. F. James Davis (1991) has argued that any changes to the one drop rule which would encourage lighter-skinned Black people to "leave" the Black community for the White community would result in significant losses for the Black population, in its political strength, its leaders, and its business and professional people. In *The New Colored People*, John Michael Spencer (1997) concurs with Davis, and is fearful that the creation of a "multiracial" box in the American Census will mean that, given this option, mixed people of Black and White heritage will *choose* to shun their Black identity in favor of a mixed identity. Spencer argues that the existence of a multiracial category in the Census could, in effect, elevate mixed people to a non-Black status, thus creating an intermediate category not unlike that of "coloureds" which existed under South African apartheid; he claims that the creation of such a category would further stigmatize monoracial Black people in the racial hierarchy.

Spencer argues that "all black people (of 'race' and 'mixed race') have come this far together and absolutely must stay together until we are all free" (1997: 52). However well intentioned this belief may be, by pleading for a unified fight against racial discrimination and oppression, such a stance may be regarded by some as an oppressive imposition of racial identity on mixed people – the forced inclusion of multiracial people under the rubric "Black." In the contemporary context, the presumption that mixed people (of Black and White heritage) who can identify as "mixed race" (as opposed to Black) will necessarily do so is unsubstantiated – as found in personal testimonies of various mixed race people such as Lisa Jones, who is clearly proud of being Black. While some mixed individuals espouse a mixed or Black identity, others claim to be *both* Black and mixed race.

Such concerns about a mixed category in the Census have also been voiced in Britain. For instance, an article about the growth of mixed race people in the *Guardian* (Younge 1997) illustrates some Black people's opposition to the recognition of a "mixed" category in the 2001 Census: "Bernie Grant, [the late, Black] Labour MP for Tottenham, objects, claiming that such a classification would give the illusion that such people make up a self-sufficient racial or ethnic group. 'Society sees mixed-race people as black, and they are treated as black. They are never accepted as white, so they have no choice', he says." Grant argues that mixed race people are not recognized as such by society. Here, Grant suggests that the one drop rule in effect applies to mixed people of Black and White heritage in Britain, just as in the USA.

However, who exactly "society" refers to is ambiguous. Is it everyone (including other Black and mixed people) or the White majority? Barbara Tizard and Ann Phoenix's findings contradict Grant's claim. These authors point out that because many of their mixed race respondents *looked* different from monoracial Black people, some individuals having very light skin, these individuals would actually be perceived as being different from other Black people by the wider population. Thus to assert a "brown" or "mixed" identity, as some respondents did, was not necessarily at odds with how they were perceived by others (1993: 163).

It is difficult to assess just how common it is for others to register the different physical appearance of mixed Black and White people, but research on skin color differences among African Americans suggests that such differences are noted and significant (see Keith and Herring 1991; Russell, Wilson, and Hall 1992). Grant and like-minded analysts may claim that the recognition of different physical features between mixed and monoracial Black people is only superficial, and does not prevent White people from stereotyping and lumping together all Black people of various shades. This may be true in various social situations. Grant denies that the assertion of a mixed identity will have any effect upon the ways in which "society" views and treats such people, and thus curtails any consideration of whether or not mixed people can or *should* be able to assert a mixed identity of their choosing.

There is no clear consensus among multiracial people or activists in either the USA or Britain about whether it is preferable to check multiple ethnic backgrounds, or to designate a single "mixed race" box in the Census. However, given the political concerns about the introduction of a mixed race category in the USA, some multiracial analysts and activists, such as Maria Root and Reg Daniels, have favored the strategy of ticking multiple boxes (the check-all-that-apply option), as opposed to one multiracial box, precisely because of their solidarity with monoracial minority communities and their wish to avoid politically undermining monoracial minority groups in any way (Spickard 2001: 84).

A multiracial panethnicity?

As suggested in the discussion of the Census above, there is now considerable evidence that there is a kind of multiracial movement afoot, especially in the USA (S. Small 2001; Mengel 2001; Spickard 2001; Spencer 1997). According to Cynthia Nakashima, three main goals are identified in the multiracial movement: (1) the struggle for inclusion and legitimacy in "traditional" racial/ethnic communities; (2) the shaping of a shared identity and common agenda among racially mixed people into a new multiracial community; and (3) the struggle to dismantle dominant racial ideology and group boundaries and to create connections across communities and so form a community of humanity (1996: 81). This movement has spawned the growth of community organizations, campus groups, university courses, magazines and newsletters, academic research and writings, and political activism, which have been created and run by multiracial people and individuals who are members of multiracial families (Nakashima 1996: 80). The 1970s witnessed the emergence of many political organizations concerning mixed race people in the USA.[14]

Much of the connective tissue binding together multiracial people is said to stem from the fact that, not only are such individuals potentially marginalized within monoracial communities (as graphically depicted in the case of Ron), but multiracial people are said to share many similar experiences and developmental concerns. For instance, George Kitahara Kich has argued that multiracial individuals tend to go through three major stages in the development and continuing resolution of their identities, including (1) an initial awareness of being different and of dissonance between self-perceptions and other people's perceptions of them; (2) a wish to be accepted by others; and (3) gradual acceptance of themselves as multiracial people. According to Kich, these three stages illustrate a multiracial person's transitions "from a questionable, sometimes devalued sense of self to one where an interracial self-conception is highly valued and secure" (1992: 305). Although not all multiracial people may experience these three stages in this order, Kich's argument that multiracial people share the task of differentiating between their own experiences and conceptions of themselves and other people's interpretations of them is important and likely to apply to many multiracial people.

Some analysts have also argued that multiracial people have in common the fact that their experiences are quite distinct from those of monoracial minorities. For instance, Laurie Mengel (2001: 107) points out that unless they are multiracial themselves, the parents of a multiracial child (though they are in a mixed relationship) cannot fully understand the experience of their offspring.

To illustrate the unique experience of being mixed, Mengel claims that a "third space" is occupied by all multiracial people, regardless of their particular mix of ancestries. Thus an important basis of a multiracial movement is said to be mixed people's consciousness of occupying this shared third space (Bhabha 1990b). In such a space, being mixed in itself constitutes an experiential link between people, and this link differs from the linkages which exist between mixed race people and monoracial individuals who share a common ancestry. Just as an Asian American panethnicity emerged in the context of their racial grouping by White American society, though Asian Americans are comprised of many different ethnicities and nationalities (Espiritu 1992), multiracial people may recognize a commonality with other multiracials, because of their common treatment (as fragmented beings) by monoracial minorities and the wider community.

Again, there is no consensus about whether multiracial people comprise a coherent group on the basis of their mixedness per se. What exactly this third space is, and whether it is a sufficient basis for a multiracial panethnicity are open to question. Some scholars have argued that a genuine and meaningful multiracial identity must be based on more than the common denominator of being mixed (see Thornton 1992, 1996). In Britain, Richard Berthoud (1998) has questioned the assumption that multiracial people of various mixes necessarily share similar experiences and views. For example, why would an individual who is White English and Black Nigerian necessarily feel a connection with someone who is White English and Chinese, particularly if their respective class backgrounds and residential locations differ markedly?

As discussed in relation to the diverse experiences of the authors of mixed race autobiographies, some empirical studies of mixed people have shown the very diverse experiences of multiracial people. Depending upon the particular mix of parental ancestries, the class backgrounds of families, the ethnic composition of neighborhoods and schools, and the ways in which they are treated by the wider local population, mixed people (even those of the same mixture) may have significantly different experiences in various spheres of their lives. What individuals are actually told about their ethnic backgrounds and communication (if any) about racism are also likely to be important in shaping the ethnic identities of mixed individuals (Waters 1990). In fact, Funderburg's interviews with individuals of Black and White parentage in *Black, White, Other* (1994) reveal that, despite a common mixed heritage, her respondents had unique lives and experiences, which could not be boiled down to broad commonalities on the basis of a shared mixed race background. Therefore, the proclamation that all multiracial people comprise a panethnic group may be premature – though this does not preclude the possibility of negotiating a common political agenda concerning their representation. Analysts such as Stephen Small (2001) have also criticized the movement for being myopically elitist and middle class in its excessive emphasis upon *individual* rights to freely assert ethnic identities of their choosing. Because the movement is peopled primarily with middle-class people, Small questions whether the key concerns identified by these people speak to the experiences and concerns of poor and working-class mixed people.

Furthermore, it is questionable whether the experiences and concerns of multiracial people are that different from those of many monoracial minorities more generally. Many of the rights specified by Root (1996) in a "bill of rights" for multiracial people could apply to the experiences of monoracial minority people. For instance, the right to identify differently from the ways in which one's parents and siblings view one and the right to have friendships and relationships with whomever one chooses are both concerns for monoracial minority individuals. It is not only multiracial people who encounter barriers or difficulties in negotiating their membership in minority communities. Monoracial minorities who veer from dominant scripts of behavior, as discussed in the last chapter, may endanger their group membership and have their ethnic or racial authenticity questioned.

Nevertheless, some multiracial analysts have celebrated the growth of mixed relationships and individuals as a hopeful sign of a more tolerant future, in which racial difference and boundaries will be of decreasing importance. According to the mission statement of *Interracial Voice*, "contemporary advocacy of a mixed-race identifier is the largest and most meaningful assault on the mythical concept of white racial purity/supremacy . . . the group most able to help this society bridge the gap between the race-obsessed present and an ideal future of racelessness is the mixed-race contingent."[15] Thus multiracial people are characterized as being in the vanguard of "an ideal future of racelessness" – if this end is indeed possible.

However, Michael Thornton, who is of Japanese and African American ancestry, characterizes some of the optimistic, celebratory assertions about mixed people as being too blithe and exaggerated, because they "view multiracial people as the hope of the future: able to freely flit across racial borders, and as a birthright to interact with assorted people and provide the seed for the destruction of race as a stratifying concept" (1996: 107). But the ability of mixed people, or minority people more generally, to "flit across racial borders" or assert their desired ethnic identities is far from unfettered, and is structured by a number of factors. There has not been enough study of the comparative experiences of different kinds of multiracial people, so we can only speculate about potential differences in the ways they work at asserting their desired identities.

Among other things, this chapter has illustrated the ways in which people with some Black ancestry in the USA may be subject to the one drop rule by White people and monoracial Black people, entailing a form of forced inclusion in the category "Black." In Britain, similar kinds of pressures seem to bear on people of White and Black ancestry to identify as Black, in comparison with the more easily achieved recognition that Anglo-Indians or Anglo-Chinese people, for example, are genuinely multiracial, and thus distinct from both monoracial Whites and minorities. As David Hollinger observes, "Asian European mixtures are highly visible because the society [U.S.] does not have a long-standing convention of concealing them by automatically consigning them to the Asian side of the descent, as it consigns black-white mixtures to the black side" (1995: 42–3).[16]

However, it would be mistaken to conclude that people of White and Asian heritage are necessarily more able to assert their desired ethnic identities than mixed people of Black and White heritage. It seems that while Eurasian people, such as Ron (discussed above), are not subject to a one drop rule (where they would be consistently categorized as Asian, as opposed to Asian and White), they are often seen as racially indeterminate and thus consigned to marginality and "otherness." Nor are mixed people with two minority heritages, such as Mexican and Chinese, or Iranian and Indian, easily able to gain recognition of their mixed status. They, too, are often subject to misrecognition and interrogation about their ethnic make-up (Mahtani and Moreno 2001).

Given the growth in many kinds of mixed relationships, including relationships between non-White people from various groups, a more diverse exploration of the ways in which mixed people conceive of and assert their ethnic identities is required. There is a need to go beyond the dualities of Black and White, not only because it's important to validate the existence of other kinds of mixed people, but also because nuanced theorizing on multiracial people cannot progress without considering the particularities of different kinds of mixed experiences.

5

The Diversification of Ethnic Groups

> Identities both reflect and potentially disrupt or recreate social and political relationships within and between groups. Examining the construction and reconstruction of identities over time contributes to our understanding of social and political processes through which individuals and groups locate themselves in relation to others, understand themselves, and define their possibilities.
>
> (Schulz 1998: 336)

The changing composition of groups

How do the changing composition and boundaries of ethnic groups shape the ways in which groups assert and negotiate their ethnic identities? In recent years, divisions have arisen among ethnic and panethnic groups, which stem from large-scale demographic and social changes in contemporary multiethnic societies such as Britain and the USA (Omi and Winant 1996). For example, the large panethnic group known as Latino or Hispanic was adopted by the US 1980 Census, and is increasingly diverse, including newly arrived Mexican immigrants, Puerto Ricans, refugees from El Salvador, and long-settled Cubans in Miami, among others (Portes and MacLeod 1996). By panethnic group, I mean "a politico-cultural collectivity made up of peoples of several, hitherto distinct, tribal or national origins" (Espiritu 1992: 2).

The emergence of these divisions is significant, because they affect the ways in which ethnic and panethnic groups go about asserting and negotiating their ethnic identities in multiethnic societies. Generally speaking, the diversification of various ethnic groups has resulted in the proliferation of the identities and images associated with each group, and this, in turn, has resulted in much contestation about each group's identity, culture, and position in relation to other groups. Given the growing diversification of ethnic groups, and their changing boundaries and memberships, tensions may develop concerning their image, cultural content, and political agenda. The meanings associated with, say, Asian American identity in the USA, or Black identity in

Britain, are increasingly contested and complicated by the changing composition and diversity of these groups and the subgroups which comprise them.

In this chapter, the diversification of groups and its implications for the negotiation of ethnic identity will be examined in relation to three particular cases: (a) class and gender-based disparities among African Americans; (b) tensions emerging between new Asian immigrants and more established Asian Americans; (c) contestations around the membership and meanings associated with the panethnic category Black in Britain.

The formation of panethnic identities

A heightened racial consciousness among ethnic minority groups has emerged, in both the USA and Britain, in the context of continuing flows of immigration and a political backlash against immigrants by the wider society. This has resulted in the institutionalization of race and ethnicity as a basis of both access to government resources and political mobilization (Kibria 1997: 526). Categories such as race and ethnicity are best understood as political resources that are used by both dominant and subordinate groups in order to legitimize and further their own social identities and interests (Solomos and Back 1996). In the process of constructing and reconstructing their ethnic identities, and what they stand for, groups must locate and define themselves in relation to other groups (Nagel 1994; Schulz 1998).

Given the current political climate, there is increased competition among ethnic minority groups for housing, employment, places in universities, and minority aid programs. The competition between groups for scarce resources means that how groups represent themselves (which inevitably involves questions of how they draw their ethnic boundaries) becomes ever more important in their quest for economic resources and/or social and political recognition (O. Patterson 1977). The strategic jockeying for particular objectives can result in the formation (or sometimes dissolution) of panethnic cooperation and alliances (Hechter 1987; Roosens 1989). According to Michael Omi and Howard Winant, "At times it is advantageous to be in a panethnic bloc, and at times it is desirable to mobilize along particular ethnic lines. Therefore both a politics of inclusion and exclusion are involved in panethnicity, as racial and ethnic definitions and boundaries are contested" (1996: 472).

Historically, panethnic groups have emerged in contexts in which there is a strategic advantage in forming large groups, so that previously distinct national and/or ethnic groups can more effectively press for political demands (Espiritu 1992; Olzak 1992). Panethnic groupings can emerge either from the imposition of a category by the state (e.g. the categorization of all Spanish-speaking people in the USA as Latino or Hispanic) or from the voluntary mobilization of various groups into a larger panethnic group. In this sense, a panethnic group can be new or "emergent" when ethnic identification, organization, and collective action are constructed around identities which did not previously exist, such as Latino or Asian American (Yancey, Ericksen, and Juliani 1976). And while such categories may be initially unwanted in some cases, groups who are categorized together within larger panethnic rubrics can, in some cases, develop a real (though not necessarily lasting) sense of kinship with one another.

For instance, because the US government lumped together various Native American tribes in the formation of their federal policies on "Indians," Native Americans gradually came to rely on a broad panethnic identity, by highlighting their pan-Indian status, in addition to their tribal affiliations. By emphasizing their pan-Indian status, not only did Native Americans stress their special status as the original inhabitants of the Americas who were largely decimated by the arrival of White Europeans; they also lobbied for various kinds of governmental resources targeted at Native Americans. In the 1960s, activist movements such as the American Indian Movement (AIM), which relied upon a collective notion of pan-Indian status, fought against the federal government's dismantling of tribal rights and worked to redefine the meanings associated with Indianness (Jarvenpa 1988; Schulz 1998). Thus broad panethnic groupings, such as "Native Americans," can make their boundaries more inclusive in order to gain particular resources or achieve political goals (see A. Cohen 1974; Olzak 1992).

For another example, in the 1960s, the political mobilization of Asian Americans was based upon the notion that Asians shared a common racial position in the USA, and included groups of diverse backgrounds, such as Japanese, Chinese, Korean, and Filipino Americans (Espiritu 1992; Takagi 1994). As various analysts have pointed out, being automatically labeled as "Oriental" or "Asian" on the basis of one's physical appearance, without regard to national or ethnic differences, is a very common experience of many Asian Americans (Espiritu 1992; Tuan 1998).

In addition to instrumental concerns about resources and political representation, emotionally charged contestations concerning a group's ethnic identity are also common because of the importance of the meanings associated with particular ethnic and panethnic groups. As discussed below, the political rubric "Black" in Britain has been the source of great debate. Exactly what kinds of identities and images are evoked by the category "Black"? Are panethnic rubrics, such as "Black," genuinely embraced by the people who are subsumed by them, or are specific ethno-national distinctions still of importance?

Panethnic formations are unstable and changeable over time, because they are highly situational. Depending upon the particular context and circumstances, national identities may be emphasized over panethnic identities, or vice versa (Nagel 1994; Kibria 1997). The degree of diversity within panethnic groupings may ultimately limit the cohesion of such entities. For instance, the groups which are included within the panethnic category "Hispanic" may be too diverse for the workings of a coherent panethnic group (Massey et al. 1993). Mexicans, Puerto Ricans, and Cubans, to name only a few, exhibit so many differences of class, history, and culture that they do not share enough in common with one another.

As will be discussed below, just as ethnic groups may make their boundaries more inclusive in order to gain certain resources or achieve political goals, so some groups may attempt to distance themselves from undesirable associations with others, by tightening or narrowing their boundaries.

Class disparities among African Americans

Class differentiation among various ethnic minority groups in Western societies has been emerging, and it suggests the inadequacy of older paradigms which stressed the collective, disadvantaged status of all ethnic minority groups and immigrants (e.g. Castles and Kosack 1973). In the USA, the class diversification of African Americans has led to debate about the nature of racial disadvantage and discrimination experienced by them (see W. J. Wilson 1978; Landry 1987; Feagin and Sikes 1994; Duneier 1992), and the implications of class diversification for the ethnic and racial identities of African Americans (see chapter 3).[1] As with any other group, different subgroups of Black people do not necessarily agree about what it means to be Black, or the political strategies and issues which should be implemented in effecting social and political change.

William Julius Wilson famously argued that the life chances of individual African Americans "have more to do with their economic class position than with their day-to-day encounters with Whites" (1978: 1). Similarly, analysts such as Thomas Sowell (1981) argued that the impact of racism per se no longer explains the disparities in outcomes among different minority groups. Pointing to the experiences of racialized groups who are generally considered successful in the USA, such as Koreans, West Indians, and Japanese, he argued that race is not an insurmountable barrier to mobility, despite its historical importance.[2] Instead, Sowell pointed to the significance of groups' differential possession of human capital.

The diversification and dispersal of African Americans has occurred primarily along class lines, leading to disparities in the experiences of the Black middle class, working class, and so-called underclass. It is ironic that, as Omi and Winant point out, "A generation after the enactment of major civil rights reforms, the African American community is both the beneficiary and victim of its own success. A community once knitted together by survival imperatives in a segregated society and bound up by the thick relationships of labor, commerce, residence, and religion within its own community has now been dispersed" (1996: 473). While many middle-class African Americans fled the inner cities in search of a better life, many poor Black people whose employment prospects were hard hit by forms of economic restructuring, particularly in the manufacturing industries, remained in urban ghettoes (W. J. Wilson 1987). Poor Black people's existence in such enclosed ghettoes has made it very difficult for them to aspire to work or to adhere to conventional ideals of success.[3] Unlike the Black middle class, which has been able to enjoy some prosperity, many poor African Americans remain in urban ghettoes, relying upon the drug trade and other aspects of the "street" economy (E. Anderson 1990; Duneier 1999).

There is now a sizeable Black middle class in the USA (Feagin and Sikes 1994; Grant, Oliver, and James 1996; Landry 1987). More than 15 percent of all African American households earn above $50,000 annually (Marable 1995: 189). On the one hand, middle-class Blacks are likely to have much more interaction with White people than do their working-class counterparts, particularly in the realms of work, school, and various public settings (Benjamin 1991; Neckerman, Carter, and Lee 1999). Outside these spheres, however, most middle-class Blacks do not socialize with White colleagues, and because of racially segregated neighborhoods, many middle-class Blacks live in predominantly Black neighborhoods. Because of their increased contact with Whites, many middle-class Black people must navigate their interactions with White people, and this can be tiring, since middle-class Black people are not necessarily immune to the everyday forms of racism which many Black people experience (Benjamin 1991).

On the other hand, middle-class Black people must negotiate tensions and difficulties which arise in the context of inter-class relations.

Because many middle-class Blacks still live near poor Blacks (Massey and Denton 1993), and because they may participate in community organizations, such as churches or civic organizations which include both working-class and middle-class people, middle-class Black people have to negotiate their relationships with poorer coethnics who may resent them or feel intimidated by their success. As a result of having relationships and contacts with both White people and poor Blacks, middle-class Black people can be said to have distinctive sorts of experiences. In fact, many middle-class minorities, including middle-class African Americans, are said to possess a "minority culture of mobility," which includes the problems of inter-racial and inter-class relations encountered by middle-class minorities and their shared interpretations of, and responses to, these problems (Neckerman, Carter, and Lee 1999).[4]

Although a strong sense of ethnic solidarity can help to bridge inter-class tensions which arise in class-heterogeneous minority groups, the problem of inter-class relations is clearly heightened in minority groups where there is a very large disparity between the richest and poorest members – a disparity which is significant in the case of affluent and poor African Americans.

Marable (1995) has also argued that the discourse of race, which lumps all Black people together, tends to obscure the growing class stratification among African Americans. While certain forms of racial discrimination remain problematic for all strata of African Americans, the nature of racial conflicts and difficulties, as well as the ways in which Black people cope with racism, can vary along class lines. The ambivalence about racial identity experienced by relatively successful middle-class Black people is likely to differ considerably from the bitter frustration felt by poor inhabitants of a segregated Black ghetto (Omi and Winant 1996: 474).

There is now substantial evidence that, as with many groups, we cannot assume a unity of vision or politics around the Black experience or identity (see chapter 3). Class differentiation among African Americans has significantly shaped the nature of these debates, including the accusation of poor, disadvantaged Black people that relatively privileged middle-class Blacks have sold out and are really acting White. One of the areas of tension stemming from the class diversification of African Americans is that of demeanor. Because many middle-class African Americans work with White people, and are cognizant of racially discriminatory beliefs about Black people, they are often anxious to prove their competence and middle-class status by, for example, speaking standard English or behaving with noticeable decorum (Benjamin 1991; E. Anderson 1990) – though consciously behaving with propriety has been found to be important to working-class Blacks as well (see Duneier 1992).

In the USA, there has been heated debate about the implications of a Black middle class for their more disadvantaged "brothers" and "sisters" and for race relations more generally. There is disagreement about whether the Black middle class, which includes Black politicians, doctors, teachers, and many public sector workers, is actually a help or a hindrance to poor, working-class Blacks and the Black urban underclass. As Stephen Small puts it, "Some Black people consider the Black 'middle class' to be a 'Talented Tenth' that will act as a vanguard for advancing the interests of all Black people; others see them simply as a 'Black Bourgeoisie', interested only in their own self-aggrandisement" (1994: 144) – a view controversially developed some decades ago by E. Franklin Frazier (1957) in his study of the Black bourgeoisie. This contentious question is important, because it is undeniable that it is middle-class Black people who hold many of the key political and economic positions in society; they are the ones who are consulted by the White establishment on a number of matters, and some of the Black elite, including the leadership of the National Association for the Advancement of Colored People or the ministers of prominent congregations throughout the country, hold considerable positions of power in terms of representing Black people's identities, needs, and agendas for the future.

Related to the class disparities among African Americans is the issue of variable skin tone (see Frazier 1957). In recent years, some analysts have punctured the taboo concerning discussions of the politics of skin color among African Americans. There is evidence that darker skin tone for Black people in the USA continues to be associated with stratification outcomes such as occupation and income. Darker Black people are likely to experience more discrimination and lower incomes than their light-skinned counterparts (Keith and Herring 1991). Some analysts argue that a Black person's position in the community "ultimately reflected the amounts of 'white blood' in his or her ancestry" (Keith and Herring 1991: 761). In *The Color Complex*, Kathy Russell and her colleagues concur: "Take a close look at Black urban professionals, or 'buppies', with their corporate salaries, middle-class values, and predominantly light-brown to medium-brown skin color. They benefit not only from their social contacts with other light-skinned Blacks but also from looks that, in a predominantly White society, are more mainstream" (Russell, Wilson, and Hall 1992: 37).[5]

However, affluent and socially prominent Black people may be viewed with distrust and suspicion and seen as elitist and out of touch (Russell,

Wilson, and Hall 1992: 39). Although their analysis is bound to be controversial (as was Spike Lee's film *School Daze*, which raised the issue of color divides in a Black university), Russell and colleagues argue that the "color complex" (or what the British MP Oona King calls "shadism") is devastating because this fixation on color and differences in color, including other phenotypical features such as hair texture and the shape of the nose and mouth, "leads Blacks to discriminate against each other" (Russell, Wilson, and Hall 1992: 2).

Furthermore, the experiences of ethnic minority people, in a number of social fields, are gendered. The nature of gendered experiences is illustrated by comparing African American men and women. In the last few decades, there has been a plethora of writing on the "crisis of Black men" in the USA, and their declining employment rate in recent decades, accompanying economic restructuring and demographic changes (see W. J. Wilson 1996; West 1994; Duneier 1992; E. Anderson 1990). While there are some shared discourses and imagery in relation to both Black men and women, many of the barriers and opportunities encountered by Black men are gender-specific (see A. Young 1999).

African American women's labor market participation has continued to increase. Unlike the case of low-skilled Black men in Los Angeles, who lost jobs, for instance, as janitors, to Latino men, Black women have moved out of domestic service (and been replaced by Latinas) into better-paying jobs in the corporate and healthcare sectors (Grant, Oliver, and James 1996). The labor force participation levels of low-skilled Black men are particularly low, in comparison with Black women, who are also benefiting from educational attainment. And in comparison with the predominantly negative perceptions held by employers of Black men in low-skill sectors, Black women were perceived as more stable, hard-working, and responsible (Shih 2002: 111).[6]

There are sources of tension arising between middle- and working-class Black people, and between Black men and women concerning the experiences, meanings, and behaviors associated with Blackness. However, awareness of these class and gender disparities may exaggerate the actual differences in the ethnic identities, norms, and life-styles among African Americans. In the case of both poor and relatively prosperous African American women and men, certain commonalities of experience which are structured by their racialization as Black people may undergird a strong sense of racial solidarity which counteracts some of the divisive effects of class and gender differentiation. Nevertheless, class differentiation, among African Americans, in particular, is significant, and it will continue to be a source of debate and discussion about what it means to be Black.

Asian Americans and the new Asian immigrants

In addition to class differentiation, another way in which the composition of an ethnic or panethnic group can change is through continuing flows of immigration. The arrival of new immigrants can result in either the inclusion and absorption of them into existing ethnic and panethnic groups or the drawing of new ethnic boundaries which distinguish the new arrivals from the older, more established population or group. While it is undeniable that the arrival of new immigrants can "replenish the ethnic community with the culture of the homeland" (Min 1999: 84), the arrival of new immigrants also changes an ethnic group's social composition and has implications for the meanings associated with its collective ethnic identity.

Recent studies of immigration to the USA have painted a complex picture of immigrant adaptation, rather than a uniform pattern of gradual assimilation into mainstream society. There is evidence of "segmented assimilation" involving disparate paths of adaptation for immigrants (Portes and Zhou 1993).[7] Differential patterns of adaptation to a new society are shaped by a number of factors, including the specific economic and labor market niches in which particular groups concentrate and the settlement patterns of more established coethnics. For instance, in recent years, while various Filipino immigrants are likely to be healthcare workers of some kind, Korean immigrants are more heavily reliant on various forms of small businesses (Cheng and Yang 1996). While immigrant adaptation can clearly differ across distinct immigrant groups, such as Cambodians or West Indians, differential paths of adapation can arise even within Asian subgroups, such as Koreans and Taiwanese.

Since the 1965 Immigration Act, most of the immigrants to the USA have been non-European and have originated from Asia and Latin America (Portes and Schauffler 1996).[8] In comparison with older waves of Asian immigration to the USA, the new wave of Asian immigration involves a higher percentage of women, greater ethnic and socioeconomic diversity, and more extensive global linkages (Cheng and Yang 1996: 308).

The ethnic diversity of Asian Americans

As a panethnic group, Asian Americans constitute a very broad group which incorporates subgroups of many different nationalities and ethnicities. The 1990 US Census categorized Asian Americans under a very wide umbrella category called "Asian and Pacific Islander" (API), which includes groups as disparate as Chinese, Filipino, Hawaiian, Samoan, Asian Indian, and Vietnamese (Kibria 1998). The question of how distinct ethno-national groups within a broad panethnic group assert their desired ethnic identities and agendas is bound to be contentious, since each subgroup can identify specific concerns and interests which pertain to them, but not necessarily to the wider pan-Asian grouping. In fact, some analysts have argued that, unlike Latino Americans (who all share the Spanish language), Asian Americans have no common language or culture to bind them together. There is also great historical enmity between certain groups, such as between Koreans and Japanese, because Japan colonized Korea from 1910 to 1945.

How did the panethnic grouping "Asian American" emerge? There were no Asian Americans, as such, before the late 1960s. In the post-Civil Rights movement era, groups with distinct ethnic and/or national identities came to be consolidated into broader racial categories (Omi and Winant 1996). From the early nineteenth century to World War II, Asians in the USA considered themselves to be distinct ethnic groups, such as Chinese, Japanese, or Filipino. Each group had been brought to the USA to meet particular labor needs, and all Asian groups had experienced various forms of discrimination, exclusion, and restriction (Cheng and Yang 1996; Espiritu 1992; Tuan 1998). However, in the 1960s, American-born Asian Americans became inspired by the Civil Rights movements occurring at that time, and many Asian American students at universities throughout the USA organized and mobilized an Asian American movement (Kibria 1998). Because anti-Asian violence cuts across particular nationalities, ethnicities, and class backgrounds, efforts to counter such violence needed to be organized at a pan-Asian level (Espiritu 1992).

However, various sources of tension and differentiation have emerged around the unifying category of Asian American. Contrary to the belief that all Asian Americans are privileged, there are significant class differences among many Asian American groups, and these may translate into constraints on racial solidarity (Espiritu and Ong 1994; Yamanaka and McClelland 1994; Hurh and Kim 1989). There can be significant class differentiation even within what is thought to be a relatively homogeneous ethnic group, such as Korean Americans in the Los Angeles area (Abelmann and Lie 1995). Class divisions among Asian Americans are likely to shape the different ways in which working- and middle-class Asians perceive and experience forms of racism, and this in turn may limit the extent to which these class groups can relate to one another (Kibria 1998).

Another source of tension within the Asian American panethnic grouping has been the assertion that certain groups' agendas (and perhaps even images and cultural symbols) have come to dominate and define the wider conception of what it means to be Asian American. For instance, Filipino Americans have complained that, despite their large numbers, Asian American organizations are dominated by Japanese and Chinese American leaders, who prioritize the needs of their own communities, thus marginalizing those of Filipinos – for instance, in relation to the provision of various social services (Espiritu 1992). In addition to the fact that, overall, Filipino Americans are more disadvantaged in socioeconomic terms than are Japanese and Chinese Americans, their cultural distance from other East Asian groups is also significant. This is because Filipinos experienced first Spanish, then American, colonial rule, and the cultural orientation of many Filipino Americans reflects their greater familiarity with Western practices and English language and laws (Espiritu 1992; Cariño 1996).

Concerns about their representation within the rubric "Asian American" have also been raised by Americans of South Asian heritage. Although South Asians now number 1.4 million in the USA, some Indian and Pakistani Americans have felt marginalized within the category "Asian American," which they claim predominantly signifies East Asian people, such as Japanese, Chinese, and Koreans (Prashad 2000: 2). Aside from the fact that many South Asians in the USA arrived with quite distinct religious affiliations (R. B. Williams 1998), it has also been noted that South Asian people look physically different from most East Asian peoples. South Asians are not (and never have been) seen as "Oriental" – a derogatory term associated with popular conceptions of the "Far East."

Within a broad panethnic group such as Asian American, some subgroups possess more political and social clout and visibility than others, and, inevitably, the smaller, less influential groups may chafe at this. Yet a key reason why Filipinos and South Asians still espouse a pan-Asian grouping for the purposes of representation is that it would be difficult for them to obtain sufficient recognition or resources at a national level without their inclusion in the broader Asian American rubric.

New Asian immigrants

The arrival of new Asian immigrants of distinct ethnic and class backgrounds can further strain the legitimacy of the broad category "Asian American." Panethnic identities, such as Asian American, are not automatically embraced by new Asian immigrants, who are much more likely to conceive of themselves initially in terms of distinct ethno-national backgrounds, such as Taiwanese, Filipinos, or Laotians (Yancey, Ericksen, and Juliani 1976). In addition to the ethnic diversity of Asian Americans, even immigrants from the same country (but from a variety of social backgrounds) may not necessarily have much in common with each other, despite being lumped together within an ethnic or racial category by the wider society. There is evidence that distinctions are recognized within ethnic groups themselves, based upon differences in length of settlement, religion, and class (Light et al. 1993). For example, among Iranian immigrants to the USA, who differ in terms of their religious affiliations, there has been the emergence of "internal ethnicity," the recognition of difference among Muslims, Jews, and Armenians, although they are all known as a recognized national group – Iranians (Bozorgmehr, Der-Martirosian, and Sabagh 1996).

Mia Tuan's (1998) study of third- and fourth-generation ("multi-generation") Chinese and Japanese Americans in the USA provides very interesting documentation of some of the tensions which can arise between multigeneration Asians who have been born and raised in the USA and newly arrived Asian immigrants, with whom multi-generation Asians have little in common. Tuan found that although many multigeneration Asian Americans had adopted largely Americanized life-styles, they still tended to be seen as foreign immigrants by many members of the White majority. As a result, in addition to resenting White people who made such assumptions about them, some multigeneration Asian Americans wanted to distinguish themselves from newly arrived Asian immigrants, who were regarded as being unfamiliar with American practices, language, and life-style. These newly arrived immigrants were seen to be perpetuating derogatory stereotypes of Asian people, thus stigmatizing the status of third- and fourth-generation Asian Americans. As illustrated in the quote below, some Asian Americans may themselves be exhibiting nativist hostility toward new Asian immigrants:

> "I thought I would never say this. But these new immigrants are ruining things for us," Jim Yamada, a third-generation Japanese American, said in disgust. "Asian Americans fought for decades against discrimination and racial prejudice. We want to be treated just like everybody else, like Americans. You see, I get real angry when people come up to me and tell me how good my English is. They say, 'Oh, you have no accent. Where did you learn English?' Where did I learn English? Right here in America. I was born here like they were. We really hated it when people assumed that just because Asian Americans looked different we were foreigners. It took us a long time to get

people to see this point, to be sensitized to it. Now the new immigrants are setting us back. People see me now and they automatically treat me as an immigrant. I really hate that. The worst thing is that these immigrants don't understand why I am angry."

(Quoted in Cheng and Yang 1996: 305)

Although he is by no means representative of most Asian Americans, established Asian Americans like Jim Yamada are frustrated by many new immigrants' lack of understanding or even concern with the racial dynamics of the wider society. Long-settled Asian Americans' distancing of themselves from new Asian immigrants may be an attempt to shield themselves from the racial abuse and taunting aimed at Asian immigrants who are characterized as foreign and speaking little English. Such efforts to disidentify with new immigrants can also be interpreted as an attempt to retain what social standing and prestige may accrue to Asian Americans who were born and raised in the USA.

More established Asians' affiliations and relationships to the wider society are likely to differ considerably from those of new Asian immigrants, and new immigrants may understand their disadvantaged or marginal status quite differently from their more settled coethnics. According to Jeremy Hein, "Where a 'native minority' can attribute inequality to a racial and ethnic hierarchy, a 'foreign minority' may attribute inequality to their status as newcomers adjusting to life in a host society" (1994: 285). A migrant orientation perceives prejudices as unintentional and the result of natives' ethnocentrism, rather than outright racism. This disparity in perception is borne out in Mary Waters's study of West Indian immigrants in New York City: "Longstanding tensions between newly arrived West Indians and American Blacks have left a legacy of mutual stereotyping. The immigrants see themselves as hard-working, ambitious, militant about their racial identities but not oversensitive or obsessed with race, and committed to education and family. They see black Americans as lazy, disorganized, obsessed with racial slights and barriers. . . . American blacks describe the immigrants as arrogant, selfish, exploited in the workplace, oblivious to racial tensions and politics in the United States" (1994: 797).

Such differences in perception arise, in part, because newly arrived immigrants and native-born minorities tend to encounter different kinds of concerns in their everyday lives. Generally speaking, recent immigrants are likely to view problems of a practical nature, such as finding housing and jobs, learning English, saving money (or sending it back to relatives), as more pressing than the racial discrimination they may encounter in the wider society (Lopez and Espiritu 1990: 206; Feagin 2000). For instance, the experiences and needs of refugees from Vietnam, Cambodia, and Laos, who started arriving in 1975, when American involvement in the Vietnam War ended, differed, not surprisingly, from those of third-generation Japanese Americans who were born and raised in California, and who, by comparison, were largely "Americanized."[9] Many of the recent immigrants from Vietnam, Cambodia, and Laos arrived as refugees of war and political persecution (see Gold 1992; Kibria 1993; Rumbaut 1996).

In effect, recent immigrants, particularly if they have come from poor countries, such as Laos, are willing to endure some racism and marginalization as the cost of being an immigrant. Thus the degree and nature of ethnic consciousness is shaped by how migrants interpret the unequal allocation of social rewards and social problems. The perception of discrimination and inequality involves a learning process which shapes a group's social identity – for example, as primarily immigrant or minority (Hein 1994). For example, Cuban and Mexican immigrants' awareness of racially and culturally based discrimination increased with their length of residence and level of education (Portes and Bach 1985).

These different understandings of racial marginalization and discrimination, in turn, affect new Asian immigrants' sense of ethnic identity, including their perception of whether a broad Asian American identity makes sense or means anything to them. Given all these potential differences, whether in terms of length of settlement or the ethnic diversity contained within the rubric "Asian American," the term "Asian American" holds no automatic resonance for many of the people officially included in this category.

Some immigrant groups may also resist inclusion in a broad panethnic category because they do not want to be associated with less privileged groups within that category (O. Patterson 1977). For example, some Cuban Americans may dispute their categorization as Latino (or Hispanic), and stress their Cuban origin because they want to distance themselves from Mexicans and Puerto Ricans, who tend to be less privileged in terms of their educational attainments and their success in the labor market (Portes and MacLeod 1996). As in the case of Black West Indian immigrants discussed by Waters (1994), Fernandez-Kelly and Schauffler (1994) found that Haitian and West Indian immigrants held on to their identities as immigrants, in order to differentiate themselves from Black Americans, who are racially stigmatized in the USA. West Indians in New York City have tried to fashion a separate cultural and political identity from "native" African Americans by creating ethnic identities via community activities and cultural celebrations such as the Labor Day Carnival (Kasinitz 1992).

While many West Indian immigrants have tried to retain their immigrant status, multigeneration Asian Americans have tried to dissociate themselves from newly arrived Asian immigrants and an immigrant status. Therefore, although panethnic groups often emerge out of instrumental concerns, such as the receipt of government resources, some subgroups within a broad panethnic group may feel that there are liabilities attached to inclusion within a panethnic group, since inclusion makes it difficult for particular subgroups to control or negotiate the specific images and identities with which they are associated.

Although I have stressed the tensions between new Asian immigrants and multigeneration Asian Americans, their relationship should not be viewed in an overly stark, oppositional way. There are interplay and forms of cultural borrowing and diffusion between recent immigrants and their more established coethnics (Neckerman, Carter, and Lee 1999). Despite all the tensions and controversies underlying the organization and cohesion of a broad panethnic group such as Asian Americans, there is no sign of this group declining in social or political significance.

Historically, the emergence of an Asian American identity is the result of a gradual process, and what it means to be Asian American (or for that matter, any other ethnic or panethnic designation) is changeable. The term "Asian American" entails changing subjectivities at different historical periods (Palumbo-Liu 1999). As the second and third generations of groups such as Korean Americans and Vietnamese Americans emerge in the USA, and as new immigrants continue to enter the USA from Asia, the meanings, behaviors, and politics associated with being Asian American will continue to be contested. Subgroups within the pan-Asian group, especially those who feel either underrepresented or marginalized, will continue to contest and negotiate issues such as leadership and the identification of core issues, as well as the question of what kind of unified public identity should be asserted.

Who is "Black" in Britain?

The kinds of panethnic terms which develop in different societies reveal a great deal about the specific histories of race relations and racial dynamics in each place. In comparison with the USA, in Britain, the term "Asian" has always referred to people of South

Asian origin, such as Indians, Pakistanis, and Bangladeshis. It has tended to exclude the Chinese population, who constitute the third largest ethnic minority group in Britain. While Americans of South Asian heritage tend to feel marginalized within dominant under-standings of "Asian American," in Britain, it is the Chinese who are not included under the rubric "Asian."

The question of who is Asian in Britain is also related to the ques-tion of who is and is not Black. The term "Black" was widely used throughout the 1970s and 1980s in reference to people of African, Caribbean, and South Asian origin in Britain, and its usage was intended to convey a sense of common interest and solidarity based upon the politics of anti-racism (Ali 1992: 105). The common usage of the term "Black" tended to highlight the discrimination and marginality faced by non-White peoples and the collective action that they could take via both law and policy measures, as well as ethnic mobilization.

This broad understanding of the category "Black" is in stark contrast with how it is conceived in the USA, where "Black" refers specifically to the experiences of people of African origin. In Britain, the inclusive usage of Black emphasizes the commonality of experi-ences of South Asian and African Caribbean people alike – whether it relates to forms of discrimination faced in the labor market or the experience of racial slurs and hostility on the street. Throughout the 1970s and 1980s, African Caribbean and Asian groups worked together in major campaigns against fascist violence, immigration controls, police harassment, and racism in employment and trade unions (Brah 1996: 106). As recently as 1994, in a widely read soci-ology textbook (see Abercrombie and Warde 1994), terms such as "ethnic disadvantage" and "the structure of the Black community" were used to refer to all non-White ethnic minorities in Britain. A survey of ethnic minorities in Britain entitled *Black and White Britain* (Brown 1984) also revealed the acceptability of using the term "Black" to refer to all non-White people, though it most commonly referred to African Caribbeans and South Asians.

The inclusion of Britons of Asian descent under the rubric "Black" reflected the prominent participation of some Asians, such as Sivanandan (1982), in the development of a Black political identity in Britain (Shukra 1996). As a basis for collective mobilization, the political identity "Black" provided a unifying basis for Asian and African Caribbean women to form the Organization of Women of African and Asian Descent (OWAAD) in their efforts to develop a Black feminist strategy in the 1970s (Shukra 1996). According to Avtar Brah, the commitment to forging unity between African, Caribbean, and Asian women was strong, but it was no easy task: "It called for an interrogation of the role of colonialism and imperialism and that of contemporary economic, political and ideological processes in sustaining particular social divisions within these groups. It required Black women to be sensitive to one another's cultural specificities while constructing common political strategies to confront patriarchal practices, racism and class inequality" (1996: 106–7).[10] A Black feminist perspective was also important in the establishment of other groups in Britain, such as Southall Black Sisters and Brixton Black Women's Group (Parmar 1990; Mirza 1997a). There were also many positive effects of the "Black power" movement for Asian communities and Asian militancy. In fact, Asian youth, and in particular Asian women, adopted militant stances, drawing on a collective Black identity, in various industrial disputes, such as in the cases of Grunwick and Imperial Typewriters (Shukra 1996: 28) and the clothing manufacturing industries, in which many Asian women worked as machinists (see Phizacklea 1990).

Within government, the Black perspectivist strategy involved the formation of an unofficial national Labour Party Black Section, aimed at uniting African Caribbean and Asian people to create a lobby which would help to produce seats for Black people on committees and in Parliament (Shukra 1996: 31). By unifying under the broad rubric "Black," it was believed that this would enable Asian and African Caribbean people to intensify the pressure they could apply within the Labour Party, in order to highlight issues of concern to them, as ethnic minorities. Furthermore, British political organizations, such as the Society of Black Lawyers, the National Black Caucus, and the Federation of Black Housing, not only rely on an inclusive understanding of "Black," they are also comprised of significant numbers of Asians, some of whom are in leadership roles (S. Small 1994: 195).

However, in recent years, there has been increased attention to the diversity of experiences of ethnicity and "race" among ethnic minority groups in Britain (Solomos and Back 1994; Song and Parker 1995). As in the case of the diversification of groups such as African Americans and Asian Americans, discussed above, the composition of both the African Caribbean and the South Asian population in Britain has changed considerably in the last few decades. For example, there is growing evidence of differences among the panethnic group known as Asians. In 1955, fewer than 8,000 people from the Indian subcontinent had entered Britain, but by 1997, Britons of South Asian heritage totaled just over 1.7 million (Anwar 1998). The historical richness of Asian settlement in Britain has resulted in commonalities, but also significant differences, among the various ethnic and religious groups comprising Asians. Generally speaking, in comparison with Pakistanis, and Bangladeshis, Indians have both lower rates of unemployment and higher incomes (Modood et al. 1997). Another key basis of division among Asians in Britain is religion, particularly between Muslims (predominantly Bangladeshis and Pakistanis) on the one hand and Hindus and Sikhs on the other hand – an issue which has gained prominence in the aftermath of September 11, because of the predominantly negative depictions of Muslims.

Some analysts now argue that ethnic minorities in Britain cannot simply be lumped together, with assumptions about certain commonalities of experience, whether they be in relation to employment, housing, or the ability to assert an identity of one's choosing. In Britain, a recent survey (Modood et al. 1997) showed that the differences between ethnic minority groups are now more important than ever, and that focusing upon the Black–White divide does little to disaggregate the varying experiences of disparate groups – for instance, in terms of education, income, family lives, and employment. There are quite diverse outcomes for ethnic minorities in the British labor market, and some analysts argue that generalized arguments about racial barriers in employment faced by all ethnic minorities are now untenable (see Iganski and Payne 1996).

Within the context of such thinking, there have been growing questions about the legitimacy and appropriateness of calling Indian or Bangladeshi Britons "Black." In what sense are they Black? And do most Asian people consider themselves to be Black? This term is allegedly not consonant with the identities of most Asian people in Britain (Modood 1994: 860). In fact, in 1988, the Commission for Racial Equality (CRE) in Britain recommended that Asians not be included under the rubric "Black," on the grounds that Black as an ethnic monitoring category did not match the self-conceptions of most Asian people.

Tariq Modood (1994, 1996) argues that "Black" connotes too narrow a conception of racial discrimination, because it is said to equate racial discrimination with color discrimination, thereby obscuring the particular kinds of racism that Asian people suffer (see chapter 7). Second, Modood has argued that the inclusiveness of "Black" is problematic because it suggests a false essentialism, that all non-White groups necessarily share something in common. He argues that, in addition to the sometimes qualitatively different kinds of racial abuse that disparate groups experience, in the case of Pakistani, Indian, or Bangladeshi people in Britain, these groups have some concerns and needs which are distinct from those of other ethnic minority groups, such as concerns about religious education in schools for Muslims. There is evidence that Asian and African Caribbean groups have been differentially affected by state policies, and their responses to forms of racial injustice and disadvantage have tended to differ. While African Caribbean communities have organized much more around the issue of the criminal justice system and the unfair treatment of Black people within it, Asian groups have been more involved in defending Asian people against violent racial attacks and in organizing campaigns against deportations and the stringent effects of immigration laws (Brah 1996).

Another reason why Modood has argued against a collective use of "Black" in relation to Asians is that it is said to be primarily evocative of people of African origin, and that this term subsumes Asian people within this category. As a consequence, this not only "smothers" Asian ethnic pride, but their inclusion in the rubric also renders them invisible. Such a claim is similar to the charge made by some Filipino leaders and activists in the USA, who argue that Filipino concerns and agendas tend to be overshadowed by those of the more dominant Chinese and Japanese Americans. According to Modood, the primary signifier of "Black" – whether it be in a news story or in popular usage – is people of African origin, not South Asians. At best, Modood argues, South Asians might get tacked onto an agenda which is centrally about African Caribbean people, with Asians a mere afterthought.

The splintering of Black identity in Britain is in part engendered by the fact that Asians and African Caribbeans are increasingly racialized in different ways in popular representations of the two groups (see chapter 2). Asians are depicted either as a hard-working entrepreneurial model minority (much in the way that Asian Americans are depicted as a "good" model minority) or in problematic terms related to their purported religious fanaticism and "backward" cultural practices (such as pressuring their children into arranged marriages), while African Caribbeans tend to be stereotyped as criminals and/or lone parents who threaten the social fabric of British society (Song and Edwards 1997).

It is difficult to assess, on the ground, and on the basis of existing empirical studies, how accurate Modood is about Asian peoples' attitudes toward their inclusion in the category "Black." Nor is there a consensus among people of African origin about whether Asian people should be referred to as "Black." The calls for narrowing and specifying the boundaries of "Blackness" in Britain do not arise only from those of South Asian heritage. Some analysts have pointed to evidence of African Caribbeans conceiving of themselves separately from Asians and other ethnic minorities, with a distinctive sense of the cultural traditions and social problems that they encounter (see Jayaweera 1993; Mama 1984).

However, some scholars such as Heidi Mirza (1992, 1997a) continue to use the term "Black" in relation to South Asian, African Caribbean, and even Chinese women in Britain. The media also often use the term "Black" to refer to both Asian and African Caribbean people. For instance, in one television report about the murder of a young South Asian prisoner by his White, racist cellmate, the news reporter referred to the safety of Black prisoners in British jails (BBC1, Southeast News, 1 Nov. 2000).

It is difficult to deny that some of the social and political agendas and needs, as identified by South Asians, may very well differ from those of African Caribbeans, especially concerns about religious practice and education in the British school system. And if, indeed, South Asian and African Caribbean people tend to experience different kinds of racial abuse and disadvantage, such differences could undermine the legitimacy of the notion of a collective Black identity, given that this term emerged out of the belief that both groups experienced much in common. These questions and the question of whether the term "Black" is primarily evocative of African Caribbean people (and only secondarily of Asians) are ones which require further empirical investigation.

Ethnic groups, and the subgroups constituting larger panethnic groups, are constantly redrawing and renegotiating their boundaries in response to ongoing forms of immigration, class differentiation, and intergroup competition, all against the backdrop of historical events and contingencies. The emergence of class differences among African Americans, continuing flows of Asian immigration, and the splintering of Black identity in Britain have all resulted in, and reflect, contestations among subgroups about their political agendas and concerns, not to mention their desired public identity and ethnicity. These three examples illustrate the internal differentiation within ethnic and panethnic groups, leading to the proliferation of diverse, increasingly nuanced, and contested ethnic options within groups.

6

The Second Generation in a Global Context

Immigrants and the second generation

Many recent studies have explored the formation of people's ethnic identities within the context of globalization and the transnational and diasporic communities associated with it. The dynamics associated with globalization are especially relevant for the experiences of the so-called second generation in Western societies. Rather than adopting only one ethnic or national affiliation, many second-generation men and women can be invested in a wide range of ethnic identities, and may want to assert their claim to more than one.

In this chapter, I draw upon both British and American studies, which share many themes and discourses about the negotiation of second-generation identity and experience more generally. Can the second generation be said to possess a greater array of ethnic options than their parents? In addressing this question, I also discuss the implications of globalization for the ways in which the second generation conceive of their ethnic identities.

While there is no one definition of "second generation," this term usually refers to the children of contemporary immigrants, who were born in the host society or who received some or a significant part of their schooling and socialization there (Zhou 1997; Portes and Rumbaut 1990; Modood, Beishon, and Virdee 1994).[1] About 15 percent of all children in the United States are immigrant children or children of immigrant parentage (Zhou 1997: 63).[2] In Britain, 90 percent of all ethnic minority people aged 0–14 were born in Britain (Scott, Pearce, and Goldblatt 2001).[3]

Recent studies of the second generation in the USA and Britain suggest a mixed picture of the kinds of opportunities and barriers encountered by this generation. Some key American scholars argue that there is a significant mismatch between the second generation's aspirations and opportunities in the labor market (see Gans 1992; Portes and Zhou 1993). However, others argue that despite economic restructuring resulting in a shift toward knowledge-intensive industries, and the fact that such jobs are quite competitive, second-generation individuals of Asian, Black, and Mexican backgrounds are not necessarily any more disadvantaged than were children from Southern and Eastern European countries emigrating to the USA at the turn of the twentieth century (Perlmann and Waldinger 1997: 895). In Britain, many recent depictions of the second generation are in marked contrast to past studies (e.g. Castles, Booth, and Wallace 1984), which painted an overly deterministic, bleak picture of second-generation offspring as replicating the disadvantaged status of their immigrant parents, who had acted as "replacement labor" in undesirable jobs vacated by the White majority.

Comparative overviews of second-generation populations show that there are diverse paths for the children of immigrants. Some achieve socioeconomic success while retaining strong ethnic attachments and identities, while others assimilate to subcultures with limited social capital and socioeconomic mobility (Portes and Zhou 1993). Still other researchers have suggested that the second generation does not necessarily assimilate straightforwardly into the mainstream, or assume a disadvantaged minority status, but may adopt a "minority culture of mobility" which is more promising (Neckerman, Carter, and Lee 1999).

By comparison with the diverse outcomes for the second generation in the labor market, there are many common themes which emerge in relation to their experiences of ethnic identity. The negotiation of ethnic identity, including the meanings associated with it, is both a more prominent and contentious issue for second-generation children and young people than it is for their immigrant parents. For many immigrant parents, particularly if they emigrated as adults, there is little question about their ethnic identities, which are largely understood in terms of ethno-national affiliations – for example, being Taiwanese or Haitian. There is no question of adopting so-called hyphenated identities such as Korean American or Black British for them (Portes and MacLeod 1996: 529). Unlike their parents, second-generation individuals are more likely to be invested in belonging in the wider society, and they are also more likely to be "deeply involved in transactions across the ethnic boundary than their parents ever were" (R. Ballard 1994: 29). As Stuart Hall puts it in relation to third-generation Black people in Britain, "Third generation young

Black men and women know that they come from the Caribbean, know that they are Black, know that they are British. They want to speak from all three identities. They are not prepared to give up on any of them" (1991b: 59).

There are various ways in which the second generation can actively work at asserting their desired ethnic identities. Although the constraints around agency and choice still apply, there is some room for maneuver (as discussed in chapter 3). Many of the issues concerning the second generation in the USA and Britain are quite similar: most second-generation individuals, in comparison with their parents, have a much greater awareness of the ways in which they may describe their ethnic identities, even if they do not always "try on" all these possibilities. For instance, many people manifest their awareness of choices when they experience shifts in their ethnic identities over time, or when they change or adjust their behaviors and practices in specific social situations, with different groups of people.

Skilled cultural navigators

The ethnic identities of second-generation individuals must be negotiated in the family context, vis-à-vis parents and siblings, as well as with their peers and in the wider society more generally (Song 1997). This is one reason why a popular way of theorizing the experiences of second-generation individuals has been to describe them as being "between two cultures" (see Watson 1977; Anwar 1998). Asian youths in Britain have been commonly depicted in these terms. For instance, Muhammad Anwar argues that "a key difficulty is a social and psychological gap between young Asians and their parents due to a difference in social environment and education. The world at home is generally different from that of school and what they see in the media. However, young Asians are part of both worlds, which sometimes leads to tensions and conflict within Asian families" (1998: 148).

However, some analysts have been very critical of the implication that second-generation young people are likely to suffer "culture conflict" (see C. Ballard 1979; R. Ballard 1994; Stopes-Roe and Cochrane 1990). In an older study of second-generation Asian adolescents in Britain, Catherine Ballard argues that the belief that Asian young people necessarily undergo forms of culture conflict is a gross oversimplification of what is actually a wide range of complex personal experiences: "It assumes a straightforward clash, a tug-of-war, between East and West, traditional and modern, rural and urban, repression and freedom, resulting in an unbridgeable gulf between the generations" (1979: 128). In fact, Ballard argues, young Asians resolve their dilemmas by working toward their own synthesis of Asian and British values and practices, rather than face an "either/or situation." The idea of culture conflict or of being between two cultures is problematic, because ethnocentric assumptions are made about young Asians wanting to be more British, if only their parents would allow it (1979: 128).

Code switching

In recent years, many studies have emphasized the great diversity of ethnic designations among young people, and the fact that they are aware of the different ways in which they can experience and assert their ethnic affiliations (see Parker 1995; R. Ballard 1994; Modood, Beishon, and Virdee 1994). Roger Ballard (1994) argues that second-generation Asians are skilled cultural navigators with a sophisticated ability to maneuver between different social worlds. According to him, switching cultural codes is not unlike being fluently bi- or multilingual: "Cultures, like languages, are *codes*, which actors use to express themselves in a given context; and as the context changes, so those with the requisite competence simply switch code" (1994: 31, emphasis original). Although code switching is not exclusive to ethnic minority people, and though not all young people engage in forms of code switching, ethnic minority young people have a greater need to develop and use such skills in comparison with the wider population.

Many studies of Asian young people in Britain illustrate the complex and diverse ethnic affiliations of the second generation. For instance, Drury's (1991) study of the ethnic practices and attitudes of Sikh girls and Knott and Khokher's (1993) study of Muslim girls' religious practices found that, rather than feeling compelled to affiliate wholly with either (White) British or Asian cultural practices and identities, these Asian girls manifested complex affiliations with both British and Asian cultures. They fashioned affiliations to both sides which suited them, and which enabled them to belong in both worlds. In another study of how respondents talked about their dress and the consumption of media, young Muslim women in Britain were found to be active in resisting dominant representations of Muslim women, which were considered crude and derogatory (see Dwyer 1998). Most of the women in this study were proud to be British, Muslim, and Asian, and sought ways to articulate these different dimensions of their identities in their own terms. They rejected the assumed polarities of, on the one hand, Asian women, who are depicted as passive victims of oppressive cultural practices, and of predominantly Westernized Asian women, who jettison what are deemed to be traditional cultural practices and mind-sets (see also Puar 1996).

Black young people can also engage in complex forms of ethnic affiliation – for instance, by code switching. In New York City, Mary Waters (1994) interviewed a second-generation Haitian woman, who reported the following: "When I'm at school and I sit with my black friends and, sometimes I'm ashamed to say this, but my accent changes. I learn all the words. I switch. Well when I'm with my friends, my black friends, I say I'm black, black American. When I'm with my Haitian-American friends, I say I'm Haitian" (1994: 807). Such an example of code switching was not uncommon among the second-generation Haitian youth that Waters studied.[4] While being bilingual can contribute to the ability to engage in code switching between different groups and situations (e.g. switching between a Chinese dialect with Chinese parents and friends and English with other British friends), being bilingual is not a prerequisite for code switching. There are other ways in which one can engage in code switching – for instance, through ways of talking, styles of presentation, and the pursuit of particular activities.

Despite the now common dismissal of the idea of being between two cultures as overly simplistic (see Parker 1995; Gardner 1995), some recent studies in both Britain and the USA continue to find that second-generation young people articulate feelings and thoughts which are similar to those evoked by this idea. The experiences of second-generation Chinese young people in Britain, for example, suggest that many of them feel, at some point in their lives, that they straddle two quite disparate worlds (Song 1999). As operators of take-away food businesses, Chinese families diverge from Western norms of family and work, in which only parents, and not children, are the providers for the family economy. Because of their hard work in the family take-away business, and because of their parents' reliance upon them for language mediation and other forms of "caring" labor, many Chinese young people tend to experience tensions between two polarized ideals of family and identity – one idealized as Chinese, one as British. These young people are highly conscious of the significant differences in attitudes between them and their immigrant parents, which they attribute to their own distinctive experiences as second-generation Chinese. They articulate a variety of understandings of what it means to be Chinese and British in Britain, and compare their senses of identity with their parents, who are regarded as straightforwardly and unproblematically Chinese.

Countering racism

Minority ethnicity is increasingly a public one, which is no longer closeted or practiced behind closed doors (Modood 1996). As illustrated by the popularity of rap music, which has addressed struggles over public space, the growing assertions of "public ethnicity," in particular by young people, are "based upon feelings of not being respected or of lacking access to public space" (Modood 1996: 10). For example, in Britain, Bengali youths' embrace of Islam demonstrates an active, politicized assertion of ethno-religious identity which attempts to invert negative meanings associated with "Islam" into positive ones. Gardner and Shukur (1994) found that these young people's growing interest in Islam emerged in a context in which they suffered persistent forms of racial prejudice and marginalization. For some, though not all, of these Bengali young people, an increased emphasis upon difference, in terms of both cultural and religious practices, has accompanied their commitment to Islam.[5]

There is substantial evidence to suggest that many second-generation individuals are relatively conscious of, and politically active in, countering various forms of racism. In Britain, this has been especially evident since the racist murder of the Black teenager Stephen Lawrence in 1993, which led to the widespread perception that there is little justice for non-White Britons, particularly in terms of their treatment by the police. In the aftermath of Stephen Lawrence's murder, much public debate has followed the release of the Macpherson Report, which put forward a particular definition of "institutional racism" and a recommendation for rooting out racism in the police force throughout Britain.

Studies of the second generation in both countries show that second-generation individuals can be active in their resistance to forms of racism, and to negative, stereotypical depictions of them (see chapter 2). For example, in the USA, because second-generation Asian Americans sometimes have to endure unappealing stereotypes such as being stolid and humorless, overly ambitious, or inscrutable, in addition to more positive characterizations, such as being intelligent and competent, Nazli Kibria (1997) suggests that they may experience their race as both a handicap and an opportunity. In fact, Kibria found that her Asian American respondents were highly aware of the unflattering aspects of the model minority image, and that they tried hard to distance themselves from such characteristics, particularly by displaying behaviors which were contrary to the stereotype. Joan, a Chinese American attorney in her late twenties, said: "I guess there's that whole Asian stereotype because of which they think I'm just going to be a meek, submissive thing, real quiet. It bothers me, but sometimes I get a kick out of surprising people. In meetings I sometimes kind of play them along, letting them think that I'm just a wallflower type. And then pow! When they least expect it I get angry or I start acting and talking in a very aggressive lawyer-type way. There have been times when I've won a point or something just because people are a little taken aback" (quoted in Kibria 2002: 143–4). This is an example of a conscious manipulation of a stereotype, which counters not only a racial, but also a gender, stereotype.

Racist experiences were commonly reported among Chinese young people who worked at their family take-away food businesses. This work typically involved taking orders from customers and assisting in cleaning, cooking, and packaging food. These young people reported that most Britons tended to associate Chinese people automatically with the running of these take-away food businesses. Because so many of these young people's social interactions with other Britons were structured by their work in the take-away (particularly across the take-away counter), many customers reportedly treated them as lesser beings who were there to serve them. Such an expectation was suggestive of a colonialist relationship between White Britons and Chinese people, most of whom emigrated from Britain's former colony, Hong Kong (Parker 1994).

Many of the Chinese young people I studied in Britain reported their resentment of stereotypes about Chinese people, which was made all the worse when such stereotypes were sexist as well. According to Sui:

> After secretarial college I went to work at a firm typing. At first I found it quite exciting. I thought, I've found what I've wanted to do. It was different, working in a different setting, and you could wear skirts, look nice [laughs]. And after a while, I got very disillusioned because I looked extremely young, compared with others, and people didn't treat me as if I had [maturity or intelligence], they were always calling, "little Sue," and "isn't she cute". And it got on my nerves. I was very competent. I was more than competent. And so I was really pissed off, and I thought, I could be as good as you, so I decided to go to university.
> (Song 1999: 182)

Sui's response to racially based stereotyping and condescension toward her as a Chinese woman was to resolve to achieve a higher level of education and labor market status than her (then) colleagues possessed.

The Chinese young people I interviewed typically reported that while their parents tended to tolerate forms of racial abuse, they themselves were much more likely to rebuke nasty or abusive customers or to refuse to serve them (Song 1999). They didn't think it was right to take it "lying down." Nor did they believe that they should be resigned about simply living with racism. However, such an assertive stance was not necessarily easily or automatically achieved, since some young people had, to varying degrees, internalized negative associations with being Chinese in Britain.

These second-generation individuals commonly redefined and revalued the meanings associated with their ethnicity, in order to counter derogatory, racialized depictions of Chinese people, which they had grown up with. Anna was typical of many Chinese young people. She was a "BBC" (a term used to refer to British-born Chinese), and she grew up working in her family's take-away business. During her adolescence, she felt ashamed of her parents' inability to speak English, and hated telling people that her family ran a take-away food business, because that was what the Chinese in Britain (of her parents' generation) typically did:

> At the time, I just thought it [the take-away] was all shit, and I wanted time, and everything was a constraint. And I was very anti-shop. There was something really humiliating at the time about, "Yeah, my dad's got a take-away", and everyone would say, "Oh, yeah", but now I actually take great pride in saying, "Yeah, my dad's in catering, and it's something we're good at. And it's something we've fallen into, out of necessity". So there are positive things about working together as a family, and I think we're more solid.
>
> (Song 1997: 354)

As in Anna's case, some second-generation minority people may experience a developmental trajectory which involves distancing themselves from, or even rejecting, their ethnic backgrounds, but which then moves on to a revaluing and embracing of their families' and their ethnic heritage. In one American study, the theme of coming to terms with one's ethnic heritage and background has been described as young people throwing off an allegedly fake White culture and embracing their ethnic heritage. One study of second-generation Vietnamese Americans found that they felt socially marginalized in childhood and adolescence, neither fully American nor fully Vietnamese (see Thai 1999). Many of these young people experienced childhood in the USA as a time when they wanted to assimilate into mainstream American society, and "acting White" was commonly reported during their childhoods. However, as they entered into young adulthood, they described a process involving the "deprogramming of the self," suggesting that they had, in effect, been brainwashed into accepting and valuing White practices and norms, at the expense of Vietnamese identity and practices. The concept of deprogramming draws on concerns about ethnic authenticity, as discussed in chapter 3, and it suggests the enduring appeal of the idea that one can discover a true, authentic self – even if this idea relies upon an essentialist, primordial understanding of ethnicity.

Panethnic identities

One way in which second-generation individuals publicly assert their ethnic identities is through a politicized adoption of a panethnic identity, particularly if they possess a heightened consciousness of racial marginalization and discrimination in the wider society. While ethno-national distinctions are not irrelevant for second-generation individuals, they are much more likely to recognize and forge panethnic identities and ties than their parents. For example, ethnic distinctions among third- and fourth-generation Asian Americans of Chinese and Japanese heritage may be diminishing, in favor of a more generalized Asian American culture and forms of panethnic association (Tuan 1998: 166; see chapter 2). Many of the young African Caribbean young men whom Alexander (1996) studied in London embraced a common sense of Black identity (though this was not the sole way in which they conceived of their ethnic identities). This was not the case with their parents, who were more likely to make distinctions, for instance, among Black Caribbeans from different islands like Jamaica or Trinidad. While inter-racial tensions can and do exist between various ethnic minority groups, there is also evidence of cultural and political dialogue, cooperation, and "cultural syncretism" among many young people (see Hewitt 1986; Back 1995).

There is also evidence of young people adopting a pan-Asian identity in Britain (see chapter 5 for Asian Americans), even though it is partly achieved through an externally imposed racial classification of Asianness. While ethno-religious differences and caste distinctions remain important among many Asians in Britain (Modood, Beishon, and Virdee 1994; Baumann 1996), there is also a sense among Asian youth of a unifying Asian culture and experience – for instance, through racialized experiences, which have been shaped by the Islamophobia following both the Salman Rushdie affair and September 11. The growing popularity of music such as Bhangra has also contributed to this awareness of an Asian popular culture. This pan-Asian identification is in sharp contrast with that of their parents: "These [parents] have no use for a category of '*Asian culture*', as if Sikhs, Hindus, Muslims, Punjabis, Gujaratis, and Bengalis were 'the same'" (Baumann 1996: 157, original emphasis). One important reason why the second generation are more likely to relate to a panethnic affiliation and identity than their parents is their tendency to militate against forms of racism by working in coalition with coethnics and other ethnic minority groups.

Ethnic identities in a global context

We live in an increasingly global world. Globalization entails increased interconnections of social and economic life. For instance, globalization has resulted in the spread of capitalist market relations and a truly interconnected global economy (Reich 1991; Boli and Thomas 1999). There are many competing arguments about the effects of globalization. Globalization is sometimes interpreted as a process of gradual homogenization dictated by the West (see Latouche 1996).[6] However, others have argued against the inevitability of homogenization: "By compressing time and space, globalization forces the juxtaposition of different civilizations, ways of life, and social practices. This both reinforces social and cultural prejudices and boundaries whilst simultaneously creating 'shared' cultural and social spaces in which there is an evolving 'hybridization' of ideas, values, knowledge and institutions" (Hall, Held, and McGrew 1992: 75; see also Pieterse 1995; Appadurai 1990).

Similarly, while refuting a simplistic notion of societal homogenization, Ulf Hannerz (1990) has argued that there is now a world culture, meaning that the world has become one network of social relationships, with a flow of meanings as well as of people and goods between various regions. As a result of these processes, more and more people are said to be involved with more than one culture (Featherstone 1990: 8). Increasingly, people's sense of their ethnic identities and affiliations are said to be relativized and shaped by their greater consciousness of the interconnections of people and societies around the world (Featherstone 1990; Robertson 1992).

How are people's ethnic identities and concerns about belonging and "home" affected by the processes of globalization? This question is especially pertinent to second-generation people born of immigrant parents in societies such as Britain and the USA. In the context of globalization, some second-generation individuals may possess an enhanced awareness of ties to their parents' homelands and of diasporic communities and cultures around the world. Although there is much debate about the concept of diaspora (see Anthias 1998), diaspora can be defined as "the (imagined) condition of a 'people' dispersed throughout the world, by force or by choice. Diasporas are transnational, spatially and temporally sprawling sociocultural formations of people, creating imagined communities whose blurred and fluctuating boundaries are sustained by real and/or symbolic ties to some original 'homeland'" (Ang 1994: 5). Diasporic people inevitably shape and transform the cultures and societies they pass through (Gilroy 1993).

Some second-generation individuals may embrace forms of diasporic cultural practices and identities. For example, young Black people may exhibit a strong identification with a global and diasporic Black culture, which traverses the "Black Atlantic" (Gilroy 1993). Certainly there has been a great deal of cross-fertilization of African American, Black Caribbean, and Black British cultural forms in the fields of music and literature. In the case of Asian Americans, in addition to trends in panethnic Asian identification and partnering, there is growing evidence of a global Asian popular culture. For example, the pan-Asian magazine *Giant Robot* is heavily plugged into youth cultures in Japan, Hong Kong, and Korea. Some Chinese young people, who were born and raised in Britain, have chosen to move to Hong Kong (from where their parents emigrated) in order to live and work there (Parker 1998). In addition to the attraction of good jobs, the BBCs (British-born Chinese) who go to Hong Kong tend to manifest a strong interest and connection with various forms of Hong Kong popular culture, such as popular films and music, which they consumed while living in Britain.

Transnational ties and communities

People's sense of "belonging" and identity are also complicated by mass migrations and multiple moves, which constitute a central dynamic of globalization. For example, it is certainly not unusual to be "twice migrants," like the people who emigrated from India to East Africa, then from East Africa to Britain (Bhachu 1985), or those who emigrated from India to the Caribbean, and then to Britain (Vertovec 1994). Given the complicated trajectories of many ethnic minorities, in terms of moving from one place to another, ethnic identity and affiliations are not necessarily bounded territorially to a person's birthplace in Britain, or say, in Pakistan.[7]

Contemporary international migration is significantly different from that of previous periods, and this is most evident in studies of transnationalism, which emphasize the economic, cultural, political, and familial networks and links between two or more locations (Gold 2000). Transnational communities refer to communities linking immigrant groups in advanced capitalist countries with their respective sending nations and hometowns. These communities are groupings of immigrants who participate on a routine basis in a field of relationships, practices, and norms that include both places of origin and places of destination (Portes, Guarnizo, and Landholt 1999). Transnational ethnic identities and networks go beyond territorially bounded notions of nation, culture, and ethnicity.

Transnational ties, networks, and identities are created in the wake of mass migrations. For instance, Ayumi Takenaka (1999) documents the experiences of Peruvians of Japanese descent. Over 20,000 Japanese people initially migrated from Japan to Peru from 1899 to the 1930s. Almost a century later, the descendants of these migrants began to migrate from Peru to Japan to work mostly as factory workers. This "return-migration" to Japan has been comprised of predominantly third-generation Peruvians of Japanese descent (aged 20–35).[8]

However, this return migration has not been easy for them. In Peru, Takenaka explains, they tend to feel "Japanese," because they look different from other Peruvians, and are effectively an ethnic minority group which encounters some discrimination. Currently, of the 80,000 to 90,000 Japanese Peruvians, one-third of them live in Japan as contract workers, while the rest live in Peru and the USA. Japanese Peruvians invoke their Japanese ancestry as a strategic resource in order to migrate to a country with a much stronger, more stable economy. Their motivation to go to Japan stems not only from their marginal status in Peru and their desire for greater social and economic mobility, but also from their ethnic attachments, both real and imagined, to Japan, as an ancestral "homeland" – even though they have never been to Japan and do not speak the Japanese language.

Upon arrival in Japan, however, these Peruvians of Japanese descent (known in Japan as "Nikkeijin") find that they are not treated as Japanese people, but rather, as "gaijin" (foreigners) and as an undesirable ethnic minority group, who are "more Peruvian" (than Japanese) in Japan, despite having a "Japanese face and name" (Takenaka 1999). The fact that many Nikkeijin do not speak Japanese, and that they engage in forms of contract labor, has also hindered their ability to mix with the wider Japanese population. As a result of their marginal status in both Japan and Peru, these Nikkeijin have forged transnational ethnic ties spanning Peru, Japan, and the

USA, to which many Nikkeijin have also emigrated. Transforming their ethnic identities from "Japanese" to "Nikkei" has been central to the maintenance and strengthening of these overseas Japanese communities.

The conceptualization of transnational ethnic identity, as with the Nikkei, is one which requires the de-coupling of cultural identity with national identity. The case of the Nikkei is interesting, because most studies thus far have shown that it is usually immigrant parents who sustain a "myth of return" to their homeland, whether it be Pakistan (Anwar 1979) or Korea (Min 1998), rather than their children or their grandchildren. It appears that, even several generations removed, disparate articulations of a myth of return can appear and motivate people to investigate an ancestral homeland. In the case of second- or even third-generation individuals, a sense of ethnicity may not be bounded to one place, or based upon any real contact with the original homeland, or even exposure to ethnic practices by parents. An awareness of global diasporas and transnational communities informs the ways in which second- (and third-) generation people conceive of their ethnic identities.

Immigrants and their children today are much more able to maintain strong transnational ties with their "homelands." Transnational ties are made possible by various factors. In many major metropolitan areas in the USA and Britain, second-generation ethnics may encounter a geographical concentration of other coethnics – for example, Asians encounter many other Asians in Bradford and Leeds, and Chinese Americans encounter many other coethnics in New York City and San Francisco. Transnational ties are also made possible by relatively inexpensive, quick air travel, and also by technological advances in communications and the mass media. For example, many groups have access to various forms of ethnic media, such as ethnic daily newspapers, weeklies, radio, and 24-hour television stations. Furthermore, second-generation children can learn their parents' ethnic languages through language programs offered on ethnic television stations, and Korean immigrant parents, for instance, commonly send their children to Korea for summer holidays in order to help them learn the Korean culture and language (Min 1999).

Rather than being a generation which will gradually but inevitably become completely acculturated into the dominant Western culture, the second generation today possesses various advantages for retaining their ethnic heritage and cultures (Min 1999). In addition to the possibility of accessing transnational ties with their parents' homelands, second-generation individuals can benefit from the implementation of multicultural policies (though these are limited in scope), especially in the form of bilingual programs and extracurricular activities which are designed to celebrate cultural diversity, such as ethnic festivals and symposia, such as the Notting Hill parade in London, which celebrates the West Indian population and culture, or the Chinese New Year's celebrations throughout Britain.

Hybridity and cultural mixing

Another way in which the identity formation of the second generation is shaped by the dynamics of globalization is the emphasis upon hybridity and various forms of mixing. For instance, Homi Bhabha (1990b) has elaborated the idea of a "third space," in which new hybrid cultural forms are emerging at the intersection of disparate cultures. Other analysts have also articulated the notions of mixing and cultural interpenetration with terms such as "inter-culturalism" (Pieterse 1995) and "cultural complexity" (Hannerz 1990).

Within multiethnic societies, such as Britain, there has been growing evidence of cultural borrowing, exchange, and "creolization" between Black and White working-class youth in London – for instance, in terms of speech, modes of dress, and music (Back 1995). Interestingly, White working-class adolescents in London and elsewhere have come to use, to varying degrees of skill, the Creole language of African Caribbean youth (Hewitt 1986). In urban areas where Black and White youth grow up together, one linguistic consequence is that both Cockney and Creole come to have an impact on the speech of both Black and White youth alike – creating a multiracial vernacular, which coexists with both friendships and racial tensions between Black and White youths.

Hybridized identities can be important for many second-generation minorities, because hybridity is said to constitute a form of resistance to the imposition of the dominant culture on minority cultures (Bhabha 1994). Given the unequal power relations which exist between dominant and subordinate populations and their respective cultures, the adoption of a hybrid identity may enable subordinate groups to subvert and to counter such imbalances of power (Lavie and Swedenburg 1996). Therefore, as a concept, hybridity suggests a positive outcome of mixing, which may increase people's repertoire of identity choices, rather than diluting cultural content.

Much of the discourse on globalization and diaspora is thus optimistic and liberating, with its emphasis on movement, fluidity, and hybridity. But how meaningful is globalization for ethnic minority groups and individuals who are subject to territorialized and localized processes of racialization? Is much of this emancipatory, celebratory discourse too optimistic and abstract?

Some analysts, such as Hamid Naficy, have argued that the celebration of hybridity will result in unattached and weightless hybrids "who are neither this nor that, neither here nor there" (Naficy 1993). A key criticism of writings on globalization and hybridity is that the concepts of hybridity, melange, and syncretism are largely meaningless to people who are rooted in their localities, and who articulate a strong sense of their "ethnic cores" (Smith 1990). In fact, globalization may simply reinforce people's localized sense of ethnic identity because global forms of belonging, including global memories and symbols, are vague and meaningless to most people (Smith 1990). A person's ethnic options are certainly likely to be significantly shaped by their locality. As Katz notes, "There must be a difference between someone who is, for instance, the only Chinese person in a small English village and someone who belongs to the Bengali community in Tower Hamlets [a part of London with a large Bengali population]" (1996: 23).

It is possible that the emancipatory tone associated with some theorizing on globalization and diaspora may over-emphasize people's ability to adopt ethnic identities which transcend territorial boundaries and to maintain multifaceted positionings and identifications. There may be too little attention paid to factors which may constrain people's experiences of identity and consciousness. In general, the discourse on globalization tends to neglect the recognition of racial difference, and experiences of racial discrimination, in the conceptualization of people's ethnic identities.

In spite of these criticisms, we should not overlook the fact that the recognition of "the third space" of hybridity can be genuinely meaningful and liberating for diasporic subjects who are constantly reinventing and renegotiating their ethnicity, and who counter and disrupt other people's categorizations of them, in relation to some original, distant homeland. Therefore, despite the constraints operating in relation to second- and third-generation individuals' ethnic options, there is substantial evidence that they possess a wider array of ethnic options than do their immigrant parents. In comparison with their parents, second- and third-generation individuals are more likely to engage in forms of code switching and ethnic reinvention, and are more likely to embrace complex diasporic identities and panethnic identities, whether they be second-generation Bengalis in Britain or third-generation Japanese Peruvians in Peru. Many second-generation individuals also work consciously at countering racism and negative representations and stereotypes of themselves.

While there is no single set of conventions which are followed by the second generation, there appear to be some significant commonalities across second-generation groups in terms of their efforts to exercise their ethnic options. It appears unlikely that the assertion of difference and the significance of ethnic identity are likely to diminish in any straightforward fashion for second-generation individuals in either Britain or the USA.

7

Debates about Racial Hierarchy

What are racial hierarchies?

It would be difficult to make sense of how ethnic minority groups negotiate and exercise their ethnic options without addressing current beliefs and understandings about groups' experiences of racism and racial disadvantage, and the opportunities and barriers they encounter more generally. Therefore, central to the question of how groups negotiate their ethnic identities (and the meanings associated with such identities) is how we perceive and map the ethnic and racial landscape, and the location of groups within it.

Even though we recognize difference and the specificities of minority experience and identity formation, we eventually confront the fact that groups do not exist in a vacuum, but in relation to one another. The notion of racial hierarchy is central to discussions about how different groups fare vis-à-vis one another in multiethnic societies. To refer to racial hierarchy is to acknowledge that we live in societies which are comprised of groups who are not on equal terms with each other. There is little doubt that racial inequalities exist in Britain and the USA, but there is little discussion of what, exactly, racial hierarchies are, and how they operate.[1] The question of whether some groups are worse off than others is highly pertinent at a time when there is growing recognition of multiple forms of racisms and racial oppression.

Does the concept of racial hierarchy illuminate our understanding of how different groups fare? The answer to this question is clearly and unproblematically "Yes" in relation to formal institutionalized systems of racial stratification, as existed in South Africa prior to 1990. In the former South Africa (though this is only the most paradigmatic and contemporary historical example of racial hierarchy), Black people were deemed inferior to both "Coloreds" and Whites, and they lived in segregated townships as lesser beings. In all aspects of their lives – economic, political, and social – Whites were undisputably at the top, Black people at the bottom, and the "Colored" population comprised a formal intermediate category (Spickard 1989).

Even today, in the USA, there is significant evidence that many non-White ethnic minorities do not have equality of opportunity in housing, labor markets, health care, education, and the criminal justice system – despite the surprisingly widespread belief, among both White and Black Americans, that there is equality of opportunity in American society (Sidanius and Pratto 1999: 107).[2] Nevertheless, the question of whether the experiences of minority groups can be understood in terms of a racial hierarchy is much more difficult to answer in relation to most contemporary multiethnic non-absolutist societies such as Britain and the USA. Forms of both overt and covert discrimination and prejudice are still all too prevalent in the USA and Europe, and race continues to play a significant role in shaping overall life chances and experiences. However, the USA and Britain are not characterized by rigid sociopolitical constraints, but rather by a gradual modification of the social and economic parameters dividing White and non-White peoples (Kilson 1975: 255), and by seemingly legitimate ideologies which enable dominant groups to maintain their hegemonic position over subordinate groups (Sidanius and Pratto 1999).[3]

Rather than provide a systematic documentation of racial disadvantage across groups, which is beyond the scope of this chapter, I will explore whether the concept of racial hierarchy helps us to understand the varied experiences and welfare of disparate groups. What makes the concept of racial hierarchy so compelling is that it is suggestive of an *overall* picture of how different groups fare in a multiethnic society. While socioeconomic disparities between Whites and non-Whites have long been acknowledged, there has been growing debate concerning the positioning of ethnic minority groups in relation to each other within the USA and Britain. Groups are invested in particular narratives about their experiences and positions in relation to others (Blumer 1958), and there is a real political stake underlying discussions about racial hierarchy. This is why debates about racial hierarchy tend to be charged with a tenor of group competition. It is difficult to divorce the personal and political investments of groups (and analysts) from the intellectual debates about racial hierarchy.

Systems of ethnic and racial stratification have differed historically, not only in terms of the groups involved, but also in terms of the complexity and the magnitude of the distinctions made between groups (Shibutani and Kwan 1965: 48). Some hierarchies are also specific to certain regions and localities within a nation. For instance, in a study of White supremacy in nineteenth-century California, Native Americans were characterized as savages, who were located at the bottom of the racial hierarchy, while Mexicans were considered to be "half civilized," and thus occupied an intermediate position on the hierarchy (Almaguer 1994; see also Loewen 1971; Twine 1998).

Beyond a general recognition of the multiple and varied manifestations of racial oppression, there is no common definition or understanding of racial hierarchy across contemporary studies. "Social dominance theory" has been influential in arguing that the means by which group-based hierarchies, including racial and ethnic hierarchies, are established and maintained are similar across social systems (Sidanius and Pratto 1999). In such group-based hierarchies, the dominant group or groups possess a disproportionately large share of "positive social value," such as political power, good food, nice homes, wealth, and high social status, while "subordinate" groups possess a disproportionately large share of "negative social value," including low social status, low power, poor health care, and high-risk, low-status jobs (Sidanius and Pratto 1999).[4]

By reviewing some of the literature in the USA and Britain, I will show that contemporary debates about racial hierarchies, including discourses about how we conceptualize the racial disadvantage and oppression of specific groups, have taken quite different forms in the two countries.[5] I will then go on to discuss some of the difficulties in constructing and asserting a racial hierarchy. First, I will argue that analysts in both countries refer to many different dimensions of well-being and disadvantage, which can be difficult to compare. Second, I will argue that a consideration of various indicators of well-being can suggest complex interstices of privilege and disadvantage among ethnic minority groups, which complicate a straightforward picture of a top-down hierarchy. Third, I will argue that the assertion of racial hierarchies can contribute to inter-ethnic tensions and divisiveness. I then conclude by questioning whether the concept of racial hierarchy should be retained in studies of racial oppression and disadvantage.

The USA: a recognized racial hierarchy

Racial awareness is very pronounced in many parts of the USA (Marable 1995). When Black West Indian immigrants in the USA complain that *both* White and Black Americans are obsessed with "racialism" – "a heightened sensitivity to race, a tendency to racialize situations and relations between people" (Waters 1999: 75) – few American social scientists or journalists would disagree with such an assessment of the American psyche. There is currently controversy surrounding the publication of two books concerning race: *Nigger* (Kennedy 2001) and *Stupid White Men* (Moore 2002).

In recognizing the multiracial diversity of the US population, some analysts, such as Michael Omi and Howard Winant (1994), delineate the historically variable processes of racialization of different minority groups, pointing to the genocide suffered by Native Americans, African American slavery, the colonization of Mexicans, and the exclusion of Asian Americans (C. Kim 1999: 105). Nevertheless, there appears to be a fairly widespread view that White Americans are at the top of a racial hierarchy, African Americans at the bottom, and groups such as Asian Americans and Latinos somewhere in between. For example, Vilna Bashi and Antonio McDaniel state: "The very idea of race assumes a hierarchy of racial groups. Within this hierarchy, Africans were [and still are] on the bottom and Europeans on top" (1997: 671). One of the few analysts who has studied the Black experience in both the USA and Britain, Stephen Small, has observed: "Black people continue to face problems which no non-Black people ever face. . . . As people of African descent, our culture, institutions, values and history still remain the most vilified of all racialised groups" (1994: 197). Small argues that in both Britain and the USA, there is an undeniable "colour line" which applies specifically to Black people, which is both "material (property, power, and privilege) and mental (attitudes, ideologies and psychology)" (1994: 180).

Many analysts in the USA believe that the historical legacy of slavery is fundamental to explaining the relatively disadvantaged status of many African Americans today.[6] In fact, there is currently a campaign by some Black activists to pay reparations to African Americans for the injuries of slavery. Joe Feagin, in *Racist America* (2000: 207), notes the "high level of white effort and energy put into maintaining antiblack racism" as one of the many reasons why African Americans are at the bottom of the racial hierarchy. In other words, White Americans have simply expended much less time and energy in exploiting and oppressing other groups such as Asian Americans and Latino Americans. Both in the past and in the present, each new non-European immigrant group in the USA is "placed, principally by the dominant whites, somewhere on a *white-to-black status continuum*, the commonplace measuring stick of social acceptability" (2000: 210, emphasis original). Feagin also argues that, viewed historically,

African Americans "have been oppressed much longer by whites than any other group except Native Americans" (2000: 206). Given the extraordinary history of enslavement and Jim Crow laws, such an experience of racial oppression and struggle is historically distinct from the kinds of racial subordination and disadvantage suffered by other groups (Woodward 1966).

In addition to arguments about their distinctive historical treatment and experiences, African Americans have fared badly according to various socioeconomic indicators (see Bonilla-Silva 1999). The following aggregate statistics illustrate how stark are the disparities in the quality of life between Black and White Americans: on average, Black families earn about 60 percent of what White families earn and survive on roughly 12 percent of the wealth of average White families. As individuals, their life spans are six to seven years shorter than Whites (Feagin 2000: 202). Furthermore, in 1995, almost one third (32.2 percent) of all African American men, aged between 20 and 29, were either in prison, in jail, on probation, or on parole (Sidanius and Pratto 1999).

Both in the past and in the present, African Americans have often been the victims of horrific racial attacks, and this is reflected in the media attention devoted to events such as the beating of Rodney King by Los Angeles police in 1992 (and, more recently, the beating of Black teenager Donovan Jackson in July 2002), and the heinous murder of James Byrd, who was tortured and dismembered by White supremacists in the South. When analysts, such as Andrew Hacker (1992), argue that forms of "racial apartheid" apply in the organization of American society, they are talking primarily about the divide between White and Black America.

So where are other minority groups positioned, in relation to African Americans? Various analysts suggest that Asian Americans are an intermediate group, between Whites at the top and Blacks at the bottom of a racial hierarchy (see Feagin 2000; Gans 1999; Kibria 1998; Matsuda 1993; Okihiro 1994). In relation to the experiences of South Asians in the USA, Vijay Prashad writes: "To be both visible (as a threat) and invisible (as a person) is a strain disproportionately borne by black America. This is not to say that we [South Asians] don't feel the edge of racism (both as prejudice and as structural violence), but we do so in a far less stark sense than do those who are seen as the detritus of U.S. civilization" (2000: 6).[7] Although C. Mathew Snipp acknowledges the historical genocide and discrimination suffered by Native Americans, he explicitly points to African Americans as the group which has endured the worst forms of racial discrimination: "It is debatable whether American Indians ever received the same measure of scorn heaped upon the African-American population. Certainly racial prejudice and discrimination have been directed at American Indians, but in recent years . . . the stigma of an American Indian identity has lessened considerably" (1997: 677).

To the extent that, historically, Latino and Asian Americans (and Jewish Americans) tried to distance themselves from the despised status of Black Americans, they bought into a system of White supremacy which firmly located African Americans as the dregs of society (Feagin 2000). Claire Kim (1999) has recently argued that Asian Americans have been "racially triangulated" in relation to Black and White Americans: Whites valorize Asian Americans in comparison with Blacks on cultural and racial grounds, enabling Whites to refute the legitimate claims and grievances of African Americans. At the same time, Whites engage in "civic ostracism" by constructing Asian Americans as alien and unassimilable. As such, White Americans manage to retain their dominant, privileged positions in society.[8]

There is also research in the USA which suggests that White Americans' "antiblack orientation" is deep and filled with fear and loathing, and that such currents of fear and hatred are not as strong in relation to other Americans of color (Feagin 2000; Feagin and Sikes 1994). In her study of White women, Ruth Frankenberg (1993) found that the White women she interviewed tended to view Asian and Latino Americans as less different from White people than Black Americans. White Americans seem to trust and feel more comfortable with Latino Americans than they do with African Americans – a key factor which accounts for the displacement of many African Americans from domestic and janitorial jobs by Latino Americans in California (J. Miles 1992). Similarly, in a study of employers' attitudes towards hiring African American and immigrant Latino low-skill workers, Shih (2002) found that many employers regarded African Americans as problematic workers with a negative attitude, especially in comparison with Latino immigrants, who were seen as more manageable, pliant, and hard-working.

Post-September 11, there has been heightened awareness of racial attacks against people deemed to be Arab or Muslim (Iganski 2000). For instance, the *New York Times* (Goodstein and Lewin 2001) reported the case of a Sikh man who was attacked for being a "dirty Arab," because he wore a turban and a beard. Racial profiling and the illegal detention of "suspects" is likely to infringe upon the civil and human rights of Arab and Muslim people (Jaggi 2002). Anti-Arab and anti-Muslim prejudice is hardly new in the USA; it has, to some extent, been simmering since the Gulf War. Nevertheless, the Middle Eastern and Arab populations in the USA are very small, and the still nascent evidence of Islamophobia is not likely to fundamentally challenge (at least for the foreseeable future) the widespread consensus that there is a racial hierarchy in the USA, with Whites at the top and African Americans at the bottom.[9]

Britain: a "hierarchy of oppression"?

In Britain, unlike the USA, most research has (until recently) stressed the *commonality* of experience of ethnic minorities in relation to the White majority, based upon a disadvantaged status in relation to the housing and labor markets, racial abuse, and certain forms of social exclusion and marginalization (but see chapter 5). Most British analysts do not conceive of ethnic minority experiences in terms of a top-down hierarchy. This may be because, in Britain, many South Asians and African Caribbeans have shared the history of British colonialism in the Indian subcontinent, the Caribbean, Africa, and South Asia (though the experiences of these populations have been clearly distinct in each of these places). Although slavery reached the shores of England during the second half of the sixteenth century, and slavery itself ended as late as 1838 (only 30 years before its abolition in the USA), slavery in the USA was more widespread and integral in economic and social terms (see Shyllon 1974; Walvin 1985).[10] Unlike many African Americans, who were direct descendants of slaves brought to the USA from the 1600s onwards, many of the African Caribbeans in Britain today emigrated to Britain from the 1950s onwards.[11]

In Britain, the stress has been on the shared experiences of many non-White immigrants, who were former colonial subjects, coming to Britain in the post-War period to work in predominantly unskilled or semi-skilled jobs as disadvantaged minorities (see Solomos 1993; Sivanandan 1982). Although state policies have impacted differently on Asian and African Caribbean populations in Britain, many Asian, Caribbean, and Chinese "subjects" emigrated to Britain in the 1950s and 1960s, and were subject to a succession of Immigration Acts which became increasingly stringent, in comparison to the easier entry afforded White Canadian and Australian Commonwealth subjects (Solomos 1993).

The stress on commonality, however, has not precluded the emergence of distinctive representations of these groups – though there are some shared discourses about the threat of unruly Asian and African Caribbean men.[12] For instance, Asian people in Britain encounter racial epithets concerning their putative foreignness, which stress, among other things, their religious beliefs and their wearing of saris, turbans, and salwar kameez. Tariq Modood (1994, 1996) has pointed to the importance of understanding the dynamics of "cultural racism," which is said to be targeted at certain groups which are seen as being assertively different from the wider society, such as South Asians – though he does not mention the visibility of Hasidic Jews.

In recent years, British Muslims have increasingly been defined negatively, drawing on notions of an emergent, alienated Pakistani and Bangladeshi underclass (Alexander 2000: 6–7). In the spring and summer of 2001, much of the media coverage of the conflicts occurring between Asian and White youths in Oldham and other cities in the Northwest was framed in terms of threatening and lawless young Asian men who were not reined in by the older generation of Asians. And since the attacks on New York City and Washington on September 11, there have been manifestations of Islamophobia, which depicts all Middle-Eastern and South Asian people (and especially young men) as fanatical and dangerous religious zealots in the British mainstream (Iganski 2000; Ray and Smith 2000). Such sentiments are also evident in the USA, but they primarily take the form of anti-Arab sentiments, aimed at Middle-Eastern people, including Iraquis, Iranians, and Libyans (Bozorgmehr, Der-Martirosian, and Sabagh 1996). This negative depiction of Asians had been preceded by their representation as foreign, but law-abiding and unproblematic – especially by comparison with the dominant representation of African Caribbeans as muggers and Rastafarian drug dealers (Alexander 2000).

While the recognition of Islamophobia has helped to broaden the frameworks for theorizing racism in Britain (Silverman and Yuval-Davis 1999), it has also engendered heated debate about racial hierarchies. The amount of media attention lavished upon the "problem" of Asian youth in recent years has led some analysts to suggest that working-class Muslims occupy the bottom of a racial hierarchy in Britain. Tariq Modood has engendered much ire by claiming, "I think it is already the case in Britain now, as it has been in Europe for some time, that the extra-European origin group that suffers the worst prejudice and exclusion are working-class Muslims. As about two-thirds of all non-white people in the European Union are Muslims, Islamophobia and the integration of Muslims will rightly emerge as key race-relations issues" (1996: 12). Arguing along similar lines, Muhammad Anwar states that "it is clear that they [Asians] face double discrimination, racial and religious. It appears that white people express more prejudice against Asians and Muslims than against [Black] Caribbeans. Recent examples include Muslim girls being refused jobs because of their dress and Sikh pupils refused school admission because of their turbans" (1998: 186).

To suggest that one ethnic minority group suffers the worst prejudice and exclusion has been unacceptable to some British analysts, on both intellectual and political grounds. Tariq Modood has been accused of positing a "hierarchy of oppression," which tends to deny the prejudicial experiences of White minorities, such as Jewish and Irish people in Britain.[13] According to Mary Hickman, "When disadvantages experienced by Irish people are acknowledged this is usually accompanied by the notion of a 'hierarchy of oppression' based on the idea that no white group could experience the level of racism which a black group can" (1998: 289).[14]

Although these analysts are sympathetic to putting Asian experiences on the map, and to conceding that race is more than about Black and White (a model which is regarded as reductive in its emphasis upon color-based racism), they resist what they perceive to be a racial landscape which is dependent upon racial victimology and which renders invisible the disadvantages experienced by White minorities in Britain. One implication of alleging a hierarchy of oppression is that it challenges the belief that all White people necessarily occupy a "location of structural advantage, of race privilege" (Frankenberg 1993).[15] By comparison, this kind of argument about White Americans is rarely made by analysts in the USA. In Britain, Whiteness is increasingly problematized in terms of class differences between working- and middle-class White Britons, and in terms of ethnic and religious differences between Jewish, Welsh, Scottish, Irish Catholics, and White English Protestants (Jenkins 1997).

One point which a number of scholars in Britain have made is that many kinds of signifiers of both phenotypical and cultural differences have been used in relation to both "people of color" and White ethnics over time (Anthias and Yuval-Davis 1992). So claims that it is people of color who *exclusively* suffer certain forms of racialization, based upon their non-White physical appearance, are contested. For instance, in relation to the racialized signifiers attributed to Semitic features (see Gilman 1985), Phil Cohen (1996) suggests that Jewish people have been racialized, and he refutes the suggestion that Asian Muslims suffer more or worse racial prejudice than Jewish and Irish people, because of the presumption that being White in Britain has shielded them from racial discrimination and prejudice.[16] Both Irish and Jewish analysts in Britain argue that it is important to remember that *visibility* (as a racialized people) is both socially constructed and changeable (Mac an Ghaill 1999).

By comparison with the USA, there is more contentiousness about whether or not it makes sense to conceive of Britain's ethnic minority experiences in terms of a racial hierarchy. However, there is growing debate in both countries about the racial order, at a time when multiple forms of racism are increasingly recognized, and when the racialization and vilification of Muslims and Arabs are more prominent (see Silverman and Yuval-Davis 1999 on Britain and France).

Many dimensions of group experience

The concept of racial hierarchy is suggestive of a big picture of how disparate groups fare. In both the USA and Britain, analysts' references to a wide range of indicators (of disadvantage and privilege) can make it difficult to assess the *overall* positions and experiences of groups, in relation to each other. For example, in a study of social change among young South Asian people and their parents in Britain, Anwar argues that "research has shown that racial attacks affect Asians more than some other groups" (1998: 14), and he goes on to suggest that Asians are especially discriminated against by the wider society. There does seem to be *some* evidence for this assertion, especially since the cataclysmic events of September 11 and the backlash against anyone vaguely deemed "Muslim" (see Ray and Smith 2000).

However, in Britain, African Caribbeans are less likely to report racial attacks than South Asians, and this is likely to be related to the fact that African Caribbeans have tended to distrust the police, who have traditionally had an antagonistic relationship with the Black population (Hall et al. 1978; Solomos 1988; Centre for Contemporary Cultural Studies 1982). The assertion that Asians are more subject to racial attacks than African Caribbeans is also more uncertain when one considers the limitations of official police data across Britain, given that there is significant variability in the recording of racially motivated incidents (see Maynard and Read 1997). Furthermore, even if there is iron-clad evidence that Asians suffer more racial attacks than African Caribbeans, is this a sufficient basis for the assertion that Asians are more discriminated against than other groups in a broader sense?

This example illustrates the lack of consensus in discussions concerning not only the criteria to be applied in constructions of racial hierarchy, but also the often murky notion of racial oppression more generally. In comparison with racial attacks, how relevant are factors such as a group's average family income, or the nature of its representation in the popular media, for the overall assessment of how a group fares? There are many and different (though in many ways related) dimensions of a group's status and experience. While a group may fare badly according to one indicator, it may be relatively privileged according to another indicator. For instance, in Britain, South Asians on the whole *may* suffer more racially motivated attacks than other groups, as discussed above. However, Indians and African Asians (who are subgroups of the rubric "Asian") have a slightly higher average total household income than the White population (Modood et al. 1997: 158). By comparison, African Caribbean, Pakistani, and Bangladeshi households report lower incomes than Indians and African Asians. This points to the importance of disaggregating the experiences of subgroups from one another.

Turning to the USA, there is evidence that, along many socioeconomic indicators, African Americans, Native Americans, and Latino Americans fare worse than Asian Americans and White Americans (Feagin 2000; Sidanius and Pratto 1999). But how should one order African Americans, Native Americans, and Latino Americans? As discussed earlier, there appears to be a fairly widespread consensus that African Americans are at the bottom of the racial hierarchy, and there is comprehensive documentation of the disadvantaged status of African Americans across many different domains, such as residential segregation and capital punishment (Bonilla-Silva 1999). By comparison with numerically small groups such as Native Americans, who constitute only 1 percent of the population (US Bureau of Census 1990), African Americans comprise 12 percent of the population, and their experiences are regarded as paradigmatic of racial oppression in the USA. However, when compared with other minority groups, African Americans fare better than some Latino subgroups and Native Americans on certain socioeconomic indicators (see table 7.1). According to the 1990 US Census (data from the 2000 Census was not yet available at the time of writing), Puerto Ricans' poverty rate was 38 percent (African Americans, 32 percent), the percentage for obtaining a university degree was 10 percent (African Americans, 12 percent), and their home ownership rate was 23 percent (African Americans, 31 percent).[17]

According to Manning Marable, "There is also substantial evidence that Latinos continue to experience discrimination in elementary, secondary, and higher education which is in many respects more severe than that experienced by African Americans" (1995: 197). Marable also notes that despite the belief that Latinos are, on the whole, more economically privileged than African Americans, when one disaggregates the large and diverse panethnic grouping "Latino," Mexican American families earn only slightly more than Black households, and Puerto Rican families earn less than Black Americans on average (1995: 196–7). Nor should nativist hostility toward vulnerable Latino immigrants be underestimated. The fact that immigrant Latinos are perceived as pliant workers doesn't mean that they are socially accepted in other spheres of life.

Yet, because there are so many different dimensions of a group's experiences, this data about Latinos does not prove that, overall, Latinos are more racially oppressed than African Americans. Furthermore, it can be difficult, if not impossible, to compare the incommensurate experiences of certain groups. Looking at the historical treatment of groups, how do we compare the genocide of Native Americans with the enslavement of African Americans? Despite the fact that it may now be "cool" to be Native American in the USA (Snipp 1997), Native Americans are still an extremely disadvantaged group. Their indicators for median family income and poverty rate are almost identical to those of African Americans, but their percentage for obtaining a university degree was only 9 percent (African Americans, 12 percent) (see table 7.1). In many parts of the USA, it is literally possible to forget about Native Americans as a disadvantaged group because there are so few of them left. Native Americans are a less visible target for abuse than African Americans, because they suffer from post-genocide invisibility. While this invisibility makes Native Americans less of a threat to White America, it doesn't lessen the "problem" of being Native American.

Yet, again, it would be unsustainable to argue that Native Americans have been more racially oppressed than African Americans, and the recognition of Native American genocide does not derogate the severity of slavery and Jim Crow. Such a comparison is akin to comparing apples and oranges.

Complex interstices of privilege and disadvantage

Another difficulty in constructing a monolithic, top-down hierarchy of groups is that while socioeconomic data regarding various groups is crucial for assessing a group's overall experience, some measures of socioeconomic well-being, in isolation from other criteria, can also obscure the multifaceted experiences of different groups. There is a tendency to extrapolate to other aspects of a group's overall experience on the basis of specific socioeconomic indicators. I argued in chapter 2 against automatically "reading off" a group's ethnic options from how it fares on key socioeconomic indicators. These indicators do not necessarily tell us about subtle and less noticeable forms of social

Table 7.1 Inequality within racial and ethnic groups, 1990

	Population share[a] (%)	Median family income ($)	Poverty rate (%)	Unemployment rate[b] (%)	College degree[c] (%)	Home ownership (%)
African American	12.0	21,423	32	14	12	31
Asian American[d]	3.0	42,240	14	6	38	51
Chinese	0.7	41,316	14	6	41	na
Filipino	0.6	46,698	6	5	39	na
Japanese	0.3	51,550	7	3	35	na
Asian Indian	0.3	na	na	na	na	na
Korean	0.3	33,909	14	6	35	na
Vietnamese	0.2	na	na	9	na	na
Other	0.5	na	na	na	na	na
Hispanic/Latino American[e]	9.0	23,431	25	10	9	39
Mexican	5.4	23,240	25	10	6	44
Puerto Rican	1.1	18,008	38	12	10	23
Cuban	0.4	31,439	13	8	20	47
Other	2.1	na	na	na	na	na
Native American	1.0	21,750	31	na	9	na
White (European American)	80.0	36,915	9	7	22	68

Note: Data for more recent years are not available for racial/ethnic subgroups.

na = not available

[a] Figures add to more than 100% because some people identify themselves as members of more than one category.

[b] 1992.

[c] 4-year degree, among persons age 25 and over. [In the USA, 4-year university degrees are the norm.]

[d] Includes Pacific Islanders.

[e] People of Hispanic descent can be members of any race.

Source: US Bureau of Census 1990

exclusion and inclusion (including social acceptance and respect), the often double-edged representation of groups in the wider society, or group members' self-esteem – all factors which impact significantly upon a group's social status and overall quality of life. Although it is undeniably important, socioeconomic well-being does not translate simply and directly into social and political forms of power and prestige.

For instance, although Asian Americans are relatively privileged according to socioeconomic indicators, "Asian-Americans as a group do not own the major corporations of banks which control access to capital. They do not own massive amounts of real estate, control the courts or city government, have ownership of the mainstream media, dominate police forces, or set urban policies" (Marable 1995: 199). In fact, they are relatively underrepresented in politics and public life more generally: Asian Americans register and vote at lower rates than White and Black Americans (Lien 1997).[18]

Far from being evidence of the unalloyed privilege of Asian Americans, or their high level of acceptance in American society, the material success of many Asian Americans has engendered resentment and rising anti-Asian violence and sentiment (Kurashige 2000; Kang 2000). For example, the anti-Japanese furore in the context of Japan's emergence as a key global economic power in the 1980s and early 1990s has engendered a climate of fear among some Asian Americans – given the common conflation of Asian Americans with Asians in Japan, Korea, and China (C. Kim 1999: 128). Asian Americans are explicitly targeted by jokes and physical intimidation in the mass media and public spaces (Tuan 1998). By comparison, it is considered politically incorrect to make racist jokes about Blacks or Latinos.

There can be significant nativist hostility toward Asian Americans – this echoes assertions by some South Asian analysts in Britain about the racialization of South Asians as foreign and alien. While some Asian Americans reify the model minority image and are racist toward Blacks and Latinos, even members of racially oppressed groups such as Latino Americans and African Americans may engage in forms of "civic ostracism" toward Asian Americans, which involves exclusionary discourses about the alien and ultimately untrustworthy nature of Asian Americans, including third- and fourth-generation Asian Americans (C. Kim 2000–1).

This kind of nativist hostility is illustrated by an example from Britain. An ethnographic study of Black, White, and Vietnamese young people in a youth club on a working-class council estate (public housing) in South London found that Vietnamese young people were socially excluded and racially taunted by both White and Black youths (see Back 1993, 1995). Although the White youths upheld an understanding of British nationalism which was reserved for Whites only, a "neighbourhood nationalism" based upon the friendships of Black and White youths also existed on the estate. Both White and Black youths participated in a very diverse mixture of popular cultural forms such as Black genres of music (such as hip-hop and rap) and White working-class idioms. Significantly, such "re-assemblage" of various cultural forms and practices enabled these youths to engage in multiracial friendships and to inhabit a "territory that is temporarily, and perhaps superficially, 'colour blind'" (Back 1993: 220; Hewitt 1986).

According to Back (1993), there was an unwritten rule that it was unacceptable to say blatantly racist things about Black people in the youth club. Many Black youths were considered to be "insiders" on the estate, especially if their families had been living there for many years. A solidarity based on being long-time residents manifested itself in opposition to newcomers, such as the Vietnamese, who were blamed for the declining conditions on the housing estate. Certainly the Vietnamese youth possessed no street cred of any value in the eyes of the White youths in South London. Unlike the Black youths on the estate, who were associated with the status and positive appeal of Black youth cultures and styles, the Vietnamese were regarded in solely negative terms, as aliens. Athough there were some instances of short-lived friendships between Vietnamese and White youth on the estate, the Vietnamese tended to suffer forms of racialized "winding-up" (aggressive teasing) – for example, in the form of Kung Fu moves or noises or hostile remarks about their "foreign"-sounding names or their alleged eating of dogs. As a result, these Vietnamese youth were excluded and tended to fall back into their Vietnamese social networks.

While there is significant empirical evidence of structured, institutionalized forms of inequality and subordination in relation to African Americans, some recent studies suggest the need to explore the various forms of cultural and social capital possessed by Black Americans (see A. Young 1999; Carter 2000). While Black Americans have endured severe discrimination, they have also had access to numerous coethnic institutions, such as colleges, churches, and powerful political associations, such as the National Association for the Advancement of Colored People. By contrast, Asians and Latinos may be subject to less segregation and less discrimination, but they are still largely culturally and institutionally invisible in the USA.[19]

It is important that generalized assertions of hierarchy, which provide an important macro picture of how groups fare, do not obscure or overlook the specificities of groups' experiences. Just as groups who are relatively well-off socioeconomically, such as Asian Americans, are not privileged in all domains, so materially disadvantaged groups, such as African Americans, may not be disadvantaged in all domains. I have shown that comparisons of the disparate experiences of groups, and their location along a hierarchy, are complicated, especially given the many dimensions of group experience discussed by analysts, some of which are not directly or easily comparable.

Inter-ethnic relations and tensions

While there is considerable agreement about the persistence of White power, privilege, and racism (though this is more contested by analysts in Britain), there is growing contentiousness among non-White minority groups in both countries about their place in the racial order. Another difficulty with the assertion of a racial hierarchy is that it can encourage invidious comparisons between groups and be politically divisive. Amidst the scramble for scarce group resources, and against a backdrop in which disparate groups may know very little about each other, there can be little room for empathy.

One source of inter-ethnic tension concerns the question of which groups do and do not constitute disadvantaged ethnic minority groups. This is contested and is not as clear as it was in the past. African Americans were at the forefront of the Civil Rights movement in the 1960s, from which all minority groups benefited. In the USA, there was some degree of "Black–Brown–Yellow" solidarity (referring to African Americans, Latinos, and Asians) in the 1960s and early 1970s, with the emergence of the Civil Rights and the Black power movements. However, in the latter part of the twentieth century, factionalism has grown concerning issues such as the continuing immigration and growth of the Latino population in the USA and contentiousness about whether all Latino Americans (such as Cubans) are indeed underprivileged, and therefore eligible for forms of state assistance (Marable 1995: 195–6).

Inter-ethnic tensions between African Americans and Latinos are emerging at a time when the Latino population has experienced huge growth (Nieman 1999). Significant demographic shifts in the USA have resulted not only in changes in size of the various minority groups, but also in increased contestation concerning the allocation of resources and groups' political interests. Early data from the 2000 Census suggests that the Hispanic population has grown by more than 60 percent in the last decade, so that it is roughly equal in number to the African American population (Schmitt 2001). The growing number of Latino and Asian immigrants in California has engendered concern about the potential economic and political marginalization of the Black population: "Blacks still enjoy sufficient political influence and power to retain a competitive advantage, but control over the portals to government employment will shift as growing naturalization rates and the advent of the second generation increase Latino and Asian electoral power" (Grant, Oliver, and James 1996: 407). The fact that much of the growth in the Latino population can be accounted for by illegal, as well as legal, immigration means that the experiences and circumstances of many Latinos are quite distinct from those of most African Americans and some Asian Americans.

Members of disparate minority groups may believe that they are more disadvantaged than others, and these competing beliefs can contribute to inter-ethnic tensions. For instance, some Hispanics may feel that they are treated as foreigners in today's anti-immigrant climate in the USA, and that African Americans hold substantial political power as an established minority group (Nieman 1999). On the other hand, some African Americans may believe that they are disadvantaged in the labor market because they are losing jobs to Hispanics, who may be favored by White employers. Thus competing narratives about which groups deserve equal or special consideration and assistance by the state have called into question dominant understandings of the existing racial order in the USA. For example, some Asian American activists have asserted that they are indeed "bona fide" minorities (like African Americans and Latino Americans), in order to counter the perception that all Asian Americans are privileged and do not require state assistance (C. Kim 2000–1).

Should we jettison the notion of racial hierarchy?

The discussion of racial hierarchy in relation to Britain and the USA has illustrated that the conceptualization of groups' disparate experiences along a racial hierarchy is specific to national contexts, and is fundamentally shaped by the histories and political climate of each country. The notion of racial hierarchy appears to make more sense in relation to the contemporary USA than to Britain, where the histories and experiences of diverse formerly colonized people – African Caribbeans, Asians, and Chinese – are more similar than are the distinct modes of incorporation of American ethnic minority groups. The arguments of some British analysts that Jewish and Irish people have suffered as White minorities are more influential in the British than the American context. This is because, for instance, as Hickman points out, "Both the colonial racism stemming from Anglo-Irish relations and the construction of the Irish (Catholic) as a historically significant Other of the English/British (Protestant) have framed the experience of the Irish in Britain" (1998: 290–91). By comparison, there is no longer such "othering" of Irish Americans in the contemporary USA (see Waters 1990).

The notion of a racial hierarchy in the USA has relied upon a rather unitary (i.e. anti-Black) understanding of racism – although this is now changing, with the growth of the non-Black minority population and the growth of Asian and Latino scholars. One of Feagin's key arguments is that "white-on-black oppression" is *fundamental* to all ethnic minority experience in the USA, and that it should underlie our understanding of racism more generally. This claim is interesting. While there is no question that the experiences of other minorities, such as those of Asian and Latino Americans, have been shaped by the laws, beliefs, and practices which were institutionalized in order to maintain and bolster the slave system, what are the implications of the "white-on-black oppression" framework for how we conceptualize and make sense of other minority groups' experiences? This question is timely and crucial, given the growing debate in the USA about exactly where other groups, such as Asian Americans and Latino Americans, fit in a racial hierarchy, with White people at the top and African Americans at the bottom (Palumbo-Liu 1999).[20]

Can Asian American and Latino American experiences be sufficiently understood in terms of Feagin's proposed "white-on-black oppression" model, in which we are to understand the racial oppression of Asian and Latino groups as derived from an older model of racism based on the historical oppression of Black people? While the racialized experiences of disparate groups have been mutually constitutive of one another (C. Kim 1999), it is also important not to lose sight of the specificity of each group's experience, which can be lost by the placement of a group within a racial paradigm, in which one group's history or experience is dominant in relation to that of other groups. It is important that the particular experiences of groups and their responses to racial oppression are investigated. In recent years, social psychologists researching the effects of racism have also begun to question whether models of racial identity based on the experiences of African Americans (the group most studied regarding the effects of racial prejudice in the USA) are adequate to understand the racial and ethnic identities of other groups, such as Latino and Asian Americans (see Murrell 1998: 194; Crocker and Quinn 1998).

In contrast to the US situation, analysts in Britain tend to identify a variety of racisms which are flourishing in contemporary Europe, including anti-Jewish, anti-Muslim, anti-Arab, anti-Turk, anti-African, and anti-Gypsy racism (Brah 1996: 167). Phil Cohen (1988) also argues that there are distinctive modalities of racism, such as anti-Semitism and "colour prejudice," which are characterized by their own histories and structures of meaning. While these analysts acknowledge that each of these racisms has its own specific history and characteristic features, the implication of such a wide-ranging list of racisms, discussed together, is that they are somehow comparable and equivalent. The coupling of anti-Jewish and anti-African racisms would rarely appear in American studies, for the dominant understanding in the USA is that such disparate forms of racism are not equivalent. In Britain, although many analysts are notably pluralistic in their identification of multiple forms of racism, tension is nevertheless emerging around the question of their comparability. This is evidenced by the assertions by Tariq Modood that Muslims in Britain are the most racially oppressed group – an argument which may receive more attention post-September 11.

How do we balance an inclusive understanding of racism (so that, for example, anti-Semitism and anti-Romany prejudice are recognized) with the identification of inequalities and historically different experiences and treatment between groups? It seems to me that we do need to consider the variable impact and intensity of racisms and racial oppression, as experienced by disparate groups. Stephen Small, for example, suggests that we must distinguish between "racialised hostility" and "ethnic antagonism": "Complications have been introduced by the confusion of racialised hostility with ethnicity and ethnic antagonism as if we are all different now, all facing obstacles and prejudices, each and every one of them meriting equal attention. In Europe, racialised hostility is being confused with ethnicity, and the 'ethnic cleansing' of Bosnia is being compared with the terror of slavery and imperialism" (1994: 192).[21] While the idea of formulating a complex, pluralistic cartography of racism is appealing and worthy (see P. Cohen 1996), we must avoid simply reducing all groups' experiences to an undifferentiated morass.

One of the key difficulties I have identified in the formulation of a racial hierarchy is that, given the numerous indicators of well-being and disadvantage discussed earlier (and their complex combination in relation to specific groups), it can be difficult to summarize groups' overall experiences along an overarching hierarchy. There is no problem with more delimited hierarchies which rank groups on the basis of specific indicators of well-being or disadvantage. By keeping specific dimensions of experience distinct (such as poverty or entrance into higher education), we do not lose information which is both analytically and politically important in the course of assessing groups' experiences.

However, it is important that we also retain a big picture understanding of racial hierarchy for a broader sense of racial disadvantage across groups, despite the problems I have just identified. Although it is difficult to evaluate claims about groups' experiences which are not directly comparable (e.g. the genocide of Native Americans versus the enslavement of African Americans), the question as to who is worse off than others should not be off limits, either politically or intellectually. A well-meaning, pluralistic understanding of racisms and racial oppression may help to avoid upsets, but it is not likely to be helpful in efforts to rectify various forms of inequality between groups. Nor can inter-ethnic tensions regarding these matters be swept neatly under the carpet.

It is important that we continue to debate assertions of racial hierarchy, whether it is an argument which suggests that African Americans are the most oppressed group in the USA or that South Asians are more discriminated against than African Caribbeans in Britain, even though these debates, regrettably, can be divisive. For example, the assertion that South Asians in Britain "face double discrimination, racial and religious" (Anwar 1998: 186), and are thus more discriminated against than are African Caribbeans, is, in my view, problematic (even post-September 11), because this formulation reflects a mechanistic understanding of racial oppression – that racial and religious oppression added together result in worse racial discrimination than that faced by other groups.[22]

Nevertheless, such an argument should be evaluated on the basis of evidence and on its intellectual merits. Even if we disagree with the reasoning underlying arguments about how different groups fare, this need not mean that we should not evaluate such arguments about racial hierarchy in the first place – though this would be only one, albeit important, way of evaluating different groups' experiences. The recognition that Muslims are the object of racial attacks in no way means that African Caribbeans, or any other minority group, now experience less racism. Unfortunately, articulations of racisms are not a zero-sum pie.

If we are to retain the concept of racial hierarchy, however, it must be qualified. The collective positioning of increasingly diverse groups within a racial hierarchy may obscure important forms of internal variation within groups and complex forms of stratification interweaving class, gender, and race (see chapter 5). Studies addressing the notion of racial hierarchy also need to pay more attention to emerging inter-ethnic relations among non-White minority poplations. The increased intermingling of groups, and the fact that it is increasingly common to possess an inter-racial heritage, also attest to the significant racial and ethnic complexity of both the American and British populations.

8

The Future of Race and Ethnic Identity

This book has explored the ways in which ethnic minority groups and individuals are able to assert and negotiate ethnic identities of their choosing and the constraints structuring such choices. The exploration of ethnic identities is important, because the significance of ethnic identity is not in decline in multiethnic societies such as the USA and Britain, particularly for non-White minority groups and individuals. Classical assimilation theorists assumed a zero-sum model of acculturation, in which immigrants' acculturation involved a gradual replacement of their ethnic identities and cultures with those of the host society. However, rather than the second (or third) generation showing a gradual assimilation into the dominant culture, with the inevitable loss of their parents' ethnicities and cultural practices, it is possible for them to retain both a minority ethnic identity and to be significantly acculturated into American and British societies.

One major reason why ethnic identities remain important for many ethnic minority people is that, in many situations, they are still subject to forms of racism and reminded of their difference. However, ethnic minority individuals and groups increasingly refuse to abide by the meanings, discourses, and stereotypes which are foisted upon them by the wider society – for instance, in the processes associated with racial assignment. Minority people are actively asserting identities, and the meanings associated with such identities, in the public sphere. Such assertions need to be understood as simultaneously a matter of pride, survival, and resistance. These claims to ethnic identity are not only political acts in themselves; they may also be a means of effecting forms of social and political change. For instance, countering the widely held stereotype that Asian Americans are conformist and not very innovative may help to bring about change in the kinds of jobs which Asian Americans may be able to obtain, as well as the treatment of Asian American students in schools and universities.

This book has demonstrated that ethnic minority individuals and groups can exercise some degree of agency and control in the assertion of their ethnic identities, including claims to belonging within the nation, on their own terms. Although significant constraints structure these processes, the conscious and deliberate choices made by minority groups and individuals regarding their ethnic identities have tended to be overlooked, particularly in the USA, where there is much emphasis on the dynamics of racial assignment by the wider society. Throughout this book, I have illustrated the many ways in which different groups contest dominant representations of themselves and work at claiming their desired identities. Minorities do have some ethnic options, but these can differ across and within groups – for instance, according to class, length of settlement, and gender.

Ethnic minorities' right to exercise or claim an ethnic identity is a highly politicized, contentious matter and cannot be taken for granted. The British Home Secretary, David Blunkett, recently made a major announcement, urging ethnic minorities in Britain to integrate and "to develop a greater sense of belonging in Britain." One major implication of the government's position is that minority groups' and individuals' rights to difference are, in practice, limited by societal expectations of what kinds of behaviors and allegiances are normatively acceptable in mainstream Britain.[1]

Groups themselves are constantly in the process of negotiating the meanings, images, and cultural practices which are associated with them. There is certainly no automatic consensus about what it means to *be* of a particular ethnicity. Claims to ethnic identity are subject to scrutiny by not only the wider society, but also by one's coethnics, and can be met by validation, denial, or disbelief. For instance, Ien Ang (1994) found that, despite her Chinese heritage, because she did not speak a Chinese dialect, she was not regarded as Chinese by the people she encountered on a trip to the People's Republic of China or by many White Dutch people she encountered in the Netherlands, where she grew up. Not speaking Chinese meant that she was not considered to be authentically Chinese.

Unfortunately, just as ethnic minority groups are constantly subject to forms of racialization by the wider society, so ethnic minority groups, and the individuals within them, are all too capable of forms of "ethnic absolutism" (Gilroy 2000). Ethnic minority groups can impose scripts of behavior or rigid formulas concerning ethnic authenticity on their members. In doing so, they keep alive the damaging belief that ethnicity and race shape and even determine (or should determine) people's sense of themselves and their behavior and interactions with others. Thus the assertion of ethnic identity is necessarily a negotiated process which engages with the dominant meanings and representations of groups, as found in the wider society, as well as with intra-group debates about the meanings and behaviors which are associated with each group.

In exploring the politicized and contested assertions of ethnic identity, I have shown how bankrupt any notions of ethnic or racial purity are, whether they are articulated in relation to gene pools and bloodlines or in essentialist understandings of a group's culture. Racial and ethnic meanings and identities are now more complex than ever, reflecting the ethnic and racial diversity of many multiethnic societies, such as the USA and Britain. The complexity of racial and ethnic identities is fostered by the fact that new inter-ethnic relations are emerging at a time when many working-class minority people's everyday interactions are with members of other minority groups, especially in multiethnic inner cities (see Rieff 1991). For example, in addition to interacting with Black customers, Korean greengrocers in New York City now rely heavily upon Mexican and Ecuadorean employees in their stores (D.-Y. Kim 1999). In such cities, certain non-White groups may have relatively little interaction with White people. For instance, Vietnamese in Southern California learn "American" culture from Mexican Americans (Gold 1992; Chang and Diaz-Veizades 1999). Furthermore, the growth of multiracial people and relationships, which challenges the legitimacy of existing ethnic and racial categories, points to the complexity and blurring of the putatively neat boundaries which are believed to separate groups.

I have argued that we must treat the formation and experience of ethnic identity as open and subject to negotiation and reinvention – as a question, rather than a primordially determined given. How important are racial and ethnic identities for people? As this book has demonstrated, they are important, but not necessarily of similar significance for everyone. Nor are the meanings associated with racial and ethnic identities necessarily shared by the people who comprise a particular ethnic group – these are and will continue to be contested. Ethnic minority people are defined not only by their ethnicity – they are complex beings with particular interests, family histories, and political views. And in noting the central place of their ethnic identities, I do not wish to deny the importance of other axes of identity, or to deny their full complexity as both individuals and members of various groups.

Some analysts have recently argued that we should transcend the language and philosophy of race and racial difference (see Appiah in Appiah and Gutmann 1996). Are we headed for a "post-ethnic" or "post-racial" world? David Hollinger (1995) argues forcefully for the desirability of a society in which people, regardless of whether they are White, Black, or Asian, are free to affiliate or disaffiliate themselves from ethnic groups at will, rather than being racially assigned according to their ethnic or racial ancestry. In a recent book, Paul Gilroy (2000) acknowledges the centrality of race in the oppositional identities which emerge among subordinated minority populations. He understands that there is a great temptation to cling stubbornly to the notion of race and racial difference. Nevertheless, Gilroy argues boldly for the "deliberate renunciation of 'race' as a basis for belonging to one another and acting in concert. They [racialized groups] will have to be reassured that the dramatic gestures involved in turning against racial observance can be accomplished without violating the precious forms of solidarity and community that have been created by their protracted subordination along racial lines" (2000: 12–13). Similarly, Kenan Malik (1996) argues that the postmodern and poststructuralist celebration and romanticizing of difference and the right to be different has led to social fragmentation and divisive competition among groups.[2] Malik refutes the philosophy and politics of difference and advocates a universal humanism which refuses to celebrate marginality and subordinated subjectivities as a good thing.[3]

Thus, in different ways, various scholars have argued for the need to transcend the discourse of race. A scenario in which we have transcended race is appealing, but we are still far off from such a society. It is difficult to imagine, at least in the foreseeable future, a "planetary humanism" (Gilroy 2000) in which notions of racial or ethnic difference do not figure centrally in people's way of thinking.

I have demonstrated that many people continue to invoke notions of race and racial difference in the articulation of their identities – albeit in different ways. To recognize this, and to document the processes and dynamics underlying these assertions, is crucial. Although calls for the renunciation of race are admirable and tempting, they are not currently plausible. As long as people in the real world continue to employ this concept in their thinking, interactions, and behaviors in their everyday lives, we as social scientists need to continue documenting such usage, alive to the fact that the concept of race and beliefs about racial difference can be reified in a damaging way.

In asking what claiming an ethnic label means for White middle-class Americans, Mary Waters (1990) concluded that ethnicity is of little consequence to most White Americans, and that it is increasingly a matter of personal choice. When they consider which of their European ancestries they may wish to embrace, most White Americans need not be "ethnic" at all – they can simply be "American." As such, ethnic heritages are of little consequence for most White Americans. The scenario in Britain is rather different: claims to distinctive White ethnicities, such as Welsh, Irish, or Scottish, are a part of an ongoing political debate. However, the mobilization of an exclusionary White, ethno-national identity is likely to gain pace in both the USA and Britain. Given the significant levels of nativist hostility in both countries toward "foreigners," whether they be legal or illegal immigrants, asylum seekers, or even second-generation Mexican Americans or Chinese Britons, the aggressive assertion of a White "American" and White "British" ethno-national identity has been emerging for some time. In this way, claims to being "authentically" American or British (or English) will remain important to some White people in both countries.

Given the political climate described above, claims by ethnic minorities to particular identities which assert ethnic and racial difference from the White majority are not likely to diminish (in any straightforward fashion) in the foreseeable future, and these assertions of difference will coincide with ethnic minorities' efforts to claim their place within the nation. Minority groups' celebration of difference is not as naive as it may appear. We should not underestimate both the social and the political importance of "new ethnicities" (Hall 1992), as assertions of difference by previously silenced sectors of the population. Such assertions constitute a form of resistance and a means of countering denigrating, dominant discourses, and infuse subordinate groups with some degree of power, self-esteem, and dignity. These claims to identity, while still using the language of race and ethnicity, are not simply and slavishly legitimizing the baggage which accompanies the use of the term race. Although there is no consensus on this issue, a number of analysts continue to defend the discourse of race as a means of countering racisms and racial inequalities. As long as racialized inequality prevails, racialized identities are likely to remain important in mobilizing against it (S. Small 1994).[4]

Another concern is that difference and the assertion of ethnic identities can fuel the flames of "identity politics," which is founded on a competitive model of group empowerment. Because racial identity politics utilizes racial consciousness or the group's collective memory and experiences as the essential framework for interpreting the actions and interests of all other groups, it tends to exacerbate areas of dissension and antagonism, rather than stress the significant parallels and common interests that exist among subordinated groups (Marable 1995).

It is undeniable that racial and ethnic identity politics and the competitive tensions between groups which characterize it can have a fragmenting effect on anti-racist politics and organization. However, recognition of the diversity and multiplicity of ethnic identifications and assertions, and the fact that competing agendas can accompany such diversity, does not necessarily mean the death knell for a politics of racial and ethnic cooperation and unity. The celebration of difference and ethnic differentiation can go hand in hand with inter-ethnic cooperation: for example, during the 1990s anti-Affirmative Action drive in California, many Asian American and Latino American students worked in alliance with Black students against the rescinding of Affirmative Action policies, emphasizing their shared status as people of color.

The assertion of ethnic and racial affiliations and identities need not necessarily and ineluctably translate into a crude, myopic racial politics. For instance, to claim a particular commitment to one's history and identity as an African Caribbean person in Britain or a Filipino American in the USA can translate into various life choices and social affiliations. There is evidence, especially among the younger generations in Britain and the USA, that particularistic claims to ethnic identity can coexist with broad panethnic identities and political affiliations which draw upon various cultural and ethnic influences and traditions.

What would be even more damaging than the acceptance of identity politics and some degree of inter-ethnic competition and divisiveness would be a romanticized, unrealized myth about inter-ethnic solidarity and cooperation, which does not concede the differences in agendas and outlooks which can emerge between groups. Such differences and divisions cannot be glossed over in the hope that no one will notice. A recognition of the multiplicity of ethnic affiliations and assertions is the starting point for a realistic commitment to inter-ethnic alliance and cooperation, because to recognize the existence of various ethnic and racial identities and voices is to take on board the whole, complex array of people and agendas in contemporary multiethnic societies. The recognition and assertion of various ethnic identities presents us with the possibility of constructing alliances which acknowledge, rather than suppress, the sometimes conflicting goals and visions of disparate groups.

Notes

Introduction

1 Long after Allan Bakke successfully sued the state of California for denying him a place in medical school in 1978 – he was a White male, and the University of California had set aside a specific number of places for which only minorities could compete – the University of California rescinded Affirmative Action policies for university entrance after a referendum was held in November 1996 (Hochschild 1999).
2 See Stephen Small's *Racialized Barriers* (1994) for a systematic comparison of the Black experience in the USA and Britain.

Chapter 1   Ethnic Identities: Choices and Constraints

1 Approximately half of the total ethnic minority population are South Asians of Indian, Pakistani, or Bangladeshi origin, one-third are people who identify themselves as Black Caribbean, Black African, or Black-Mixed, and Chinese and Other Asians comprise 10 percent of the minority population (Scott, Pearce, and Goldblatt 2001).
2 Social constructionist understandings of ethnicity are now widespread in sociology and in other disciplines. In addition to refuting essentialist conceptions of identity, such that individuals can possess singular, integral, and unproblematic identities, or that groups of people can be defined by some "essence" or set of core features, social constructionism challenges the notion that identity is given, naturally, and the idea that it can be produced simply by acts of individual will (Calhoun 1994).
3 In Britain, there has been a tendency in much scholarship to use scare quotes around "race." However, in the USA, there is still widespread acceptance of "race" (a term rarely placed in scare quotes), as a system of power, in both ideological and material terms.

4 The discourse of "difference" and of "othering" often involves asymmetrical power relations between dominant and subordinate groups within a society. The recognition of difference is the main practice of classification systems, which divide people and all their characteristics in such a way that we can make sense of their identities (Hall 1997). Without the recognition of difference, racial and ethnic categories could not exist. For example, the meanings associated with "Black" are usually dependent upon the oppositional binary of Black/White. Rather than there being an essence to Blackness, the meaning of Black derives from the way in which it is opposed to its putative opposite – White (L. Gordon 1997).

5 Of course, racial differences need not be the sole basis of the relative privilege and oppression experienced by various groups in a society. For instance, Catholics, who comprise the majority in Northern Ireland, have tended to be a disadvantaged group in relation to the Protestant minority there. In addition to religious differences, ethnic differences can form the basis for the differential status and well-being of groups. In Japan, following Japan's colonization of Korea, which lasted from 1910 to 1945, Koreans in Japan continue to be treated as second-class citizens.

6 Generally speaking, the move away from more deterministic analyses of race and ethnicity accompanies the postmodern turn and the highlighting of the unstable meanings and effects of not only race and ethnicity but also class. For instance, in discussing how trapped the protagonist, Renton, felt in his Scottish hometown and his circle of old friends, the filmmaker who made *Trainspotting*, Danny Boyle, observes: "That's an interesting thing about class, your own private relationship with it, what you do with it. Not just 'it' as a monumental force controlling everyone" (O'Hagan and Macnab 1996: 11).

7 According to two influential scholars on race and race relations, Michael Omi and Howard Winant, "Since the ambiguous triumph of the civil rights movement in the mid-1960s, clarity about what racism means has been eroding" (1994: 69). Omi and Winant's (1994: 162) understanding of racism is "a fundamental characteristic of social projects which create or reproduce structures of domination based on essentialist categories of race." And, as Robert Miles (1989) has argued, broad understandings of racism and persistent forms of racial inequality have tended to "inflate" the concept of racism in such a way that the term has lost its precise meaning – so that racism is both everything and nothing, so wide and vague is the usage of this term.

Chapter 2   Comparing Minorities' Ethnic Options

1 One difficulty with the enterprise of comparing minority groups' ethnic options is that it presupposes a degree of homogeneity for each group, when, in fact, various subgroups can comprise such groups (see chapter 5). Differences within a recognized group, according to length of

settlement, sex, religion, and class, among other issues, contribute to divisions within them.

2 Tuan argues that the issue of racial options – the ability to choose whether to be identified in racial terms – is what is relevant for African Americans. She concludes that African Americans cannot escape the racial marker of being Black.

3 However, some analysts, such as Hurh and Kim (1989), have argued that such generalized statistics can give a false impression about how well Asian Americans fare in the labor market. They claim that when one considers other factors, such as working hours, the number of workers in the household, and education, the individual earnings ratio for Asian Americans (especially the foreign-born) are lower than those of White people with equivalent conditions of investment in education and the labor market.

4 In the case of the celebrated success of South Asian Americans, for instance, it is largely forgotten that the reason why so many South Asians seem to possess advanced degrees and professional jobs is that such immigrants from the Indian subcontinent are favored by immigration procedures, thus creating a wholly artificial community of high-flyers (Prashad 2000: 169). The model minority image also fails to acknowledge real differences in the alleged success of various East Asian groups in the USA (Espiritu 1992; Yamanaka and McClelland 1994; Cheng and Yang 1996; Wong et al. 1998). Not all Asian Americans are "successful." For Asian Americans of both sexes and various ethnic backgrounds, differences in class backgrounds and native, versus foreign-born, status result in different structures of opportunity and outcomes.

5 Tizard and Phoenix found that more boys than girls reported experiences of racist name calling and aggression in their schools. The authors suggest that one reason why boys may be more subject to racial slurs and violence is that, particularly in working-class schools, such behavior is an accepted part of masculine youth culture.

6 There may be differences among minority groups and their methods of dealing with racism. In one of the few recent studies about Asian Americans coping with racial discrimination, Wen Kuo (1995) found that they primarily relied upon "emotion-focussed coping," which involved cognitive reconceptualization of problems, avoidance, and optimistic comparison, in contrast with African Americans, who employed forms of "problem-focussed" coping, such as seeking advice from a friend or relative, or seeking organizational redress. Kuo's study focuses on individualistic, psycho-social coping with racism, and seems to confirm existing stereotypes about Asian Americans as meek and nonconfrontational (though there is also evidence of Asian Americans in active and vocal protest and forms of political organization – see Espiritu 1992). Interestingly, Crocker and Quinn (1998) found that the perception that one is personally disadvantaged was related to lower self-esteem among Asian American students, who were more likely to attribute this disadvantage to personal failings on their part, in comparison with African American

students, who were more likely to attribute their disadvantage to racial discrimination. Such an understanding of their disadvantaged status helped to protect African Americans' self-esteem.

7 Some American analysts, such as Toni Morrison (1993), have argued, however, that African Americans are often made to feel alien or as outsiders in relation to mainstream American society. Interestingly, in Britain, Black people's status as "real" Britons is sometimes called into question, as is pointed out in Paul Gilroy's evocative title *There Ain't No Black in the Union Jack* (1987). This may stem, in part, from the fact that African Americans have been part of American society since the inception of slavery, whereas many Black Britons emigrated to Britain in the mid-twentieth century. In Britain, both African Caribbean and South Asian people have also been subject to discourses of repatriation.

8 The "model minority" stereotype (which is a relatively recent one), and its assumptions of social acceptance, also endanger the memory of historical discrimination against Asian Americans. Fears about the "Yellow Peril" were reflected in the Chinese Exclusion Act, which prohibited Chinese immigration to the USA until 1943 (Daniels 1988; Espiritu 1992), and Japanese Americans were interned in camps during World War II, as a result of the Japanese bombing of Pearl Harbor (Daniels 1988; Takaki 1989).

9 One issue which arises in the discussion of Black oppositional cultures and identities is how they should be regarded. While some American analysts and policymakers have regarded the emergence of Black English in racially segregated black ghettoes as problematic, in terms of further disadvantaging Black people in schools and the labor market, some British analysts, such as Claire Alexander (1996), have stressed the reinventions of identity which are lived out by young Black men in London, in which identities are based upon both unwitting and deliberate inversions of meaning or exaggerations of racial stereotype.

10 It should be noted that middle-class African Americans possess their own forms of cultural capital, which have arisen from their interactions with both the White middle class and the Black working class (see Neckerman, Carter, and Lee 1999).

Chapter 3   Negotiating Individual and Group Identities

1 An exception to this may be a persecuted minority group such as the Kurds, whose political oppression may result in a strong and unified sense of Kurdish identity, at least vis-à-vis the outside world.

2 Sidanius and Pratto (1999: 51) argue that the psychology of intergroup conflict is connected to the male predisposition for group boundary maintenance, territorial defence, and the exercise of dominion.

3 Although I'm focusing here upon the boundary-keeping activities of ethnic minority groups, this is not to deny that dominant groups object to

intermarriage as well (and have historically banned it in various places). See Spickard 1989 and Spencer 1997.

4 The controversial nature of inter-racial relationships has been addressed in forms of popular culture, such as in the films *Jungle Fever* and *Mississippi Masala*. In Spike Lee's *Jungle Fever*, the African American male protagonist, named Flipper, is seemingly happily married to a beautiful Black woman, is a doting father, and a successful architect (albeit rather frustrated by his lack of promotion) in a predominantly White firm. Flipper engages in an illicit relationship with his attractive, single Italian American secretary. In the course of the film, he is thrown out of the house by his wife, and Flipper undergoes a journey of discovery, in which he seems to rediscover and revalue his "true" self as a Black man.

5 Women tend to be placed in a generically familial relationship to the male members of a community; for instance, women are referred to as the men's "sisters" (Alexander 1998: 448). Perceived attacks or insults on their womenfolk can be the basis for male group members to exact revenge.

6 Although Hollinger acknowledges the continuing significance of ethno-racial distinctions as they apply to many disadvantaged ethnic minority people, he argues that a person who is classified as a member of a disadvantaged minority group "may have no interest whatsoever in the culture popularly associated with that group" (1995: 128).

7 Some scripts of behavior associated with particular groups or subgroups (e.g. in certain ethnic religious groups) may be more stringent than others. For instance, Orthodox Jews and Nation of Islam members are expected to follow very explicit scripts of behavior. Such scripts are formally prescribed, and members of these groups often embrace such scripts precisely to underline their separateness from other groups in the wider society.

8 Generally speaking, because of the disconnection of African diasporas from Africa, proponents of Afrocentrism such as Molefi Asante (1998) have advocated forms of Black cultural reconstruction drawing upon African traditions and cultures (particularly those of the ancient Egyptian civilization and the Nile Valley), as well as establishing a world view about the writing and speaking of historically oppressed people such as African Americans.

9 In the early 1990s, a young Black woman in New York City, Tawana Brawley, claimed that a gang of White men had raped her and dumped her in the street. Although there was much shock and outrage from all quarters to this reportedly heinous act, it soon became apparent that Brawley had fabricated the story in order to provide an alibi for having gone out (against her mother's violent boyfriend's orders). Even when more evidence began to emerge, which put Brawley's claims in doubt, relatively few Black figures were willing to condemn the web of lies which were spun not only by Brawley, but also by some of the high-profile Black lawyers and ministers who supported her case.

10 Drawing on Herder, Charles Taylor discusses the idea of being true to oneself: "There is a certain way of being human which is *my* way. I am called upon to live my life in this way, and not in imitation of anyone else's life. . . . If I am not [true to myself], I miss the point of my life; I miss what being human is for *me*" (1994: 78, emphasis original).

11 Nevertheless, as Lisa See, the author of *On Gold Mountain* (who has some Chinese ancestry in her family tree) has noted, "Although I don't look physically Chinese, like my grandmother, I am Chinese in my heart" (1995: p. xx).

Chapter 4 The Growth of Mixed Race People

1 Neither term is less problematic or more preferable than the other, and the debates about terminology are ongoing (see Parker and Song 2001a).

2 According to a special report in *USA Today*, inter-racial dating is increasingly common among teenagers in the USA, who hold more liberal views about mixed relationships than their parents (Peterson 1997). Despite the general consensus that inter-racial unions are on the rise, it is difficult to assess just how common these relationships are, particularly for the less common mixes of people (S. Small 2001).

3 However, the lack of sufficient blood quantum is now used to renege on treaties and to prohibit the reclamation of land by Native Americans in the USA. In this way, although they are not considered White, many Native Americans cannot prove enough Native ancestry to claim rights and resources earmarked for them (Mengel 2001).

4 Some of these "marginal men" were seen to be educated colonial intellectuals with unrealistic aspirations for a better life. Not only were they race-conscious, but these allegedly maladjusted individuals were said to be doomed to a life of instability, unable to live on either side of the cultural divide. Ultimately, these men posed a threat to the maintenance of existing racial lines and were seen as "troublemakers" in anti-colonial struggles (Furedi 2001).

5 However, to be accused of passing could have a different resonance for the mixed individual, depending on whether the accusation was made by a White person or someone she considered to be a coethnic.

6 Instances of passing have been recognized in relation to some light-skinned Hispanics passing as Whites and Jewish people passing as Gentiles.

7 The racial classification of Hispanics in the USA is complicated, because Hispanics constitute a very diverse group which includes Brown, Black, and White people (Nelson and Tienda 1988).

8 In *Repossessing Ernestine* Marsha Hunt (1996) documents her elderly grandmother's history, which included more than 52 years in mental institutions. In particular, Hunt explores the key role that racial ancestry and skin color played on her father's side of the family, in the American Deep South. As a very light-skinned woman (which has traditionally connoted higher social status in Black America), Ernestine (the author's

grandmother) was prized as a bride precisely because she was so light-skinned. But Ernestine's history is tragic, as she was forcibly (as it transpires) institutionalized shortly after the successive births of her three sons. Hunt suggests that because Ernestine could pass as White, this made her particularly vulnerable to resentment and forms of abuse by others.

9　A term used to refer to people with part Asian ancestry, whether they be White and Japanese, or Korean and African American, among other possible combinations.

10　Historically, Jewish people were key supporters of the Black Civil Rights movement in the USA, until the early 1970s. Two major factors chilled this once amicable relationship: some members of the Black power movement in the late 1960s espoused revolutionary action against all White people (including Jews), and Afrocentric leaders who espoused a kinship between African Americans and Third World peoples in general increasingly saw Israel's treatment of the Palestinians as racist (Zack 1996).

11　See also *Native Speaker* by Chang-Rae Lee (1995) and *My Year of Meat* by Ruth Ozeki (1998).

12　These categories were "White, Black Caribbean, Black African, Black other, Indian, Pakistani, Bangladeshi, Chinese, and any other ethnic group."

13　In order to avoid the possibility that multiracial people will conflate the question of their own ethnic *identity* with the question of their ethnic *ancestry*, Berthoud suggests a simple solution: a census question which asks for the ethnic origin of each parent, with separate columns for "your mother" and "your father." Below these two columns would be an instruction: "Please explain your family origins in more detail, if the boxes above are not appropriate to your particular situation."

14　Many of these early American organizations, such as PROJECT RACE (Reclassify All Children Equally) and The Interracial Family Circle of Washington DC, are family and children-oriented, with some being support groups, while others lobbied for changes in the registration of mixed race people (usually children) in schools, employment, and on medical forms requiring information on racial background (Mengel 2001). More recently, various kinds of organizations led by multiracial individuals have sprung up, such as the Association of Multi-Ethnic Americans and the Hapa Issues Forum (http://www.hapaissuesforum.org). Although the on-line journal *Interracial Voice* may not be representative of the views of all multiracial people, it seems to be an important forum for debate and discussion among them. In Britain, organizations such as People in Harmony, an organization which supports mixed couples and people of mixed race, and Intermix are also increasingly common.

15　Editorial in http://www.webcom.com/intvoice.

16　Hollinger goes on to note that because Asians tend to be regarded as a more distinct race than Latinos in the USA, Latino-European mixtures may not represent dramatic examples of mixedness. Many Mexican Americans, for example, have embodied and taken for granted a mixed ancestry (Hollinger 1995: 43).

Chapter 5 The Diversification of Ethnic Groups

1 The relationship between class and ethnic identity is by no means straight-forward. Classic assimilation theorists looking at American society would have believed that the children of immigrants from lower-class back-grounds (who have tended to grow up in close proximity with other coethnics) were more likely to retain their ethnic identities and to retain language skills than children from middle-class backgrounds who were more likely to have grown up in White middle-class neighborhoods. Such middle-class children were expected to be highly assimilated into Amer-ican culture, with little ethnic attachment to their parents' cultures. How-ever, some recent research challenges this expectation. For example, Min and Kim (2000) found that even highly educated second-generation Asian Americans tended to retain a strong sense of ethno-national identity, such as Japanese American (and sometimes a panethnic Asian identity), despite their links with the White middle class. Jobs in predominantly White professional milieus and friendships and intimate relationships with Whites did not necessarily result in the erosion of ethnic attachment. In fact, many of their respondents were found to possess bicultural orientations. This is aided by the fact that middle-class parents have more resources which are instrumental in encouraging their children's identification and attachment to their "home" cultures.
2 Phil Kasinitz (1992) refutes the image of West Indians as ghetto entrepren-eurs, or as being generally more successful (in business terms) by com-parison with African Americans (as suggested by Glazer and Moynihan 1963 and Sowell 1981). While the first wave of West Indian immigrants set up some successful businesses in Harlem, the post-1965 Caribbean immigration to New York has predominantly entered into relatively low-level jobs in the service sector, not in the small business sector.
3 In an important debate about the origins of the Black underclass in the USA, Douglas Massey and Nancy Denton (1993) have taken issue with Wilson's thesis, and have argued that the key missing element in making sense of the Black underclass is the persistence of residential racial segregation.
4 Such a "minority culture of mobility" is said to include "symbolic ele-ments, particularly those relevant to problems of ambiguous identity and affiliation – will one identify (or be identified) in terms of class, ethnic group, or both? – that often accompany minority middle class status" (Neckerman, Carter, and Lee 1999: 949). The minority culture of mobil-ity is said to be "assembled from ethnically distinctive cultural idioms, practice and institutions" in relation to each group (p. 951).
5 Their analysis stresses the importance of the intersection of class privilege and light skin tone for African Americans versus the consistent link found between dark skin tone and class disadvantage. For instance, they note that when one drives through most Black urban ghettoes, it is hard to miss the fact that many of their residents are very dark-skinned.

6 Black women's status in Britain appears to be more mixed. Black British women stay on longer at school in order to achieve their long-term educational aspirations. Since they encounter both sexism and racism in their schooling, young Black women strategically opt for gendered and racialized occupations such as nursing and social work, which provide them with opportunities to study in higher education (Mirza 1997b). Black women's labor in Britain has been historically devalued, however, and their reliance upon jobs in the caring professions, such as nursing, teaching, and social work, is restrictive. Furthermore, these jobs are vulnerable to cutbacks accompanying privatization and economic crises (Mama 1984).

7 One path involves their acculturation and integration into the White middle class; the second leads immigrants into poverty and assimilation into an underprivileged underclass; and the third path involves selective or delayed assimilation, so that immigrants may take advantage of the social capital and support afforded by their ties to their ethnic communities (but see also Neckerman, Carter, and Lee 1999).

8 Min Zhou reports: "According to the Immigration and Naturalization Service (INS), of the 7.3 million immigrants admitted to the United States during the 1980s (not counting undocumented immigrants), 87 percent came from Asia and the Americas, compared to the 8.8 million admitted during the 1910s who were predominantly from Europe. In the past decade, Mexico, the Philippines, China/Taiwan, South Korea, and Vietnam were the top five sending countries, followed by the Dominican Republic, India, El Salvador, and Jamaica" (1997: 65).

9 Even among immigrants from Southeast Asia, there were two waves of immigration: the first, from 1975 to 1980, was comprised primarily of South Vietnam's elites, whereas the second included the "boat people" who had escaped from concentration camps and great economic hardship (Cheng and Yang 1996).

10 One tension which emerged concerned how the organization could combine a focus on the Black political struggle in Britain with one on the African continent (Brixton Black Women's Group 1984). Furthermore, tensions emerged around the issue of recognizing the specificities of Asian women's experiences of racism and oppression in Britain. In a well-known intervention in feminist debate and scholarship, Floya Anthias and Nira Yuval-Davis (1983) noted the problematic usage of terms such as "Black" pointing to the netherworld occupied by neither White nor Black women in Britain, such as Cypriot or Middle Eastern women.

Chapter 6 The Second Generation in a Global Context

1 Individuals who immigrate to the USA as children have also been called the "one and a half generation" (a term coined by Ruben Rumbaut) to characterize those who straddle the old and the new worlds but are not wholly integrated into either (Zhou 1997: 65; see also K. Y. Park 1997).

2 59 percent of Latino American children and 90 percent of Asian American children are members of the first or second generation, compared to 6 percent of African American children and 5 percent of European American children.

3 There is some variability across groups, of course. For instance, while 95 percent of Black Caribbean children aged 0–14 were born in Britain, 81 percent of Chinese children in the same age group were born in Britain. In the 15–29 age group, 73 percent of Indian people in this age group were born in Britain, but only 33 percent of Bangladeshi people (and 60 percent of Pakistanis) in this age group were born there (Scott, Pearce, and Goldblatt 2001).

4 However, problems can arise for an individual when they are known to have switched codes, and "where behaviour in the second arena takes a form which is regarded as unacceptable from the perspective of the first" (R. Ballard 1994: 31).

5 It would be mistaken, however, to assume that followers of Islam in Britain are necessarily a homogeneous group (R. Ballard 1994; Alexander 2000). In recent years, sectarian interests have grown, and British Islamic organizations have mounted campaigns to win the allegiance of young Muslims. For instance, in comparison with the more moderate Islamic Forum Europe, Hizb ut Tahrir is known for attracting young Muslims with a more militant anti-Western stance (Bunting 1995).

6 Serge Latouche notes with great dismay that "Today, and even more tomorrow, the world is doomed to uniformity. And tomorrow has already begun. The telecommunications satellites have been launched. The channels that will allow financial markets to function as a single market-place round the clock in all time-zones are already in place. Information, entertainment, fashions, instructions and all that these imply move instantaneously from north to south and from west to east, by fax, telephone, telex, tele-everything. No political barriers can resist them; Third-World poverty and dereliction offer no obstacle" (1996: 1–2).

7 White people, too, are said to possess enhanced ethnic options in the context of globalization. A few years ago, the *Wall Street Journal* (7 Jan. 1999) ran a story about Barry Cox, a 21-year-old working-class White Briton from Liverpool, who has become a local celebrity because of his ability to sing in perfect Cantonese and because of his aspirations to become a Chinese pop star, in Hong Kong (Zachary 1999). As discussed in chapter 1, White people are motivated to adopt ethnic identities or practices to feel special and to escape the humdrum anonymity of being White (Waters 1990). As Barry Cox notes, "If I didn't mix with Chinese and speak Chinese and sing Chinese, what would I be doing now? I'd just be a normal person, nothing special about me." According to the *Wall Street Journal*, "That a working-class bloke from Liverpool would cherish a Chinese persona is a consequence of the increasing migration of different cultures around the world and a deepening awareness of the film, music and art of Asia, Africa and Latin America. That exposure gives young people looking to revamp their identities a much larger menu to choose from."

8 In the early 1990s, the Japanese government needed contract laborers and allowed Peruvians with Japanese ancestry (going back up to three generations) entry to work in Japan on a temporary basis. The preferential treatment of Japanese Peruvians as contract workers was based upon an essentialist assumption that, because of their Japanese heritage, such workers would be relatively easily assimilated into Japanese society (Takenaka 1999).

Chapter 7   Debates about Racial Hierarchy

1 Even Paul Gilroy (2000), who argues forcefully against the concept of race, points to the stubborn existence of racial hierarchies.
2 According to Sidanius and Pratto (1999: 107), in 1997, the Gallup organization announced the first results of a major study on race relations in the USA. Gallup asked a large number of White and Black Americans to indicate the degree to which they believed that "Blacks in your community have as good a chance as Whites" to get (a) "any kind of job," (b) "education," and (c) "housing." Most Whites felt that Black people had the same opportunities as Whites in jobs (79 percent), education (79 percent), and housing (86 percent). Interestingly, a majority (albeit a much smaller majority than Whites) of Blacks also believed that Black people had equal opportunities in these three areas: jobs (46 percent), education (63 percent), and housing (58 percent).
3 People's perceptions of how groups fare are also significantly shaped by historical circumstances and events. At particular historical moments, different groups are targeted and vilified as enemies within. For example, in the aftermath of the attacks on New York and Washington, there is greater awareness of the prejudice against many people of Middle Eastern and South Asian heritage in the USA and Britain.
4 According to social dominance theory (SDT), an "arbitrary-set system," which is one type of stratification system, is filled with socially constructed groups based on race, ethnicity, nation, caste, social class, religion, and the other socially relevant distinctions that the human mind is capable of imagining. An arbitrary-set system is characterized by a high degree of arbitrariness, flexibility, and situational and contextual sensitivity in determining which group distinctions are socially salient and the way in which in-groups and out-groups are defined (Sidanius and Pratto 1999: 33).
5 See e.g. R. Miles 1989 and the special issue of *Patterns of Prejudice* (1996) for Britain, and Sears 1988 and Bonilla-Silva 1999 for the USA.
6 John Ogbu (1990) has argued that African Americans', Native Americans', and Mexican Americans' success in the educational system has been compromised by the fact that they are "involuntary" minorities – that is, they were incorporated into American society against their will, as slaves, or as a conquered people subject to genocide. In contrast, Ogbu argues that "voluntary" minorities, including many immigrants to the USA,

such as the Punjabis and the Chinese, perform better because they came with expectations of improving their status through the American educational system and other institutions.

7 Prashad (2000: 160) observes that Whites' relationship to India, historically, was more nuanced than their relationship to Africa; for instance, there was acknowledgment that the ancient Indian civilization had produced ideas and artifacts which were considered to be of some intellectual and aesthetic value.

8 This triangulation of Asian Americans is illustrated in depictions of the Black–Korean conflicts concerning businesses owned by Korean immigrants in New York City and Los Angeles. There has been much media coverage of the Black–Korean conflict in these cities, with most of the coverage depicting Korean store owners as the hapless victims of Black anger and resentment (see Min 1996). There are a number of dangers resulting from an emphasis upon this inter-ethnic conflict. For one thing, this frame of analysis simply reifies both African Americans and Korean Americans, and fails to recognize the heterogeneity of these two groups. Second, the depiction of this inter-ethnic conflict relies on an ideological opposition of Asian Americans as the model minority and African Americans as an urban underclass (Abelmann and Lie 1995: 149).

9 We do need to be careful about how we use the term "Islamophobia." Various issues of conflict concerning Islam have arisen across different Western societies: Rushdie in the UK, the headscarf in France, anti-Arab sentiment in the USA. Nor is Islamophobia something which is perpetrated solely by a unified Western world – look at India (Halliday 1999).

10 From 1787 onward, Parliament and many British people came to view slavery as both wrong and possibly economically irrational. Between 1807, when the slave trade was abolished, and 1838, when slavery itself was abolished, there existed an "apprenticeship" system, which involved slaves working free for their former masters for a certain number of hours before being free to work for themselves (Walvin 1985).

11 Unlike the African American population, which comprises about 12 percent of the total population (US Census 1990), the African Caribbean population in Britain is much smaller and relatively recently settled (see Pryce 1979; Goulbourne 1990; Cashmore and Troyna 1982). According to the Office for National Statistics (1998), there are an estimated 1,150,000 Black Caribbeans, Black Africans, and "Black Other" people, together comprising about 2 percent of the British population. By comparison, there are about 1,746,000 South Asians, which is about 3 percent of Britain's population, and almost 53 million White Britons.

12 Some analysts have suggested that studies of African Caribbeans in Britain are more likely to focus on their experiences of racism, while studies of Asians have focused more on their cultural practices (see Benson 1996).

13 In the American context, Irish Americans' status as bona fide Whites differs considerably from that of Irish people in England and Northern Ireland, where they are unquestionably a disadvantaged minority group,

who are subject to continuing forms of discrimination, such as in the labor market or in their indiscriminate branding as terrorists (Mac an Ghaill 1999).

14 Historically, before the mass migration of people from the new Commonwealth countries, such as Pakistan and Jamaica, to Britain, both Irish migrant workers and Jewish immigrants from Eastern Europe encountered hostility from many White Britons. Although most studies of migration, ethnicity, and racial discrimination in Britain tend to ignore the Irish, according to Mary Hickman (1998), they constitute the largest ethnic minority group in Britain's workforce, and have provided the most important source of migrant labor in Britain for the past 200 years. In the earlier parts of the twentieth century, "No Irish" signs were common throughout England, for instance, in relation to obtaining lodgings (see Hickman 1998; Mac an Ghaill 1999).

15 There is growing interest in Whiteness more generally in both Britain and the USA (see Waters 1990; Roediger 1991; Ware 1992; Frankenberg 1993; Dyer 1997; Ferber 1998; Bonnett 1998).

16 Even today, the hyper-visibility of orthodox Jews in the USA and Britain means that they are vulnerable to attacks and ridicule for their distinctive cultural practices and modes of presentation.

17 The only data for 2000 for racial inequality currently available come from the March 2000 Current Population Survey (CPS) and can be accessed at: http://www.census.gov/population/www/socdemo/race/ppl-142.html.

18 Some recent electoral gains for Asian Americans include the election of Gary Locke as the governor of Washington State in 1996, making him the first Asian American governor in the USA. Also, Norman Mineta became the first Asian American to hold a cabinet position as the US Secretary of Commerce in July 2000 (Xu 2002).

19 This observation was made by Steve Gold in January 2002.

20 According to David Palumbo-Liu, "The occasional absence of 'Asian American' from racial categories in America reflects the undecidability of the term. Asia/America resides *in transit*, as a point of reference on the horizon that is part of *both* a 'minority' identity and a 'majority' identity" (1999: 5, emphasis original).

21 Is hostility toward Kosovan refugees in Britain comparable to the racialized hostility experienced by some African Caribbean, Asian, and Chinese Britons? The hostility and prejudice experienced by Kosovan refugees may be motivated by their status as political refugees and foreigners (and the belief that they are recipients of special treatment by the British state). This kind of hostility may be qualitatively different from racial hatred premised upon beliefs about the superiority and inferiority of disparate races.

22 Such a conceptualization of discrimination is rather reminiscent of the now criticized conceptualizations of ethnic minority women as suffering from triple forms of oppression: gender + class + race.

Chapter 8 The Future of Race and Ethnic Identity

1 This announcement was made on 9 December 2001. Blunkett stated that there had to be a two-way street when it came to the right to assert difference; minorities had to make an effort to learn English, and to fit into British ways of doing things. This would include discouraging forced marriages in the South Asian community.

2 Such a postmodern celebration of difference is exemplified, for instance, by Stuart Hall (1992), among others.

3 Analysts such as Homi Bhabha have warned that the difference of cultures cannot be unproblematically accommodated within a universalist framework, and involves forms of "incommensurability": "it is actually very difficult, even impossible and counterproductive, to try and fit together different forms of culture and to pretend that they can easily coexist. The assumption that at some level all forms of cultural diversity may be understood on the basis of a particular universal concept, whether it be 'human being', 'class' or 'race', can be both very dangerous and very limiting in trying to understand the ways in which cultural practices construct their own systems of meaning and social organisation" (1990b: 209).

4 Others, such as Michael Dyson, argue that "The goal should not be to transcend race, but to transcend the biased meanings associated with race. Ironically, the very attempt to transcend race by denying its presence [the old color-blind approach] reinforces its power to influence perceptions because it gains strength in secrecy" (1994: 227).

References

Abelmann, Nancy and Lie, John 1995: *Blue Dreams: Korean Americans and the Los Angeles Riots*. Cambridge, MA: Harvard University Press.

Abercrombie, Nicholas and Warde, Alan 1994: *Contemporary British Society*. Cambridge: Polity.

Alba, Richard 1988: The twilight of ethnicity among Americans of European ancestry: the case of Italians. In R. Alba (ed.), *Ethnicity and Race in the U.S.A.*, New York: Routledge & Kegan Paul, 134–58.

—— 1990: *Ethnicity in America: The Transformation of White Ethnicity*. New Haven: Yale University Press.

Alexander, Claire 1996: *The Art of Being Black*. Oxford: Clarendon Press.

—— 1998: Re-imagining the Muslim Community. *Innovation*, 11 (4), 439–50.

—— 2000: *The Asian Gang*. Oxford: Berg.

Ali, Yasmine 1992: Muslim women and the politics of ethnicity and culture in northern England. In G. Sahgal and N. Yuval-Davis (eds), *Refusing Holy Orders*, London: Virago, 101–23.

Alibhai-Brown, Yasmin and Montague, Anne 1992: *The Colour of Love*. London: Virago.

Almaguer, Tomas 1994: *Racial Fault Lines*. Berkeley: University of California Press.

Anderson, Benedict 1983: *Imagined Communities*. London: Verso.

Anderson, Elijah 1990: *Streetwise*. Chicago: University of Chicago Press.

Ang, Ien 1994: On not speaking Chinese. *New Formations*, 24 (Nov.), 1–18.

Anthias, Floya 1998: Evaluating diaspora: beyond ethnicity? *Sociology*, 32 (3), 557–80.

Anthias, Floya and Yuval-Davis, Nira 1983: Contextualizing feminism – gender, ethnic and class division. *Feminist Review*, 15, 62–75.

—— 1992: *Racialized Boundaries*. London: Routledge.

Anwar, Muhammad 1979: *The Myth of Return*. Oxford: Oxford University Press.

—— 1998: *Between Cultures*. London: Routledge.

Appadurai, Arjun 1990: Disjuncture and difference in the global cultural economy. In M. Featherstone (ed.), *Global Culture*, London: Sage, 295–310.

Appiah, Kwame Anthony 1990: Racisms. In David Goldberg (ed.), *Anatomy of Racism*, Minneapolis: University of Minnesota Press, 3–17.

Appiah, Kwame Anthony and Gutmann, Amy 1996: *Color Conscious*. Princeton: Princeton University Press.

Asante, Molefi 1998: *The Afrocentric Idea*. Philadelphia: Temple University Press.

Back, Les 1993: Race, identity and nation within an adolescent community in South London. *New Community*, 19 (2), 217–33.

—— 1995: *New Ethnicities*. London: UCL Press.

Bakalian, Anny 1993: *Armenian-Americans: From Being to Feeling Armenian*. New Brunswick, NJ: Transaction.

Ballard, Catherine 1979: Conflict, continuity and change. In V. Saifullah Khan (ed.), *Minority Families in Britain*, London: Macmillan, 109–29.

Ballard, Roger (ed.) 1994: *Desh Pardesh: The South Asian Presence in Britain*. London: Hurst & Company.

Banton, Michael 1997: *Ethnic and Racial Consciousness*. Harlow: Addison Wesley Longman.

Barker, Martin 1981: *The New Racism*. London: Junction Books.

Barot, Rohit, Bradley, Harriet, and Fenton, Steve (eds) 1999: *Ethnicity, Gender and Social Change*. Basingstoke: Macmillan.

Barth, Frederik 1969: Introduction. In F. Barth (ed.), *Ethnic Groups and Boundaries*, Boston: Little & Brown, 9–38.

Bashi, Vilna 1998: Racial categories matter because racial hierarchies matter. *Ethnic and Racial Studies*, 21 (5), 959–68.

Bashi, Vilna and McDaniel, Antonio 1997: A theory of immigration and racial stratification. *Journal of Black Studies*, 27 (5), 668–82.

Baumann, Gerd 1996: *Contesting Culture*. Cambridge: Cambridge University Press.

Benjamin, Lois 1991: *The Black Elite: Facing the Color Line in the Twilight of the Twentieth Century*. Chicago: Nelson-Hall Publishers.

Benson, Susan 1981: *Ambiguous Ethnicity*. Cambridge: Cambridge University Press.

—— 1996: Asians have culture, West Indians have problems. In T. Ranger, Y. Samad, O. Stuart (eds), *Culture, Identity and Politics*. Aldershot: Avebury.

Berthoud, Richard 1998: Defining ethnic groups. *Patterns of Prejudice*, 32 (2), 53–63.

Bhabha, Homi 1990a: The postcolonial prerogative. In D. Goldberg (ed.), *Anatomy of Racism*, Minneapolis: University of Minnesota Press, 183–209.

—— 1990b: The third space. In Jonathan Rutherford (ed.), *Identity: Community, Culture, Difference*, London: Lawrence & Wishart, 207–21.

—— 1994: *The Location of Culture*. London: Routledge.

Bhachu, Parminder 1985: *Twice Migrants*. London: Tavistock.

Blauner, Robert 1972: *Racial Oppression in America*. New York: Harper & Row.

Blumer, Herbert 1958: Race prejudice as a sense of group position. *Pacific Sociological Review*, 1, 3–7.

Boli, John and Thomas, George 1999: *Constructing World Culture*. Stanford, CA: Stanford University Press.

Bonilla-Silva, Eduardo 1999: The new racism. In Paul Wong (ed.), *Race, Ethnicity and Nationality in the United States*, Boulder, CO: Westview Press, 55–101.

Bonnett, Alistair 1998: Who was white? *Ethnic and Racial Studies*, 21 (6), 1029–55.

Bourdieu, Pierre 1984: *Distinction*. London: Routledge.

Bozorgmehr, Mehdi, Der-Martirosian, Claudia, and Sabagh, George 1996: Middle Easterners: a new kind of immigrant. In R. Waldinger and M. Bozorgmehr (eds), *Ethnic Los Angeles*, New York: Russell Sage Foundation, 345–78.

Bradley, Harriet 1996: *Fractured Identities*. Cambridge: Polity.

Brah, Avtar 1996: *Cartographies of Diaspora*. London: Routledge.

Brixton Black Women's Group 1984: Black women organizing. *Feminist Review*, 17, 90–9.

Brown, Colin 1984: *Black and White Britain*. London: Heinemann.

Bulmer, Martin 1986: Ethnicity and race. In R. Burgess (ed.), *Key Variables in Social Investigation*, London: Routledge, 54–75.

Bunting, Madeleine 1995: Muslim extremists challenged for hearts of youth. *Guardian*, Aug. 5, 1995.

Calhoun, Craig 1993: Nationalism and ethnicity. *Annual Review of Sociology*, 19, 211–39.

—— 1994: Social theory and the politics of identity. In C. Calhoun (ed.), *Social Theory and the Politics of Identity*, Oxford: Blackwell, 9–36.

Cariño, Benjamin 1996: Filipino Americans. In S. Pedraza and R. Rumbaut (eds), *Origins and Destinies*, Belmont, CA: Wadsworth Publishing, 293–301.

Carter, Prudence 2000: It's all in the "act": the substance of black cultural capital among low-income African American youth. Paper presented at the 95th annual meeting of the American Sociological Association, Washington, DC.

Cashmore, Ellis 1997: *The Black Culture Industry*. London: Routledge.

Cashmore, Ellis and Troyna, Barry (eds) 1982: *Black Youth in Crisis*. London: Allen & Unwin.

Castles, Stephen and Kosack, Godula 1973: *Immigrant Workers and Class Structure in Western Europe*. Oxford: Oxford University Press.

Castles, Stephen, Booth, Heather, and Wallace, Tina 1984: *Here for Good: Western Europe's New Ethnic Minorities*. London: Pluto Press.

Centre for Contemporary Cultural Studies 1982: *The Empire Strikes Back*. London: Hutchinson.

Chang, Edward and Diaz-Veizades, Jeannette 1999: *Ethnic Peace in the City*. New York: NYU Press.

Chavira, Victor and Phinney, Jean 1991: Adolescents' ethnic identity, self-esteem, and strategies for dealing with ethnicity and minority status. *Hispanic Journal of Behavioral Sciences*, 13, 226–7.

Cheng, Lucy and Yang, Philip 1996: Asian Americans: the model minority deconstructed. In Roger Waldinger and Mehdi Bozorgmehr (eds), *Ethnic Los Angeles*, New York: Russell Sage Foundation, 305–44.

Cohen, Abner 1974: The lesson of ethnicity. In A. Cohen (ed.), *Urban Ethnicity*, London: Tavistock, pp. ix–xxiv.

Cohen, Phil 1988: The perversion of inheritance. In P. Cohen and H. Bains (eds), *Multi-Racist Britain*, London: Macmillan Education, 9–118.

—— 1996: A message from the other shore. *Patterns of Prejudice*, 30 (1), 15–22.

Collins, S. 1957: *Coloured Minorities in Britain*. Guildford: Lutterworth Press.

Cornell, Stephen and Hartmann, Douglas 1998: *Ethnicity and Race*. Thousand Oaks, CA: Pine Forge Press.

Crocker, J. and Quinn, D. 1998: Racism and self-esteem. In J. Eberhardt and S. Fiske (eds), *Confronting Racism: The Problem and the Response*, Newbury Park, CA: Sage, 169–87.

Daniels, Roger 1988: *Asian America*. Seattle: University of Washington Press.

Davis, F. James 1991: *Who is Black?* University Park: Pennsylvania State University Press.

Dominguez, Virginia 1998: Exporting U.S. concepts of race. *Social Research*, 65 (2), 369–99.

Douglas, Mary 1966: *Purity and Danger*. London: Ark Paperbacks.

Dover, C. 1937: *Half Caste*. London: Secker and Warburg.

Drury, Beatrice 1991: Sikh girls and the maintenance of an ethnic culture. *New Community*, 17 (3), 387–401.

D'Souza, Dinesh 1995: *The End of Racism*. New York: Free Press.

Duneier, Mitchell 1992: *Slim's Table*. Chicago: University of Chicago Press.

—— 1999: *Sidewalk*. New York: Farrar, Straus and Giroux.

Dwyer, Claire 1998: Challenging dominant representations of young British Muslim women. In Tracey Skelton and Gill Valentine (eds), *Cool Places: Geographies of Youth Cultures*, London: Routledge, 50–65.

Dyer, Richard 1997: *White*. London: Routledge.

Dyson, Michael 1994: Essentialism and the complexities of racial identity. In D. Goldberg (ed.), *Multiculturalism*, Oxford: Blackwell, 218–29.

Espiritu, Yen 1992: *Asian-American Panethnicity*. Philadelphia: Temple University Press.

Espiritu, Yen and Ong, Paul 1994: Class constraints on racial solidarity among Asian Americans. In Paul Ong, Edna Bonacich, and Lucie Cheng (eds), *The New Asian Immigration in Los Angeles and Global Restructuring*, Philadelphia: Temple University Press, 295–321.

Fanon, Frantz 1963: *The Wretched of the Earth*. New York: Grove Press.

Feagin, Joe 1991: The continuing significance of race: antiblack discrimination in public places. *American Sociological Review*, 56, 101–16.

—— 2000: *Racist America*. New York: Routledge.

Feagin, Joe and Sikes, Melvin 1994: *Living with Racism*. Boston: Beacon Press.

Featherstone, Mike 1990: Global culture: an introduction. In M. Featherstone (ed.), *Global Culture*, London: Sage, 1–14.

Ferber, Abby 1998: Constructing whiteness. *Ethnic and Racial Studies*, 21 (1), 48–63.

Fernandez-Kelly, Patricia and Schauffler, Richard 1994: Divided fates: immigrant children in a restructured U.S. economy. *International Migration Review*, 28 (4), 662–89.

Frankenberg, Ruth 1993: *White Women, Race Matters*. Minneapolis: University of Minnesota Press.

Frazier, E. Franklin 1957: *The Black Bourgeoisie*. New York: Free Press.

Funderburg, L. 1994: *Black, White, Other: Biracial Americans Talk about Race and Identity*. New York: Morrow.

Furedi, Frank 1998: *The Silent War*. London: Pluto Press.

—— 2001: How sociology imagined "mixed race." In D. Parker and M. Song (eds), *Rethinking "Mixed Race"*, London: Pluto Press, 23–41.

Gans, Herbert 1979: Symbolic ethnicity: the future of ethnic groups and cultures in America. *Ethnic and Racial Studies*, 2 (1), 1–20.

—— 1992: Second generation decline. *Ethnic and Racial Studies*, 15 (2), 173–92.

—— 1999: The possibility of a new racial hierarchy in the twenty-first-century United States. In Michele Lamont (ed.), *The Cultural Territories of Race*, Chicago: University of Chicago Press, 371–90.

Gardner, Katy 1995: *Global Migrants, Local Lives*. Oxford: Clarendon Press.

Gardner, Katy and Shukur, Abdus 1994: I'm Bengali, I'm Asian, and I'm Living Here. In R. Ballard (ed.), *Desh Pardesh*, London: Hurst & Company, 142–64.

Gates, Henry Louis 1988: *The Signifying Monkey*. New York: Oxford University Press.

Geertz, Clifford 1963: The integrative revolution: primordial sentiments and civil politics in the new states. In C. Geertz (ed.), *Old Societies and New States*, New York: Free Press, 105–57.

Gibbs, J. and Moskowitz-Sweet, G. 1991: Clinical and cultural issues in the treatment of biracial and bicultural adolescents. *Families in Society: Journal of Contemporary Human Services*, 72, 579–92.

Giddens, Anthony 1984: *The Constitution of Society: Outline of the Theory of Structuration*. Berkeley: University of California Press.

—— 1991: *Modernity and Self-Identity*. Cambridge: Polity.

Gilman, Sander 1985: *Difference and Pathology*. Ithaca, NY: Cornell University Press.

Gilroy, Paul 1987: *There Ain't No Black in the Union Jack*. London: Hutchinson.

—— 1993: *The Black Atlantic*. London: Verso.

—— 2000: *Between Camps*. London: Penguin.

Glazer, Nathan 1993: Is assimilation dead? *Annals of the American Academy of Political Sciences*, 530 (Nov.), 122–38.

Glazer, Nathan and Moynihan, Daniel 1963: *Beyond the Melting Pot.* Cambridge, MA: MIT Press.

——(eds) 1975: *Ethnicity: Theory and Experience*, Cambridge, MA: Harvard University Press.

Goffman, Erving 1963: *Stigma.* Englewood Cliffs, NJ: Prentice-Hall.

Gold, Steve 1992: *Refugee Communities.* Newbury Park, CA: Sage.

—— 2000: Transnational communities: examining migration in a globally integrated world. In Preet Aulakh and Michael Schechter (eds), *Rethinking Globalization(s)*, New York: St. Martin's Press, 73–90.

Gold, Steve and Phillips, Bruce 1996: Mobility and continuity among Eastern European Jews. In Sylvia Pedraza and Ruben Rumbaut (eds), *Origins and Destinies*, Belmont: Wadsworth Publishing, 182–94.

Goldberg, David (ed.) 1990: *Anatomy of Racism.* Minneapolis: University of Minnesota Press.

—— 1992: The semantics of race. *Ethnic and Racial Studies*, 15 (4), 543–65.

Goodstein, Laurie and Lewin, Tamar 2001: Victims of mistaken identity, Sikhs pay a price for turbans. *New York Times on the Web*, Sept. 19, 2001.

Gordon, Lewis 1997: *Her Majesty's Other Children.* Lanham, MD: Rowman & Littlefield.

Gordon, Milton 1964: *Assimilation in American Life.* New York: Oxford University Press.

Goulbourne, Harry (ed.) 1990: *Black Politics in Britain.* Aldershot: Avebury Press.

Grant, David, Oliver, Melvin, and James, Angela 1996: African Americans: social and economic bifurcation. In Roger Waldinger and Mehdi Bozorg-mehr (eds), *Ethnic Los Angeles*, New York: Russell Sage Foundation, 379–412.

Hacker, Andrew 1992: *Two Nations.* New York: Scribners.

—— 1997: Introduction. In Richard Delgado, *The Coming Race War*, Phila-delphia: Temple University Press, pp. xviii–xxv.

Haizlip, Shirlee 1994: *The Sweeter the Juice: A Family Memoir in Black and White.* New York: Simon and Schuster.

Haley, Alex 1976: *Roots.* London: Hutchinson.

Hall, Stuart 1987: Minimal selves. In "Identity the real me", ICA document no. 6, London: ICA.

—— 1990: Cultural identity and diaspora. In Jonathan Rutherford (ed.), *Identity, Community, Cultural Difference*, London: Lawrence and Wishart, 222–37.

—— 1991a: The local and the global: globalisation and ethnicity. In Anthony King (ed.), *Culture, Globalisation and the World-System*, Basingstoke: Macmillan, 19–39.

—— 1991b: Old and new identities, old and new ethnicities. In Anthony King (ed.), *Culture, Globalization and the World-System*, Basingstoke: Macmillan, 40–68.

—— 1992: New ethnicities. In J. Donald and A. Rattansi (eds), *"Race", Culture and Difference*, London: Sage, 252–9.

—— (ed.) 1997: *Representation.* London: Sage.

Hall, Stuart, Critcher, C., Jefferson, T., Clarke, J., and Roberts, B. 1978: *Policing the Crisis*. London: Macmillan.

Hall, Stuart, Held, David, and McGrew, Tony (eds) 1992: *Modernity and its Futures*. Milton Keynes: Open University Press.

Halliday, Fred 1999: Islamophobia reconsidered. *Ethnic and Racial Studies*, 22 (5), 892–902.

Hannerz, Ulf 1990: Cosmopolitans and locals in world culture. In M. Featherstone (ed.), *Global Culture*, London: Sage, 237–52.

Hechter, Michael 1987: *Principles of Group Solidarity*. Berkeley: University of California Press.

Hein, Jeremy 1994: From migrant to minority: Hmong refugees and the social construction of identity in the United States. *Sociological Inquiry*, 64 (3), 281–306.

Hewitt, Roger 1986: *White Talk, Black Talk*. Cambridge: Cambridge University Press.

—— 1992: Language, youth and the destabilisation of ethnicity. In C. Palmgren, K. Lovgren, and G. Bolin (eds), *Ethnicity in Youth Culture*, Stockholm: Stockholm University Press.

Hickman, Mary 1998: Reconstructing deconstructing "race": British discourses about the Irish in Britain. *Ethnic and Racial Studies*, 21 (2), 288–307.

Hochschild, Jennifer 1999: Affirmative action as culture war. In M. Lamont (ed.), *The Cultural Territories of Race*, Chicago: University of Chicago Press, 343–68.

Hollinger, David 1995: *Postethnic America*. New York: Basic Books.

hooks, bell 1992: Representing whiteness in the black imagination. In Lawrence Grossberg, Cary Nelson, and Paula Treichler (eds), *Cultural Studies*, London: Routledge, 338–46.

Hunt, Marsha 1996: *Repossessing Ernestine*. New York: Harper Collins.

Hurh, Won Moo and Kim, Kwang Chung 1989: The "success" image of Asian Americans: its validity, and its practical and theoretical implications. *Ethnic and Racial Studies*, 12 (4), 512–38.

Ifekwunigwe, Jayne 1999: *Scattered Belongings*. London: Routledge.

—— 2001: Re-Membering "Race." In D. Parker and M. Song (eds), *Re-thinking "Mixed Race"*, London: Pluto Press, 42–64.

Iganski, Paul 2000: Introduction: the problem of hate crimes and hate crime laws. In P. Iganski (ed.), *The Hate Debate*, London: Profile Books, 1–14.

Iganski, Paul and Payne, Geoff 1996: Declining racial disadvantage in the British labour market. *Ethnic and Racial Studies*, 19 (1), 113–34.

Jaggi, Maya 2002: Civil Wrongs. *The Guardian Weekend*, 22 June, 54–60.

Jarvenpa, Robert 1988: The political economy and political ethnicity of American Indian adaptations and identities. In Richard Alba (ed.), *Ethnicity and Race in the U.S.A.*, New York: Routledge & Kegan Paul, 29–48.

Jayaweera, Hiranthi 1993: Racial disadvantage and ethnic identity. *New Community*, 19 (3), 383–406.

Jenkins, Richard 1997: *Rethinking Ethnicity*. London: Sage.

Jewel in the Crown 1984: Granada Television. Produced by Christopher Morahan, directed by Christopher Morahan and Jim O'Brien.

Johnson, Kevin 1999: *How did you Get to be Mexican?* Philadelphia: Temple University Press.

Jones, Lisa 1994: *Bulletproof Diva: Tales of Race, Sex, and Hair.* New York: Doubleday.

Jones, S. 1988: *White Youth, Black Culture.* Basingstoke: Macmillan.

Joppke, Christian 1996: Multiculturalism and immigration. *Theory and Society*, 25 (4), 449–500.

Josephides, S. 1988: Honor, family and work: Greek Cypriot women before and after migration. In S. Westwood and P. Bhachu (eds), *Enterprising Women*, London: Routledge, 34–57.

Kalra, Virinder and Hutnyk, John 1998: Brimful of agitation, authenticity and appropriation: Madonna's "Asian Kool." *Postcolonial Studies*, 1 (3), 339–55.

Kang, Connie 2000: U.S. Asians seen as "alien", study finds. *Los Angeles Times*, 2 March, p. A3.

Kao, Grace 2000: Group images and possible selves among adolescents, *Sociological Forum*, 15 (3), 407–30.

Kasinitz, Phil 1992: *Caribbean New York.* Ithaca, NY: Cornell University Press.

Katz, Ilan 1996: *The Construction of Racial Identity in Children of Mixed Parentage.* London: Jessica Kingsley Publishers.

Keith, Michael 1995: Making the street visible. *New Community*, 21 (4), 551–65.

Keith, Verna and Herring, Cedric 1991: Skin tone and stratification in the black community. *American Journal of Sociology*, 97 (3), 760–78.

Kennedy, Randall 2001: *Nigger.* Cambridge, MA: Harvard University Press.

Khan, Yasmine 2001: Mixed-race Britons: people, problems, possibilities. Presentation at "Mixed: a new category for the census" conference, 19 March, The Institute of Education, University of London.

Kibria, Nazli 1993: *Family Tightrope.* Princeton: Princeton University Press.

—— 1997: The construction of "Asian American": reflections on intermarriage and ethnic identity among second-generation Chinese and Korean Americans. *Ethnic and Racial Studies*, 20 (3), 523–44.

—— 1998: The contested meanings of "Asian American": racial dilemmas in the contemporary U.S. *Ethnic and Racial Studies*, 21 (5), 939–58.

—— 2000: Race, ethnic options and ethnic binds: identity negotiations of second generation Chinese and Korean Americans. *Sociological Perspectives*, 43 (1), 77–95.

—— 2002: *Becoming Asian American.* Baltimore: Johns Hopkins Press.

Kich, George Kitahara 1992: The developmental process of asserting a biracial, bicultural identity. In Maria Root (ed.), *Racially Mixed People in America*, Newbury Park: Sage, 304–17.

Kilson, Martin 1975: Blacks and neo-ethnicity in American political life. In N. Glazer and D. P. Moynihan (eds), *Ethnicity: Theory and Experience*, Cambridge, MA: Harvard University Press, 236–66.

Kim, Claire Jean 1999: The racial triangulation of Asian Americans. *Politics and Society*, 27 (1), 105–38.
—— 2000/1: Playing the racial trump card. *Amerasia Journal*, 26 (3), 35–66.
Kim, Dae-Young 1999: Beyond co-ethnic solidarity. *Ethnic and Racial Studies*, 22 (3), 581–605.
King, James 1981: *The Biology of Race*. Berkeley: University of California Press.
Kirton, Derek 2000: *"Race", Ethnicity and Adoption*. Buckingham: Open University Press.
Knott, Kim and Khokher, Sajda 1993: Religious and ethnic identity among young Muslim women in Bradford. *New Community*, 19 (4), 593–610.
Kuo, Wen 1995: Coping with racial discrimination: the case of Asian Americans. *Ethnic and Racial Studies*, 18 (1), 109–27.
Kurashige, Scott 2000: Beyond random acts of violence. *Amerasia Journal*, 26 (1), 208–33.
Kureishi, Hanif 1991: *The Buddha of Suburbia*. London: Faber & Faber.
Kymlicka, Will (ed.) 1995: *The Rights of Minority Cultures*. Oxford: Oxford University Press.
Lal, Barbara 2001: Learning to do ethnic identity. In D. Parker and M. Song (eds), *Rethinking "Mixed Race"*, London: Pluto Press, 154–72.
Landry, Bart 1987: *The New Black Middle Class*. Los Angeles: University of California Press.
Latouche, Serge 1996: *Westernization of the World*. Cambridge: Polity.
Lavie, Smadar and Swedenburg, Ted 1996: *Displacement, Diaspora and Geographies of Identity*. Durham, NC: Duke University Press.
Lee, Chang-Rae 1995: *Native Speaker*. New York: Riverhead Books.
Lee, Sharon 1996: *Unraveling the "Model Minority" Stereotype*. New York: Teachers College Press.
Leonard, Karen 1992: *Making Ethnic Choices: California's Punjabi Mexican Americans*. Philadelphia: Temple University Press.
Lewontin, R. C., Rose, Steven, and Kamin, Leon 1984: *Not in Our Genes*. New York: Pantheon.
Lieberson, Stanley 1988: Unhyphenated whites in the United States. In Richard Alba (ed.), *Ethnicity and Race in the U.S.A.*, New York: Routledge & Kegan Paul, 159–80.
Lien, Pei-Te 1997: *The Political Participation of Asian Americans*. New York: Garland Publishing.
Light, Ivan, Sabagh, George, Bozorgmehr, Mehdi, and der-Martirosian, Claudia 1993: Internal ethnicity in the ethnic economy. *Ethnic and Racial Studies*, 16 (4), 581–97.
Loewen, J. W. 1971: *The Mississippi Chinese: Between Black and White*. Cambridge, MA: Harvard University Press.
Lopez, David and Espiritu, Yen 1990: Panethnicity in the United States: a theoretical framework. *Ethnic and Racial Studies*, 13 (2), 198–224.
Lott, Tommy 1994: Black vernacular representation and cultural malpractice. In David Goldberg (ed.), *Multiculturalism*, Oxford: Blackwell, 230–58.

Lowe, Lisa 1996: *Immigrant Acts: On Asian American Cultural Politics*. Durham, NC: Duke University Press.

Lyles, M., Yancey, A., Grace, C., and Carter, J. 1985: Racial identity and self-esteem: problems peculiar to biracial children. *Journal of the American Academy of Child and Adolescent Psychiatry*, 24, 150–3.

Mac an Ghaill, Mairtin 1999: *Contemporary Racisms and Ethnicities*. Buckingham: Open University Press.

Mahtani, Minelle 2001: I'm a blonde-haired, blue-eyed Black girl. In D. Parker and M. Song (eds), *Rethinking "Mixed Race"*, London: Pluto Press, 173–90.

—— 2002: Interrogating the hyphen-nation. *Social Identity*, 8 (1), 67–90.

Mahtani, Minelle and Moreno, April 2001: Same difference: towards a more unified discourse in "mixed race" theory. In D. Parker and M. Song (eds), *Rethinking "Mixed Race"*, London: Pluto Press, 65–75.

Malik, Kenan 1996: *The Meaning of Race*. Basingstoke: Macmillan.

Mama, Amina 1984: Black women, the economic crisis and the British state. *Feminist Review*, no. 17 (July), 21–35.

Marable, Manning 1995: *Beyond Black and White*. London: Verso.

Mass, Amy 1992: Interracial Japanese Americans. In M. Root (ed.), *Racially Mixed People in America*, Newbury Park: Sage, 265–79.

Massey, Douglas and Denton, Nancy 1993: *American Apartheid*. Cambridge, MA: Harvard University Press.

Massey, Douglas, Arango, J., Hugo, G., Komouci, A., Pellegrino, A., and Taylor, J. E. 1993: Theories of international migration. *Population and Development Review*, 19 (3), 431–66.

Matsuda, Mari 1993: We will not be used. *UCLA Asian American Pacific Islands Law Journal*, 1, 79–84.

Maynard, Warwick and Read, Tim 1997: *Policing Racially Motivated Incidents*, Crime Detection and Prevention Series Paper 84. London: Home Office.

Mengel, Laurie 2001: Triples – the social evolution of a multiracial panethnicity. In D. Parker and M. Song (eds), *Rethinking "Mixed Race"*, London: Pluto Press, 99–116.

Merton, Robert 1941: Intermarriage and the social structure: fact and theory. *Psychiatry*, 4 (Aug.), 361–74.

Miles, Jack 1992: Blacks vs. Browns. *Atlantic Monthly*, Oct., pp. 41–5.

Miles, Robert 1989: *Racism*. London: Routledge.

Min, Pyong Gap 1996: *Caught in the Middle*. Berkeley: University of California Press.

—— 1998: *Changes and Conflicts: Korean Immigrant Families in New York*. Boston: Allyn & Bacon.

—— 1999: A comparison of post-1965 and turn-of-the-century immigrants. *Journal of American Ethnic History*, 18 (3), 65–94.

Min, Pyong Gap and Kim, Rose 2000: Formation of ethnic and racial identities: narratives by young Asian-American professionals. *Ethnic and Racial Studies*, 23 (4), 735–60.

Mirza, Heidi 1992: *Young, Female, and Black*. London: Routledge.

—— (ed.) 1997a: *Black British Feminism*. London: Routledge.

—— 1997b: Black women in education. In H. Mirza (ed.), *Black British Feminism*, London: Routledge, 269–77.

Modood, Tariq 1994: Political blackness and British Asians. *Sociology*, 28 (4), 859–76.

—— 1996: The changing context of "race" in Britain. *Patterns of Prejudice*, 30 (1), 3–13.

Modood, Tariq, Beishon, Sharon, and Virdee, Sharon 1994: *Changing Ethnic Identities*. London: Policy Studies Institute.

Modood, Tariq, Berthoud, Richard, Lakey, Jane, Nazroo, James, Smith, Patten, Virdee, Satnam, and Beishon, Sharon 1997: *Ethnic Minorities in Britain*. London: Policy Studies Institute.

Montero, D. 1981: The Japanese Americans: changing patterns of assimilation over three generations. *American Sociological Review*, 46 (Dec.), 829–39.

Moore, Michael 2002: *Stupid White Men*. New York: Harper Collins.

Morris, Lydia 1994: *Dangerous Classes: The Underclass and Social Citizenship*. London: Routledge.

Morrison, Toni 1993: On the backs of blacks. *Time*, special issue, Fall, p. 57.

Murrell, Audrey 1998: To identify or not to identify. In J. Eberhardt and S. Fiske (eds), *Confronting Racism*, Thousand Oaks, CA: Sage, 188–201.

Myrdal, Gunnar 1944: *An American Dilemma*. New York: McGraw-Hill.

Naficy, Hamid 1993: *The Making of Exile Cultures*. Minneapolis: University of Minnesota Press.

Nagel, Joanne 1986: The political construction of ethnicity. In Susan Olzak and J. Nagel (eds), *Competitive Ethnic Relations*, New York: Academic Press, 93–112.

—— 1994: Constructing ethnicity: creating and recreating ethnic identity and culture. *Social Problems*, 41 (1), 152–76.

Nakashima, Cynthia 1996: Voices from the movement: approaches to multiraciality. In M. Root (ed.), *The Multiracial Experience*, Thousand Oaks, CA: Sage, 79–100.

Neckerman, Kathryn, Carter, Prudence, and Lee, Jennifer 1999: Segmented assimilation and minority cultures of mobility. *Ethnic and Racial Studies*, 22 (6), 945–65.

Nelson, Candace and Tienda, Marta 1988: The structuring of Hispanic ethnicity. In R. Alba (ed.), *Ethnicity and Race in the U.S.A.*, New York: Routledge & Kegan Paul, 49–74.

Nieman, Yolanda 1999: Social ecological contexts of prejudice between Hispanics and Blacks. In Paul Wong (ed.), *Race, Ethnicity and Nationality in the United States*, Boulder, CO: Westview Press, 170–90.

Office of Management and Budget 1997: Federal Register 62 (131) (9 July), 36874–946.

Office for National Statistics 1998: Newport, England.

Ogbu, John 1990: Minority status and literacy in comparative perspective. *Daedalus*, 119, 141–69.

O'Hagan, Andrew and Macnab, Geoffrey 1996: The boys are back in town. *Sight and Sound*, 6 (2), (Feb.), 8–11.

Okihiro, Gary 1994: *Margins and Mainstreams: Asians in History and Culture*. Seattle: University of Washington Press.

Olzak, Susan 1992: *The Dynamics of Ethnic Competition and Conflict*. Stanford, CA: Stanford University Press.

Omi, Michael and Winant, Howard 1994: *Racial Formation in the United States*. New York: Routledge.

—— 1996: Contesting the meaning of race in the post-civil rights movement era. In S. Pedraza and R. Rumbaut (eds), *Origins and Destinies*, Belmont, CA: Wadsworth Publishing, 470–8.

Ortner, Sherry 1996: *Making Gender*. Boston: Beacon Press.

Owen, Charlie 2001: Mixed race in official statistics. In D. Parker and M. Song (eds), *Rethinking "Mixed Race"*, London: Pluto Press, 134–53.

Ozeki, Ruth 1998: *My Year of Meat*. London: Picador.

Palumbo-Liu, David 1999: *Asian/American*. Stanford, CA: Stanford University Press.

Park, Kye Young 1997: *The Korean American Dream*. Ithaca, NY: Cornell University Press.

Park, Robert 1928: Human migration and the marginal man. *American Journal of Sociology*, 33, 881–90.

Parker, David 1994: Encounters across the counter: young Chinese people in Britain. *New Community*, 20 (4), 621–34.

—— 1995: *Through Different Eyes: The Cultural Identities of Young Chinese People in Britain*. Aldershot: Avebury Press.

—— 1998: Rethinking British Chinese identities. In T. Skelton and G. Valentine (eds), *Cool Places*, London: Routledge, 66–82.

Parker, David and Song, Miri 2001a: Introduction: rethinking "mixed race". In D. Parker and M. Song (eds), *Rethinking "Mixed Race"*, London: Pluto Press, 1–22.

Parker, David and Song, Miri (eds) 2001b: *Rethinking "Mixed Race"*. London: Pluto Press.

Parmar, Pratiba 1990: Black feminism: the politics of articulation. In J. Rutherford (ed.), *Identity, Community, Cultural Difference*, London: Lawrence & Wishart, 101–26.

Patterns of Prejudice 1996: 30 (1).

Patterson, Orlando 1975: Context and choice in ethnic allegiance. In Nathan Glazer and Daniel Moynihan (eds), *Ethnicity: Theory and Experience*, Cambridge, MA: Harvard University Press, 305–49.

—— 1977: *Ethnic Chauvinism*. New York: Stein and Day.

Patterson, Sheila 1963: *Dark Strangers*. Harmondsworth: Penguin.

Perlmann, Joel and Waldinger, Roger 1997: Second generation decline? Children of immigrants, past and present – a reconsideration. *International Migration Review*, 31 (4), 893–922.

Peterson, Karen 1997: Interracial dating is no big deal for teens. *USA Today*, 3 Nov., 10A.

Phizacklea, Annie 1990: *Unpacking the Fashion Industry*. London: Routledge.

Phoenix, Ann and Owen, Charlie 1996: From miscegenation to hybridity: mixed relationships and mixed-parentage in profile. In B. Bernstein and

J. Brannen (eds), *Children, Research, and Policy*, London: Taylor & Francis, 111–35.

Pieterse, Jan N. 1995: Globalization as hybridization. In M. Featherstone, S. Lash, and R. Robertson (eds), *Global Modernities*, London: Sage, 45–68.

Portes, Alejandro and Bach, Robert 1985: *Latin Journey: Cuban and Mexican Immigrants in the United States*. Berkeley: University of California Press.

Portes, Alejandro and MacLeod, Dag 1996: What shall I call myself? Hispanic identity formation in the second generation. *Ethnic and Racial Studies*, 19 (3), 523–47.

Portes, Alejandro and Rumbaut, Ruben 1990: *Immigrant America*. Berkeley: University of California Press.

Portes, Alejandro and Schauffler, Richard 1996: Language acquisition and loss among children of immigrants. In S. Pedraza and R. Rumbaut (eds), *Origins and Destinies*, Belmont, CA: Wadsworth Publishing, 432–43.

Portes, Alejandro and Zhou, Min 1993: The new second generation: segmented assimilation and its variants. *Annals of the American Academy of Political and Social Science*, 530, 74–96.

Portes, Alejandro, Guarnizo, Luis, and Landholt, Patricia 1999: Introduction. Special issue on transnational communities. *Ethnic and Racial Studies*, 22 (2), 217–37.

Prashad, Vijay 2000: *The Karma of Brown Folk*. Minneapolis: University of Minnesota Press.

Pryce, Kenneth 1979: *Endless Pressure*. Harmondsworth: Penguin.

Puar, Jasbir 1996: Resituating discourses of "Whiteness" and "Asianness" in Northern England: second-generation Sikh women and the construction of identity. In M. Maynard and J. Purvis (eds), *New Frontiers in Women's Studies*, London: Taylor & Francis, pp. 127–50.

Ray, Larry and Smith, David 2000: Hate crime, violence and cultures of racism. In Paul Iganski (ed.), *The Hate Debate*, London: Profile Books, 88–102.

Raz, Joseph 1994: Liberal multiculturalism. *Dissent* (Winter), 67–79.

Reed, Ishmael, Wong, Shawn, Callahan, Bob, and Hope, Andrew 1989: Is ethnicity obsolete? In Werner Sollors (ed.), *The Invention of Ethnicity*, Oxford: Oxford University Press, 226–36.

Reich, Robert 1991: *The Work of Nations*. New York: Knopf.

Rieff, David 1991: *Los Angeles*. New York: Touchstone.

Robertson, Roland 1992: *Globalization*. London: Sage.

Roediger, David 1991: *The Wages of Whiteness*. New York: Verso.

Roosens, Eugene 1989: *Creating Ethnicity*. Newbury Park: Sage.

Root, Maria 1992: *Racially Mixed People in America*. Thousand Oaks, CA: Sage.

—— 1996: A Bill of Rights for racially mixed people. In M. Root (ed.), *The Multiracial Experience*, Thousand Oaks, CA: Sage, 3–14.

Rumbaut, Ruben 1996: A legacy of war: refugees from Vietnam, Laos, and Cambodia. In S. Pedraza and R. Rumbaut (eds), *Origins and Destinies*, Belmont, CA: Wadsworth Publishing, 315–33.

Russell, Kathy, Wilson, Midge, and Hall, Ronald 1992: *The Color Complex*. New York: Doubleday.

Said, Edward 1978: *Orientalism*. London: Penguin.

Schmitt, Eric 2001: Census figures show Hispanics pulling even with Blacks. New York Times on the Web, 8 March.

Schulz, Amy 1998: Navajo women and the politics of identity. *Social Problems*, 45 (3), 336–55.

Schuman, Howard and Steeh, Charlotte 1996: The complexity of racial attitudes in America. In S. Pedraza and R. Rumbaut (eds), *Origins and Destinies*, Belmont, CA: Wadsworth Publishing, 455–69.

Scott, Anne, Pearce, D., and Goldblatt, P. 2001: *Population Trends*, no. 105. London: The Stationery Office.

Sears, D. O. 1988: Symbolic racism. In P. A. Katz and D. A. Taylor (eds), *Eliminating Racism*, New York: Plenum, 53–84.

See, Lisa 1995: *On Gold Mountain: The One-Hundred-Year Odyssey of my Chinese-American Family*. New York: Vintage.

Sharma, A., Hutnyk, John, and Sharma, S. (eds) 1996: *Dis-Orienting Rhythms: The Politics of the New Asian Dance Music*. London: Zed Press.

Shibutani, Tamotsu and Kwan, Kian 1965: *Ethnic Stratification*. New York: Macmillan.

Shih, Johanna 2002: "Yeah, I could hire this one, but I know it's gonna be a problem": how race, nativity, and gender affect employers' perceptions of the manageability of job seekers. *Ethnic and Racial Studies*, 25 (1), 99–119.

Shukra, Kalbir 1996: A scramble for the British pie. *Patterns of Prejudice*, 30 (1), 28–36.

Shyllon, Folarin 1974: *Black Slaves in Britain*. Oxford: Oxford University Press.

Sidanius, Jim and Pratto, Felicia 1999: *Social Dominance*. Cambridge: Cambridge University Press.

Silverman, Max and Yuval-Davis, Nira 1999: Jews, Arabs and the theorisation of racism in Britain and France. In A. Brah, M. Hickman, and M. Mac an Ghaill (eds), *Thinking Identities*, Basingstoke: Macmillan, 25–48.

Sivanandan, A. 1982: *A Different Hunger*. London: Pluto Press.

Small, J. 1986: Transracial placements: conflicts and contradictions. In S. Ahmed, J. Cheetham, and J. Small (eds), *Social Work with Black Children and their Families*, London: Batsford, 81–99.

Small, Stephen 1994: *Racialised Barriers*. London: Routledge.

—— 2001: Colour, culture and class. In D. Parker and M. Song (eds), *Rethinking "Mixed Race"*, London: Pluto Press, 117–33.

Smith, Anthony 1990: Towards a global culture? In M. Featherstone (ed.), *Global Culture*, London: Sage, 171–92.

Snipp, C. Mathew 1997: Some observations about racial boundaries and the experiences of American Indians. *Ethnic and Racial Studies*, 29 (4), 667–89.

Sollors, Werner (ed.) 1989: *The Invention of Ethnicity*. Oxford: Oxford University Press.

—— 1997: *Neither Black Nor White Yet Both: A Thematic Analysis of Interracial Literature*. New York: Oxford University Press.

Solomos, John 1988: *Black Youth, Racism and the State*. Cambridge: Cambridge University Press.

—— 1993: *Race and Racism in Britain*. London: Macmillan.

Solomos, John and Back, Les 1994: Conceptualising Racisms. *Sociology*, 28 (1), 143–62.

—— 1996: *Racism and Society*. London: Macmillan.

Song, Miri 1997: "You're becoming more and more English": investigating Chinese siblings' cultural identities. *New Community*, 23 (3), 343–62.

—— 1999: *Helping Out: Children's Labor in Ethnic Businesses*. Philadelphia: Temple University Press.

Song, Miri and Edwards, Rosalind 1997: Comment: raising questions about perspectives on black lone motherhood. *Journal of Social Policy*, 26 (2), 233–44.

Song, Miri and Parker, David 1995: Commonality, difference, and the dynamics of disclosure in in-depth interviewing. *Sociology*, 29 (2), 241–56.

Sowell, Thomas 1981: *Ethnic America*. New York: Basic Books.

Soysal, Yasemin 1994: *Limits to Citizenship*. Chicago: University of Chicago Press.

Spencer, John Michael 1997: *The New Colored People*. New York: New York University Press.

Spickard, Paul 1989: *Mixed Blood: Intermarriage and Ethnic Identity in Twentieth Century America*. Madison: University of Wisconsin Press.

—— 1992: The illogic of racial categories. In M. Root (ed.), *Racially Mixed People in America*, Thousand Oaks, CA: Sage, 12–23.

—— 2001: The subject is mixed race: the boom in biracial biography. In D. Parker and M. Song (eds), *Rethinking "Mixed Race"*, London: Pluto Press, 76–98.

Spickard, Paul and Fong, Rowena 1995: Pacific Islander Americans and multiethnicity. *Social Forces*, 73, 1365–83.

Steinberg, Stephen 1981: *The Ethnic Myth: Race, Ethnicity, and Class in America*. Boston: Beacon Press.

Stonequist, E. V. 1937: *The Marginal Man*. New York: Russell & Russell.

Stopes-Roe, Mary and Cochrane, Raymond 1990: *Citizens of this Country*. Clevedon: Multilingual Matters.

Stout, Mira 1997: *One Thousand Chestnut Trees*. London: Flamingo.

Swidler, Ann 1986: Culture in action: symbols and strategies. *American Sociological Review*, 51 (Apr.), 273–86.

Takagi, Dana 1992: *The Retreat from Race*. New Brunswick, NJ: Rutgers University Press.

—— 1994: Post-civil rights politics and Asian American identity: admissions and higher education. In Steven Gregory and Roger Sanjek (eds), *Race*, New Brunswick, NJ: Rutgers University Press, 229–42.

Takaki, Ronald 1989: *Strangers from a Different Shore*. New York: Penguin.

Takenaka, Ayumi 1999: Transnational community and its ethnic consequences. *American Behavioral Scientist*, 42 (9), 1459–74.

Taylor, Charles 1994: On the politics of recognition. In D. Goldberg (ed.), *Multiculturalism*, Oxford: Blackwell, 75–106.

Taylor, Ronald 1979: Black ethnicity and the persistence of ethnogenesis. *American Journal of Sociology*, 84 (6), 1401–23.

Thai, Hung 1999: "Splitting things in half is so white!": conceptions of family life and friendship and the formation of ethnic identity among second generation Vietnamese Americans. Paper given at the American Sociological Association, Chicago, 6–10 August.

Thompson, Becky and Tyagi, Sangeeta (eds) 1996: *Names We Call Home: Autobiography on Racial Identity*. New York: Routledge.

Thornton, Michael 1992: Is multiracial status unique? In M. Root (ed.), *Racially Mixed People in America*, Thousand Oaks, CA: Sage, 321–5.

—— 1996: Hidden agendas, identity theories, and multiracial people. In M. Root (ed.), *The Multiracial Experience*, Thousand Oaks, CA: Sage, 101–20.

Tizard, Barbara and Phoenix, Ann 1993: *Black, White, or Mixed?* New York: Routledge.

Tuan, Mia 1998: *Forever Foreigners or Honorary Whites?* New Brunswick, NJ: Rutgers University Press.

Twine, France Winddance 1998: *Racism in a Racial Democracy: The Maintenance of White Supremacy in Brazil*. New Brunswick, NJ: Rutgers University Press.

US Bureau of Census 1990: Inequality within racial and ethnic groups, 1990. Washington, DC: US Government Printing Office.

Van den Berghe, Pierre 1978: Race and ethnicity. *Ethnic and Racial Studies*, 1 (4), 401–11.

Vertovec, Steven 1994: Caught in an ethnic quandary. In Roger Ballard (ed.), *Desh Pardesh: The South Asian Presence in Britain*, London: Hurst & Company, 272–90.

Wallman, Sandra 1978: Boundaries of "race": processes of ethnicity in England. *Man*, 13, 200–17.

Walvin, James 1985: Freeing the slaves: how important was Wilberforce? In Jack Hayward (ed.), *Out of Slavery*. London: Frank Cass, 30–46.

Ware, Vron 1992: *Beyond the Pale*. London: Verso.

Warner, W. L. and Srole, Leo 1945: *The Social Systems of American Ethnic Groups*. New Haven: Yale University Press.

Waters, Mary 1990: *Ethnic Options*. Berkeley: University of California Press.

—— 1991: The role of family lineage in identity formation among Black Americans. *Qualitative Sociology*, 14 (1), 57–76.

—— 1994: Ethnic and racial identities of second-generation black immigrants in New York City. *International Migration Review*, 28 (4), 795–820.

—— 1996: Ethnic options: for whites only? In S. Pedraza and R. Rumbaut (eds), *Origins and Destinies*, Belmont, CA: Wadsworth Publishing, 444–54.

—— 1999: Explaining the comfort factor: West Indian immigrants confront American race relations. In M. Lamont (ed.), *The Cultural Territories of Race*. Chicago: University of Chicago Press, 63–97.

Watson, James (ed.) 1977: *Between Two Cultures*. Oxford: Oxford University Press.

Weber, Max 1968: *Economy and Society*. Berkeley: University of California Press. Orig. pub. 1921.

Weeks, Jeffrey 1990: The value of difference. In Jonathan Rutherford (ed.), *Identity, Community, Cultural Difference*, London: Lawrence and Wishart, 88–100.

Weisman, Jan 1996: An "other" way of life. In M. Root (ed.), *The Multiracial Experience*, New York: Routledge, 152–64.

West, Cornel 1994: *Race Matters*. New York: Vintage.

Williams, Gregory Howard 1995: *Life on the Color Line*. New York: Dutton.

Williams, Raymond Brady 1998: Asian Indian and Pakistani religions in the United States. *Annals, AAPSS*, 558 (July), 178–95.

Wilson, Anne 1987: *Mixed Race Children*. London: Allen & Unwin.

Wilson, W. J. 1978: *The Declining Significance of Race*. Chicago: University of Chicago Press.

—— 1987: *The Truly Disadvantaged*. Chicago: University of Chicago Press.

—— 1996: *When Work Disappears*. New York: Knopf.

Wolfe, Tom 1998: *A Man in Full*. London: Jonathan Cape.

Wong, Paul (ed.) 1999: *Race, Ethnicity, and Nationality in the United States*. Boulder, CO: Westview Press.

Wong, Paul et al. 1998: Asian Americans as a model minority. *Sociological Perspectives*, 41 (1), 95–118.

Woodward, C. Vann 1966: *The Strange Career of Jim Crow*. New York: Oxford University Press.

Xu, Jun 2002: Why do Asian Americans register less? Paper submitted to the American Sociological Association, Asia and Asian American Section Student Paper Competition, July.

Yamanaka, Keiko and McClelland, Kent 1994: Earning the model-minority image: diverse strategies of economic adaptation by Asian-American women. *Ethnic and Racial Studies*, 17 (1), 79–114.

Yancey, William, Ericksen, Eugene, and Juliani, Richard 1976: Emergent ethnicity. *American Sociological Review*, 41 (3), 391–403.

Yinger, Milton 1994: *Ethnicity*. Albany: State University of New York Press.

Young, Alford, Jr. 1999: Navigating race: getting ahead in the lives of "rags to riches" young black men. In M. Lamont (ed.), *The Cultural Territories of Race*, Chicago: University of Chicago Press, 30–62.

Younge, Gary 1997: Beige Britain. *Guardian*, 22 May, p. G2.

Zachary, G. Pascal 1999: I'd like to teach the world to sing in perfect Cantonese. *Wall Street Journal*, 7 January.

Zack, Naomi (ed.) 1995: *American Mixed Race: The Culture of Microdiversity*. Lanham, MD: Rowman & Littlefield.

—— 1996: On being and not-being Black and Jewish. In M. Root (ed.), *The Multiracial Experience*, London: Sage, 140–51.

Zenner, Walter 1988: Jewishness in America: ascription and choice. In Richard Alba (ed.), *Ethnicity and Race in the U.S.A.*, New York: Routledge & Kegan Paul, 117–33.

Zhou, Min 1997: Growing up American. *Annual Review of Sociology*, 23, 63–95.

Zhou, Min and Bankston, Carl 1994: Social capital and the adaptation of the second generation: the case of Vietnamese youth in New Orleans. *International Migration Review*, 28 (4), 821–45.

Index